THE CHALLENGES OF GLOBALIZATION: *RETHINKING NATURE, CULTURE, AND FREEDOM*

Edited by
Steven V. Hicks

and
Daniel E. Shannon

Blackwell Publishing

350 Main Street, Malden, MA 02148-5020, USA
9600 Garsington Road, Oxford OX4 2DQ, UK
550 Swanston Street, Carlton, Victoria 3053, Australia

First published 2007 by Blackwell Publishing Ltd.

Library of Congress Cataloging-in-Publication Data

International Society for Universal Dialogue. World Congress
(6th : 2006 : Helsinki, FInland)
   The challenges of globalization : rethinking nature,
culture, and freedom / edited by Steven V. Hicks and
Daniel E. Shannon.
      p.   cm. — (The American journal of economics and
sociology ; v. 66, Jan. 2007, no. 1)
   Papers presented at 6th World Congress of the International
Society for Universal Dialogue, held in Helsinki, 2006.
   ISBN 978-1-4051-7357-5 (hardcover)
   ISBN 978-1-4051-7356-8 (pbk.)
   1. Globalization—Congresses.   2. Social justice—Congresses.
3. Pluralism (Social sciences)—Congresses.   4. Environmental
protection—International cooperation—Congresses.   I. Hicks,
Steven V., 1939–   II. Shannon, Daniel E., 1955–   III. Title.
   JZ1318.I5585   2007
   303.48′2—dc22
                                                2007003760

A catalogue record for this title is available from the Library of Congress.

Set in 10 on 13pt Garamond Light
by SNP Best-set Typesetter Ltd., Hong Kong

For further information on
Blackwell Publishing, visit our website:
http://www.blackwellpublishing.com

Contents

Preface and Acknowledgments

STEVEN V. HICKS *and* DANIEL E. SHANNON, *Editors*

THE ESSAYS INCLUDED in this volume were originally presented at the Renvall Institute for Area and Cultural Studies, University of Helsinki, Finland, on the occasion of the Sixth World Congress of the International Society for Universal Dialogue (ISUD). Most were either keynote addresses or prize-winning papers at the Congress, and all are focused on a central theme: namely, the need to rethink our concepts of nature, culture, and freedom in an age of increased globalization.

In his introductory essay "Rethinking Nature, Culture, and Freedom," Steven V. Hicks sets the tone for the volume by arguing that humanity at the beginning of the 21st century faces some ominous challenges that call for a radical rethinking and repositioning of several basic ideas and relations that define modern society. In particular, he focuses on three broad areas of concern: the problem of the physical sustainability of the natural world, the problem of inter-cultural dialogue and coexistence, and the problem of promoting freedom and human rights in a world of economic and corporate globalization. He also discusses the need to find creative ways of breaking the current cycle of dominance and economic/ecological/ cultural destruction in order to build a more peaceful and just world through universal dialogue and collaboration.

Part I of the volume is entitled "Global Justice, Democracy, and Universal Dialogue." In this section, four contemporary political philosophers—Edward Demenchonok, Karl-Otto Apel, James P. Sterba, and Alyssa R. Bernstein—discuss the important issues of global justice, peace, democracy, and international law. Demenchonok's essay "From a State of War to Perpetual Peace" establishes the groundwork for the discussion that follows in Part I by carefully examining the problems of war, peace, and the future of human rights protection in a global context. His essay also explores some competing contemporary approaches to these difficult problems, specifically highlighting the "democratic peace" theories and new "cosmopolitan democracy" theories of Doyle, Habermas, Apel, Rawls, and others.

American Journal of Economics and Sociology, Vol. 66, No. 1 (January, 2007).
© 2007 American Journal of Economics and Sociology, Inc.

Demenchonok concludes his essay by arguing for the ongoing relevance of Immanuel Kant's political philosophy to current and future discussions concerning global peace, justice, and human rights. The German philosopher Karl-Otto Apel, in his essay "Discourse Ethics, Democracy, and International Law," also argues for the contemporary relevance of Kant's philosophy for meeting the ethical challenges posed by globalization. Professor Apel explores the foundational relation between human rights, democracy, and international law (or *jus gentium*); he takes issue with both Jürgen Habermas's and John Rawls's approaches to implementing a just global system of law; and he argues that a rational solution to the current problems of international law and justice is only possible through a critical transformation of Kant's practical philosophy via a "transcendental-pragmatic" conception of "discourse ethics." By contrast, James P. Sterba, in his essay "Rethinking Global Justice from the Perspective of All Living Nature," considers traditional libertarian and utilitarian approaches to justice and argues, instead, for a more adequate conception of "global justice" that takes into account all living beings and that imposes some additional obligations on us that are absent from less defensible "human-centered" (e.g., Rawlsian) notions of global justice, although not as many as we might initially think. Finally, Alyssa R. Bernstein, in her essay "Human Rights, Global Justice, and Disaggregated States," concludes this section by defending a Rawlsian approach to a just global system of public law (a "law of peoples") against Apel, Sterba, and others. In particular, she is concerned with arguing against Onora O'Neill and Anne-Marie Slaughter and their recent claims that transformations in the concept of state sovereignty due to globalization require significant modifications in Rawls's conception of human rights. Bernstein concludes this section by arguing that globalization has not rendered obsolete Rawls's conception of human rights and the "law of peoples," and that we therefore have some reason to hope that a just world order is a realistic possibility.

Part II, entitled "Rethinking Nature: Globalization and the Challenges of Environmental Ethics," examines some of the ethical challenges posed by globalization to current environmental thinking. Charles S. Brown, in his essay "Beyond Intrinsic Value: Undermining the Justification of Ecoterrorism," takes issue with certain radical approaches to environmental ethics, in particular, Aldo Leopold's "land ethics" and Arne Naess's "deep ecology." Brown argues, instead, for an alternative pragmatic conception of value that, he thinks, can better guide environmental thinking on matters of law, policy, and activism, and that undercuts the intellectual, psychological, and ethical justification for either ecofascism or ecoterrorism. Marc Lucht also looks to an alternative, and often neglected, resource for creative environmental thinking in a global context, namely, Kant's aesthetics. Lucht, in his essay "Does Kant Have Anything to Teach Us about Environmental Ethics?," argues that Kant's aesthetic categories of the beautiful and the sublime, when rightly understood, help reorient investigations in environmental philosophy by providing a more realistic view of the relationship between human beings and nature than one finds in most traditional dualistic or monistic theories.

Part III is entitled "Rethinking Culture: Globalization and the Challenges of Interculturality." As the title implies, the essays in this section focus attention on understanding different aspects of culture in the context of increased globalization. Xiaorong Li, in her essay "A Cultural Critique of Cultural Relativism," explores a certain line of critical analysis that, she thinks, undercuts the claim that judgments approaching freedom, and standards upholding human rights, are culturally relativistic and, as such, cannot possibly have any universal validity. She argues that a "cultural critique," rightly understood, dissolves the presumed problem of morality's relativity to culture or the cultural relativity of morality. As she sees it, there is no real ethical problem of cultural relativity as such, though there may well be problems of cultural misunderstanding, insensitivity, discrimination, and denial of inner-culture differences and/or similarities between cultures in our increasingly "creolized" and "hybridized" world. Li concludes by arguing that in such a hybrid world, cultures are indeed internally divided, but they are also mutually commensurable, penetrable, and therefore comprehensible. As such, multicultural societies and the individuals who inhabit them have a responsibility for promoting universalistic ethical principles of rational dialogue, human rights, and freedom. While Li would agree with Apel, Demenchonok, and others in this volume in claiming that the cultural challenges posed by globalization can be effectively met within the "modernist" framework of a universalistic social ethics and a liberal/cosmopolitan politics, Paul Santilli argues, by contrast, that globalization is already part of a "postmodern, liquid, and messy" ethical and social condition. As Santilli sees it, for modern ethicists (Apel, Habermas, Rawls), such a "liquid, messy condition" is a thing of "horror" to be somehow controlled or overcome by appeal to practical reason. For the "postmodernists," however, it is something elemental to our very being, and so, of course, to any successful approach to ethics. Thus, in his essay "Culture, Evil, and Horror," Santilli explores in some detail this concept of "existential horror" and contends that it is an important concept for helping us come to grips with the modern and postmodern world. While acknowledging the need for modernist ethical institutions of "international law, human rights, and basic justice to resist the evils done to persons displaced by globalization," Santilli also reflects on the need for a "postmodern ethics" that takes responsibility for the hybrid "monstrosities," ambiguities, and "horrors of being" generated by modernity's globalization. He concludes his essay by speculating on the way in which such a "postmodern ethics" (which has yet to be written) may have to accept the experience of horror as "that which one must pass through in order to remember and redeem the slaughtered millions of modernity."

Part IV is called "Rethinking Freedom: Persons and the Challenges of Autonomy." This section begins with John P. Lizza's essay, "Persons: Natural, Functional, or Ethical Kind?," in which he considers alternative views on the nature of the person, the subject of freedom. Very much in the spirit of the social theorist G. H. Mead, Lizza argues for the advantages of what he calls a substantive view of persons (or a social constitutive view) that treats persons as largely constituted by their (moral, social, and cultural) relational properties. He argues that such a view provides the best theoretical grounding for dealing with the complex practical and bioethical questions that arise in our increasingly global society. This section concludes with John Sanbonmatsu's essay, "The Subject of Freedom at the End of History." Taking his cue from the work of Eric Fromm, Herbert Marcuse, and Ernst Bloch, among others, Sanbonmatsu tries to recuperate a specifically "socialist humanism" that, he hopes, will provide the ground for a comprehensive new theory and practice of liberatory politics. "Metahumanism" is the term he coins for this "emergent social movement" toward social equality, justice, reconciliation with nature, and universal freedom.

Part V is entitled "The Challenges of Globalization: A Non-Western Perspective." In this concluding section, Professor Keping Wang of Beijing International Studies University examines the history of a core conception of Chinese intellectual thought, namely, *tian ren heyi,* or "heaven-and-human oneness." In his essay, "A Rediscovery of Heaven-and-Human Oneness," Wang argues that this complex and subtle concept embodies the general ethos or spirit of Chinese philosophy, even in the contemporary world. Having explored the detailed history of the concept, Wang then looks at some contemporary pragmatic applications and implications of the concept, specifically with reference to the urgent ecoenvironmental concerns in modern China as well as in the rest of the world. He concludes his essay by arguing that this traditional ethical concept from Chinese philosophy can be creatively developed and reinterpreted into a modern, pragmatic alternative for human fulfillment and ecoenvironmental protection.

The editors of this volume would like to thank Sonja Servomaa and the staff of the Renvall Institute for Area and Cultural Studies, University of Helsinki, for their many efforts in making the ISUD Sixth World Congress such a success. We would also like to thank the estate of the late Jens A. B. Jacobsen for its generous financial support of the Congress and of the work for this volume. Finally, we would like to thank Laurence S. Moss, editor-in-chief of *The American Journal of Economics and Sociology,* for his patience, encouragement, and support of our editorial work on this special supplemental issue.

Editorial Introduction

Rethinking Nature, Culture, and Freedom

By STEVEN V. HICKS*

ON JULY 15, 2005, scholars from around the world gathered together at the University of Helsinki, Finland, for the Sixth World Congress of the International Society for Universal Dialogue (ISUD). This special invited issue of the *American Journal of Economics and Sociology* is derived, in part, from a select group of papers that were originally presented at this World Congress. For those readers who may be unfamiliar with the work of the ISUD, the main purpose of this international philosophical society is to promote, both in theory and in practice, the ideals of universal dialogue as the most effective means for promoting the gradual realization of a more decent, peaceful, and just world order. Founded at the University of Warsaw, Poland, on November 9, 1989 (the day of the collapse of the Berlin Wall), the ISUD now includes more than 300 scholars and educators from Africa, Asia, and the Americas, as well as Europe. In the words of its constitution, the ISUD was created "in order to investigate and articulate the basic principles of universality [and dialogue], systematically, rationally, and comprehensively—with an effort to promote a global understanding of these principles, striving to help generate [a] universal world consciousness towards the gradual emergence of a decent world order, and aspiring to actualize the highest and richest

*Steven V. Hicks is Professor and Chair of Philosophy at Queens College of the City University of New York. He is the author of numerous articles on Hegel, Nietzsche, and 19th-century German philosophy and literature. His books include *International Law and the Possibility of a Just World Order* (1999), *Mythos and Logos: How to Regain the Love of Wisdom* (2004), and *Reading Nietzsche at the Margins* (forthcoming 2007). He has served on the board of editorial consultants for the *History of Philosophy Quarterly* (2001–2004), and he is currently the editor of the special book series *Universal Justice* of Editions Rodopi. From 2003–2005 he served as president of the ISUD. An earlier version of this essay was presented as the Presidential Address at the inaugural session of the ISUD Sixth World Congress, University of Helsinki, Finland, July 15, 2005.

American Journal of Economics and Sociology, Vol. 66, No. 1 (January, 2007).

human values" in the arts, natural and social sciences, politics, education, and social and cultural life.[1] To help achieve these lofty goals, the members of the ISUD strive by means of their scholarly efforts—via regional and international conferences and symposia, via individual and collective works—to "explore and share important areas of human knowledge and experience." We do this in order to "evoke and invigorate a global consciousness," that is, an "existential awareness that all of the peoples of the world belong to one species, the human species, and accordingly, have the same fundamental stock of needs, aspirations, and capacities."[2] The ISUD is committed to promoting the recognition that these shared "needs, aspirations, and capacities cannot be adequately realized under [the current] conditions of selfish competition, violence, and exploitation," but only under conditions of "peace, cooperation, and freedom." We also acknowledge our responsibility to other species and to future generations, and "to the preservation and restoration of the health and beauty of all eco-systems on the planet."[3]

Since 2004, the ISUD has been one of 103 full members of the International Federation of Philosophical Societies (FISP), a nongovernmental organization that unifies various national and international philosophical organizations and that is linked with the International Council for Philosophy and Humanistic Studies (ICPHS) and with UNESCO. The goals of the ISUD are very much in line with the main objectives of FISP, ICPHS, and UNESCO: namely, to promote philosophical education on a global scale, and to generate a greater awareness of the social and global problems that confront us in order to break through the impasse in which humanity finds itself in the early 21st century. But what are the main world problems that we face today?

This question brings us to the theme of this special issue of the *AJES*: "The Challenges of Globalization: Rethinking Nature, Culture, and Freedom." As the title of this volume implies, humanity at the beginning of the 21st century faces serious global challenges that call for a radical rethinking and repositioning of many basic ideas that influence personal, governmental, and natural relationships that, in turn, define modern society. Escalating social and global problems—such as the proliferation of wars in a world full of weapons of mass destruction, the neglect of the developing world and the pressing needs of those living in extreme poverty, and ecological degradation—threaten the future of humanity; the solution to such problems clearly requires the joint efforts of all of the nations of the world. Yet the current policies of so many of the main players on the international scene—policies of preemptive wars in the name of freedom and democracy, confrontation, and polarization—threaten to destabilize the world rather than to offer solutions to our current difficulties. Humanity must find creative ways to break the vicious cycle of dominance and (economic/ ecological/cultural) destruction and to build a more peaceful and prosperous world through dialogue and collaboration. But how should we proceed in the face of the enormity of these problems?

In pondering these questions, I am reminded of the young Friedrich Nietzsche who, following his "ghastly" experiences in the Franco-Prussian war in 1870, wrote to his friend Gersdorff, "I am terribly concerned about the impending state of [modern] culture. . . . Between you and me, I now consider [Prussian nationalism] a power that is extremely dangerous for [contemporary] culture."[4] Contemplating the collapse of the traditional supports of value and the "crisis of modern ethics" that he identified with the "Death of God," the mounting belief in "social Darwinism" (which blurred the distinction between human and animal), and the uncritical faith in the human species' unchecked technological capabilities, Nietzsche predicted disaster: "Our whole European culture has been moving towards a disaster, with a tortured tension that is growing decade to decade."[5] Moreover, he boldly predicted that power politics, brutal "constructs [and ideologies] of domination," and vicious "wars the like of which have never yet been seen on earth" would be the wave of the future (20th) century.[6] Sadly, he was not entirely mistaken in his dire predictions.

In part, Nietzsche's diagnosis of our modern societal ills was similar to that of Schiller, Hölderlin, Hegel, and Marx, among others in the 19th century: namely, that life in the modern (post-Enlightenment) world lacked a kind of unity, coherence, and meaning that life in earlier cultures had possessed. Modern individuals had used their freedoms to develop their talents, capabilities, and powers in an overspecialized, one-sided way. As a result, their lives were fragmented, not integrated, and they lacked the ability to identify with their society in a natural way, to feel "at home" (*bei sich*) in that society, and to play the social and cultural roles assigned to them in the world whole-heartedly. Thus, they could not see the lives they led as genuinely meaningful, free, and good.[7] To this general diagnosis, however, Nietzsche would also add:

> our whole [modern] attitude toward nature, the way we violate her with the aid of machines and the heedless inventiveness of our technicians and engineers, is *hubris*; our attitude toward God as some alleged spider of purpose and morality behind the great captious web of causality, is *hubris*. . . . our attitude toward *ourselves* is *hubris*, for we experiment with ourselves in a way we would never permit ourselves to experiment with animals . . . we cheerfully vivisect our souls.[8]

Once again, Nietzsche predicted dire consequences. As he writes in a late note from 1887–1888:

> Once we possess that common economic management of the earth that will soon be inevitable [what we would now call "economic globalization"], humankind will be able to find its best meaning as a machine in the service of this [global] economy—as a tremendous clockwork, composed of ever smaller, ever more subtly "adapted gears"; as an ever-growing superfluity of all dominating and commanding elements; as a whole of tremendous force, whose individual factors represent only *minimal forces, minimal values.*[9]

Anyone familiar with Nietzsche's writings knows that he deeply appreciated the natural (as well as the cultural and artistic) world, and that he defined humankind, at least partly, in terms of naturalistic categories. Yet in the 1880s, few people (including Nietzsche) believed that humans could actually destroy the natural conditions for human life and culture. Nuclear weapons were not on the conceptual horizon (much less on the warheads of ICBMs); the human population was a fraction of what it is today; despite the remarkable achievements of 19th-century European industry, industrialization had not spread far beyond Europe and parts of North America; the rapid species extinction that we see today was only beginning; the terms "acid rain," "global warming," and "climate change" had not yet entered into the popular lexicon; and vast areas of land and "wilderness habitat" were not only largely uncharted but also regarded, however naively, as virtually "untouched" by human hands.[10] And while Nietzsche's alter ego and "prophet" of a future, higher, and freer humanity, Zarathustra, would proclaim, "Remain faithful to the Earth," Nietzsche himself would probably have some serious misgivings about certain aspects of contemporary environmentalism. For example, he would probably be deeply suspicious of the romantic yearnings of some environmentalists to "re-enchant nature," or as Nietzsche would say, to impose "the breakshoe on the wheel of time," to "will backwards," and to try to restore a supposed Edenic past.[11] He would likely criticize the seriousness, the "spirit of gravity," and the idealized asceticism discernable in many contemporary environmentalists. And perhaps most importantly, as Michael Zimmerman notes, he would criticize the kind of anti-anthropocentrism that guides so much of today's environmentalism:

> In his "modest" attempt to naturalize humankind, and in his critique of shame about the human body and its natural demands, Nietzsche did *not* make the mistake of overlooking how dramatically *different* man is from other animals! Man is the "over-animal" because he has developed an exceptional moral and evaluative capacity. Real "progress," we are told, would occur if man left behind the instinct for violence and lust for punishment—"gifts" bestowed on humans by *other* animals—and developed instead a greater capacity for justice.[12]

And while Nietzsche often criticized arrogant (anti-naturalistic) anthropocentrism, his major concern was about the health and destiny of humanity. Man may not be "the measure of all things," but what man does *is* to measure, and that means to give value to himself or herself, to others, and to the world. Thus Nietzsche's major theme was how to avoid decadence (or the inability to generate new values), cultural degeneration, and the "advent of nihilism," and not specifically how to avoid environmental destruction and "ecocide."

And yet for those of us who confront with a real comprehension today's ecological, as well as social, cultural, and political crises—especially in light of the tragic events of the 20th century—Nietzsche's work remains a source of inspiration. For he urges us to continue to strive to find new ways to say "yes" to life in the face of so much senseless suffering, even as we sail out upon the "uncharted," "horizon-less sea," the infinite universe "de-deified" by post-Enlightenment science and "disenchanted" by the "Death of God."[13] I suspect that, had Nietzsche witnessed some of the tragic events of the 20th century, especially the astonishingly evil purposes to which National Socialists used the late 19th-century European "politics of nature" (which blended racism, social Darwinism, doctrines of "physiological degeneration," and frequent talk of breeding "nobler" races), he would have renounced certain aspects of his anti-democratic elitism as well as his talk of a "Grand Politics." And had he seen how the genetic revolution in Darwinism, as well as empirical and comparative anthropological research, undermined central aspects of the doctrines of race and breeding that were common in his age, he would have tempered some dimensions of his aristocratic anti-modernism. But even as things stand, his writings strike a cautionary note for those of us who strive to rethink and possibly reenchant our relationship to nature in light of its complete de-deification and modern disenchantment. As Nietzsche asks: "When may we begin to *'naturalize'* humanity in terms of a pure, newly discovered, and newly redeemed nature?"[14]

By "de-deifying" and "disenchanting" the world, post-Enlightenment modernity made possible advances in science, technology, and industry, the remarkable success of which contributed to eradicating deadly diseases (such as smallpox and polio), and to legitimating and spreading democratic ideals and institutions. Moreover, its methodological principles opened up a space for freedom of inquiry and dialogue that was protected from the dogmatism and intrusions of religious authority. Thus any credible alternatives to modernity's current discontents will need to explicitly affirm and integrate modernity's noblest achievements, especially the freedoms of thought, inquiry, and dialogue, which always threaten conventional mores and traditional institutions. If we are to seriously rethink, redeem, and possibly reenchant our relationship to the natural and cultural world—and thus to restore a profound dimension of significance to it—then, like Schiller, Hegel, and Nietzsche, we must adopt simultaneously an affirmative *and* a critical stance toward modernity. While denouncing with Nietzsche the dark side of modernity, for example, its tendency toward cultural nihilism and ecological degradation, we ought also to emphasize its many important contributions—scientific, technological, educational, political, economic, social, cultural, and personal. One of modernity's most defining achievements was to differentiate among domains that fold in upon one another in premodern cultures: science, politics/religion/morality, and art/subjectivity. In premodern culture, establishing and defending truth were not independent enterprises, but instead were inextricably related to political and religious authority as, for example, Galileo discovered already in the 16th century. Moreover, individuals were not free to develop their own aesthetic taste and subjective preferences; instead they had to conform to communal practices that were, in turn, consistent with prevailing cultural, religious, and political norms. By contrast, "modernity's nobility lies in the fact that it differentiates among science, morality/politics, and art/subjectivity."[15]

However, having paved the way for material prosperity, political democracy, individual liberty, and the rights of difference and diversity, modernity took a number of wrong turns and soon arrived at the kind of social and political impasse that we face today. Philosophers as diverse as Heidegger, Habermas, and Foucault, among many others, have spent a considerable amount of time and effort discussing modernity's mistakes; for example, how modern post-Enlightenment science became scientism, which, in turn, colonized the world of everyday life, transforming political decisions into technocratic ones. To even touch upon their analyses is far beyond the scope of this essay. My point for now is simply this: the solution to modernity's shortcomings and discontents—including its degradation of the natural environment and denigration of certain valid aspects of more traditional, premodern cultures—is not to "will backwards" and to regress to premodern social formations (as, e.g., in the case of National Socialism and its politics of *Blut und Boden*, or in the case of certain contemporary fundamentalist/theocratic regimes); instead, it is to be found in an effort to develop a form of postmodernity that integrates what is valid and noble about modernity, while moving beyond its current limitations and impasses.[16] And this brings us, once again, to the theme of this volume: rethinking nature, culture, and freedom. Let me briefly focus on three general aspects of this theme.

1. The problem of the physical sustainability of the natural world. Human beings at the beginning of the 21st century continue to exhaust, at an ever-increasing rate, the most accessible but nonrenewable natural resources, and they do so without being capable of replacing them with renewable resources. Likewise, they exploit these exhaustible natural resources through production methods that often destroy the natural conditions for human life without enabling us to restore those conditions. As a result, we see an unprecedented increase in concentrations of carbon dioxide, methane, and nitrous oxide in the atmosphere produced by human activities such as the burning of fossil fuels at greater rates and the clearing of rainforests and vegetation from wilderness areas, leading to global warming, rising sea levels, extinction of species, and the loss of entire ecosystems. As Peter Kemp rightly notes: "We may therefore leave future generations a world with material conditions inferior to those known to us. We need education for responsibility towards the Other in a world of the future where our descendents would not have to blame us for our exploitation of physical capital."[17]

In this volume, Professor Keping Wang reminds us of the rich Chinese ethical tradition in which human and environmental interaction is considered, discussed, and valued. He further suggests that something like this *ethos*, creatively developed and reinterpreted into a modern pragmatic alternative for human fulfillment and eco-environmental protection, is what the West now requires if the natural world is to be sustained. Along similar lines, James P. Sterba urges us to rethink the requirements of "global justice" in such a way that "all living beings," and not just human beings, are taken into account. Only in doing so, he argues, can we begin to fashion geopolitical policies that will favor the long-term survival of the human species as well as the return of humans to their proper environmental niche where, unlike now, they will be in balance with the rest of the biotic community. Finally, Charles S. Brown and Marc Lucht offer up some pragmatic as well as aesthetic insights that, they believe, can better help to situate us within, rather than pit us against, the natural world. It is their hope that such alternative pragmatic, ethico-aesthetic concepts of value will begin to reorient investigations in environmental philosophy by providing a more realistic view of the relation between human beings and nature than one finds in so many contemporary environmental theories, such as "land ethics" theories, "deep ecology" theories, and "earth first" theories. If successful, their new "pragmatic realism" can perhaps better guide our future environmental thinking on matters of law, policy, and activism.

2. The problem of intercultural dialogue and coexistence. In his recent book *One World*, Peter Singer observes that "for most of the eons of human existence, people living only short distances apart might as well, for all the differences they made in each other's lives, have been living in separate worlds. A river, a mountain range, a stretch of forest or desert, a sea—these were enough to cut people off from each other."[18] However, over the past century this isolation has dwindled with increasing rapidity, and people from different cultures are discovering and interacting with each other in ways previously unimaginable. Modern technologies—jet planes, the telephone, fax, e-mail, the Internet, instant digital communication—have overcome the physical distances that once separated us. Economic globalization has followed, but the "human globalization," the universal dialogue, has only just begun. Many long-standing animosities, prejudices, and biases must be reexamined if this dialogue is really to get going and to be successful. Moreover, as Peter Kemp notes, "reconciliation between cultures, especially between Islamic and Judeo-Christian cultures, will never take place unless both sides refrain from trying to solve their differences by violence. We need education for peace, and this must include tolerance of local and national cultures that must be protected in every [regional and] transnational political union that may be established."[19] In the present volume, Xiaorong Li and Paul Santilli make the case for such intercultural tolerance, mutual recognition, and reconciliation. However, the approaches they advocate are radically different. In Li's case, the focus of analysis is on a culturally based "critique" of the claims of normative cultural relativism. Li tries to demonstrate how certain common misunderstandings of culture have, in the past, provided ammunition to the cultural relativists. She argues persuasively, however, that in our increasingly globalized and hybrid-ized world, cultures may indeed clash, but they are nonetheless mutually commensurable, penetrable, and comprehensible; and as such, moral judgments approving freedom, and standards upholding human rights, can lay claim to a certain universal validity. Paul Santilli, on the other hand, expresses serious reservations toward all such "modernist" cosmopolitan attempts to assimilate cultural ambiguities and ambivalences under supposed universal norms and rational principles. He argues, instead, that a better philosophical understanding of such "horrifying" cultural anomalies and ambiguities, in the context of a late modern global economy and culture, may point the way toward a new "postmodern ethics"—one that will accept, love, and take responsibility for the "monstrous Other" generated, in large measure, by globalization (but not yet slotted into any particular cultural schema). Santilli argues that such a "postmodern ethics" is more suited to the emerging "liquid, global phase of late modernity" than the classical liberal, Enlightenment ethics of rational subjects attuned to universal, rational principles.

   3. **The problem of freedom in a world of economic and corporate globalization.** As previously noted, the increasing degree to which there is a single global market and world economy is due, in large part, to the enormous growth in international telecommunication systems (e-mail, Internet) as well as intercontinental jet travel. For example, in New York, where I live, grocery markets offer for sale fresh fruits and vegetables from Chile and Holland alongside those grown in nearby Long Island. On a daily basis, jet planes arriving at Kennedy airport bring in immigrants seeking liberty and the betterment of their own lives in a country they have long admired; but in the wrong hands, those same planes become deadly weapons that bring down the World Trade Center. The increasing degree to which there is economic globalization is also reflected in the development of certain nascent forms of global governance, the most controversial being the World Trade Organization (WTO), International Monetary Fund (IMF), and World Bank. A more or less open struggle currently exists between the declining power of the individual nation-states and the increasing power of this global system of transnational corporations and international banks. And at the center of the struggle, as Edward Demenchonk stresses in Chapter 1 of this volume, is the unresolved issue of the status of international law and the uncertain role of the United Nations as its "legitimate" political representative. Certainly, the dynamics of the current economic and corporate-driven globalization have been steadily undermining the nation-state as an instrument of human well-being, often subordinating it to

multinational or supranational corporate forces. This has forced even some of the better (liberal, democratic) states to dilute the security and welfare programs serving their own citizens and has hampered the ability of many states to perform their traditional ethical function: namely, providing their citizens with basic human rights and liberties, as well as "political democracy, a sense of community and tradition, and overall security."[20] It is not too far-fetched to imagine a summit conference a few years from now in which representatives of these multinational/transnational corporations, cartels, and international banks give the rest of the world its marching orders. As Marx might observe, this situation would epitomize humanity living, not in a state of freedom, but in a state of alienation: in other words, living in a world in which, instead of ruling ourselves, we are ruled by our own creation—the global economy. We therefore need "education attuned to global life where international encounters and connections go hand in hand with a more democratically controlled world economy" and where there is social and political accountability beyond the corporate boardroom.[21] This will require vision, social initiative, mobilization, and even activism across borders in order to institute a more "human-driven" (or "people-oriented") globalism to counterbalance or neutralize the current "corporate-driven" globalism. As the political scientist Richard Falk once observed:

> The decisive challenge of the moment is Hegelian in character. What is required is the formation of a [universal] consciousness capable of generating ideas and mobilizing support in a manner that facilitates transition to a new stage of . . . globalization. . . . Without the ideational stage-setting, structural solutions will not be politically feasible or will be misappropriated by oppressive, [anti-democratic] anti-ecological tendencies.[22]

We urgently need to engage in that "ideational stage-setting" in order to seek concrete structural solutions to the enormous new problems that confront all people on the globe. By rethinking nature, culture, and freedom—and by having a real dialogue concerning what these issues might entail—we can perhaps contribute to finding the necessary solutions to many of our current global problems and to goading our political leaders into carrying them out. For their part, the contributors to the present volume attempt to provide just such an "ideational stage-setting" for future global dialogue. Karl-Otto Apel, for example, tries to establish a foundational "architectonic" relation between basic human rights and democracy, and international law or *jus gentium*; while Edward Demonchonok tries to promote a "properly reformed" United Nations Organization as the appropriate vehicle for implementing and enforcing the legal status of human rights internationally, thus paving the way for the more peaceful socioeconomic and political advancement of humanity on the planet. Alyssa R. Bernstein, for her part, strives to formulate a "Rawlsian" political conception of the moral basis of a just system of international law, including a justification of enforceable basic human rights that meet the requirements of public reason; while Charles S. Brown, Marc Lucht, and James P. Sterba all urge us, in various ways, to consider the intrinsic value of nonhumans in nature when assessing the requirements of global justice. John P. Lizza argues persuasively that our modern self-identities as autonomous subjects is defined and sustained by our ever-expanding interactions with others around the globe. Finally, while Keping Wang tries to creatively develop and reinterpret traditional Chinese ethical thinking into a modern cosmopolitan alternative for human fulfillment and eco-environmental protection, John Sanbonmatsu advocates a new "socialist humanism" in which the liberation of nonhuman animals from human oppression, and the emancipation of our sensuous embodied selves *as* human animals, become central features of a new global movement for civil and cultural reform based in social equality, justice, and reconciliation with nature.

It goes without saying that there are serious problems impeding progress toward these lofty goals. Much of the contemporary world remains divided into armed sectarian (ethnic and religious) enclaves (in Iraq, Afghanistan, Lebanon, Sudan, etc.) or hostile nationalistic camps (Palestine and Israel, North and South Korea, India and Pakistan, China and Taiwan). Many regional conflicts (e.g., in the Middle East, in Africa) are likely to figure in the world of the immediate future. More often than not, these hostilities are based on longstanding historical grievances and contrary interpretations of past political events. It is often difficult to know how to resolve these disputes or how to determine which side (if either) is right. Indeed, as Hegel once observed, there are very few conflicts in which the "rightness" or "justice" of one side is clear and unambiguous.[23] And this is why war is so tempting: "to see which claim to right will give way."[24] But this is also why war is ultimately unacceptable. For in addition to the suffering and death it causes, war typically does nothing to resolve the festering historical grievances; it merely creates new grievances and resentments. Thus the only reasonable course of action is to try to envision a global society and political environment in which the hostile parties, despite their differing perspectives, would be willing and able to make acceptable compromises and concessions.[25] We need to envision and pursue rules, principles, and institutional applications of "global justice" in which the basic moral objectives (of individual freedom, the rights of persons, the values of communities, peaceful resolutions of conflicts, ecological sustainability, etc.) are promoted on a global scale. Important among these are respect for the independence of national peoples, respect for the freedoms of dialogue, association, and communication, respect for basic human rights, and the observation of a "duty" of nonintervention as well as a "duty" to assist others who may be living "under unfavorable conditions that prevent their having a just or decent political and social regime" and to accept responsibility to protect the citizens of states that cannot (or will not) protect them from massacres or genocide.[26] Other important and related institutional amplifications of "global justice" include building "secondary" transnational associations and organizations of an international "civil society," encouraging the political and judicial structures of a global "political authority," strengthening existing international bodies and procedures for settling disputes, and fostering global democratic reforms and democratically structured regional alliances.[27]

Still, it must be recognized that not all developments of transnational interdependence and global interconnection are positive ones. Many WTO and World Bank policies have benefited the "ruling" elites as opposed to ordinary citizens. NAFTA and other international "free trade" agreements (such as the recently proposed CAFTA accord) have been opposed by many labor unions and environmental groups as being bad for workers and harmful to the global environment. And while advances in telecommunication and information technologies have helped to forge new transnational associations as well as a huge single world economy, they have also helped to amplify and exacerbate many of our current international problems. They have often created wider gaps between rich and poor, between the powerful and the powerless. They have driven a "high-tech" wedge between those who have access to information technologies and those who do not. Moreover, the combination of a global market with advanced digital communication technologies has created a small minority of "high-tech" informational and corporate elites and a large majority of "low-tech" laborers who are working long hours for low wages. This is causing greater divisions, dislocations, hardships, and fragmentations, greater exclusions for the poor and uneducated, and the gradual erosion of many local communities and settled forms of social life. As Paul Santilli observes in Chapter 8 of this volume:

> In the liquid era of digital information, telecommunication, and deregulated markets, there are no fixed territories for manufacture and distribution and no permanent set of rules or norms to limit the harsher effects of capitalism. The global economy and the weakening of the welfare state bring a multitude of material benefits that stimulate and gratify (temporarily) the desires of consumers, who are (momentarily) succeeding in the new order. But its unregulated freedoms also bring new forms of insecurity, misery, and violence, as evidenced by the millions of unemployed, abandoned in the rush to "downsize" and "outsource," and the millions of refugees, asylum seekers, and so-called illegal economic migrants who are left homeless in city streets, in camps, in holding cells, and prisons, as the financial, managerial, and intellectual elite whiz around the globe in constant motion.

Advances in information technology are also allowing more self-enclosure and isolation for the elites by, for example, allowing them to build "high-tech" walls around themselves to keep the excluded poor at bay. As the new corporate and informational elites are less able to see beyond themselves, they will be less inclined to distribute resources in a way that benefits the least well off. They will be less inclined and less prepared to regard sharing as a duty of justice owed to other community members. It is not hard to imagine an ominous future where political and economic power is centralized in a few "high-tech" transnational (and perhaps virtual) corporate centers, and where the corporate elites are answerable to no one (e.g., no democratic procedures, no regulatory oversight, no rational governance) beyond the corporate boardroom. Thus, if it turns out that economic and informational connectedness is the only "social glue" holding us together as a world community, then the new "globalization" will likely lead to new inequalities, more impoverishment, more exclusions, fewer individual freedoms, and greater injustices. In the face of such a failed global culture, it is likely that we will continue to see extremist revivals of radical nationalism, sectarianism, anti-secular fundamentalism, and even global terrorism as "cynical" attempts to fill the global ethical and cultural void. In short, the new "globalization" may herald a new "dark age" for many of the world's citizens.

Yet for those of us in the ISUD who are concerned to promote a more decent, peaceful, and just world, we will continue to look for new ideas and new sources of inspiration. We will continue to work for a more just international legal and political framework as well as for a more rational, and democratically oriented, world governance. And we will continue to strive to discover how we can have participation in the best of local, national, and regional cultures and traditions, as well as location in much broader cultural and historical contexts—including, perhaps, a cosmopolitan world culture and an emerging global, ethical community.

Notes

1. For the complete ISUD Constitution, see http://www.isud.org/isud_general_information/isud_constituti.html.
2. ISUD Constitution, Article IV.
3. ISUD Constitution, Article IV.
4. Nietzsche, *B* 3, 155.
5. Nietzsche, *WP*, "Preface," §2.
6. See *WP*, §12; *EH*, "Why I am a Destiny," §1.
7. See Geuss, xii.
8. Nietzsche, *GM*.III.9.
9. Nietzsche, *WP*, §866.
10. See Zimmerman, "Nietzsche and Ecology."
11. See Nietzsche, *Z*.II.20.
12. See Zimmerman, "Nietzsche on Ecology"; see also *AC*, §14; *WS*, §183; *HAH*, §§43–44, 452. Some examples of the kind of anti-anthropocentrism that would bother Nietzsche, and that he would regard as nihilistic, would be the claim advanced by Paul Taylor that the earth would be largely unaffected by human annihilation, except insofar as this would enable the earth to heal itself

after millennia of human abuse (see Taylor, 76–77), or the call of "Earth Firsters" for eliminating layers of civilization and for returning to hunter-gatherer times.

13. See Nietzsche, *GS*, §343.
14. *GS*, § 109.
15. See Zimmerman, "Re-Enchanting the World: Proceed with Care."
16. See Zimmerman, "Re-Enchanting the World: Proceed with Care."
17. Kemp, 1.
18. Singer, 9.
19. Kemp, 1.
20. See Falk, *Explorations at the Edge of Time*, 204.
21. See Kemp, 1.
22. Falk, "An Inquiry into the Political Economy of World Order."
23. See Hegel, 540–541.
24. Hegel, 541.
25. See Thompson, 194.
26. See Rawls, 37; see also Thompson, 167–187; for more on the controversial issue of "nonintervention" and "assistance" under "unfavorable conditions," see Rawls, 105–120.
27. For more detailed discussion on these issues, see Hicks (1999, 2002).

References

Falk, Richard. (1992). *Explorations at the Edge of Time: The Prospects for World Order*. Philadelphia: Temple University Press.
———. (1994). "An Inquiry into the Political Economy of World Order." Paper presented at the Portrack Seminar, Dumfries, Scotland (June).
Geuss, Raymond. (1999). "Introduction." In *The Birth of Tragedy and Other Writings*, eds. R. Geuss and R. Speirs. Cambridge: Cambridge University Press.
Hegel, G. W. F. (1970). "Die Verfassung Deutschlands." In *Frühe Schriften*. Frankfurt am Main: Suhrkamp Verlag.
Hicks, Steven V. (1999). *International Law and the Possibility of a Just World Order*. Amsterdam: Rodopi.
———. (2002). "Regionalism, Globalism, and the Prospects for World Order: An Hegelian Approach." *Interpretation: A Journal of Political Philosophy* 30(1): 49–78.
Kemp, Peter. (2004). "Message from the President." FISP Newsletter (Summer/Fall). For the complete message, see http://www.fisp.org/newsletters.
Nietzsche, Friedrich. ([1888] 1954). *Der Antichrist* [*The Antichrist*]. In *The Portable Nietzsche*, trans. Walter Kaufmann. New York: Viking Penguin. Abbreviated as *AC*.
———. ([1888] 1968). *Ecce Homo*. In *Basic Writings of Nietzsche*, trans. Walter Kaufmann. New York: Random House. Abbreviated as *EH*.

———. ([1887] 1968). *Zur Genealogie der Moral* [*On the Genealogy of Morals*]. In *Basic Writings of Nietzsche*, trans. Walter Kaufmann and R. J. Hollingdale. Abbreviated as *GM*.

———. ([1882; Part 5, 1887] 1974). *Die fröhliche Wissenschaft* [*The Gay Science*], trans. Walter Kaufmann. New York: Random House (Vintage). Abbreviated as *GS*.

———. ([1878] 1986). *Menschliches, Allzumenschliches* [*Human, All Too Human*], trans. R. J. Hollingdale. Cambridge: Cambridge University Press. Abbreviated as *HAH*.

———. (1986). *Sämtliche Briefe*, 8 vols, eds. G. Colli and M. Montinari. Munich: Deutscher Taschenbuch Verlag. Abbreviated as *B*.

———. (1968). *Der Wille zur Macht* [Notes from the 1880s: *The Will to Power*], trans. Walter Kaufmann and R. J. Hollingdale. New York: Vintage Books. Abbreviated as *WP*.

———. ([1879] 1986). *Der Wanderer und sein Schatten* [*The Wanderer and His Shadow*], trans. R. J. Hollingdale. In *Human, All Too Human*, vol. 2. Cambridge: Cambridge University Press. Abbreviated as *WS*.

———. ([1883–1885] 1954). *Also Sprach Zarathustra* [*Thus Spoke Zarathustra*]. In *The Portable Nietzsche*, trans. Walter Kaufmann. New York: Viking Penguin. Abbreviated as *Z*.

Rawls, John. (1999). *The Law of Peoples*. Cambridge: Harvard University Press.

Singer, Peter. (2002). *One World: The Ethics of Globalization*. New Haven, CT: Yale University Press.

Taylor, Paul. (2001). "The Ethics of Respect for Nature." In *Environmental Philosophy: From Animal Rights to Radical Ecology*, eds. Michael E. Zimmerman, et al. (pp. 71–86). Upper Saddle River, NJ: Prentice Hall.

Thompson, Janna. (1992). *Justice and World Order: A Philosophical Inquiry*. London: Routledge.

Zimmerman, Michael E. (Forthcoming). "Nietzsche and Ecology: A Critical Inquiry." In *Reading Nietzsche at the Margins*, eds. Steven V. Hicks and Alan Rosenberg. Purdue University Press.

———. "Re-Enchanting the World: Proceed with Care." Unpublished ms.

PART I: GLOBAL JUSTICE, DEMOCRACY, AND UNIVERSAL DIALOGUE

1

From a State of War to Perpetual Peace

By EDWARD DEMENCHONOK*

ABSTRACT. This essay examines current debates in political philosophy regarding the problems of war and peace and of human rights
protection. Two contrasting approaches are analyzed: one represented
by "democratic peace" theories, and the other by the movement for a
cosmopolitan order. At the heart of both approaches are conflicting
interpretations of Kant's political philosophy, especially his project of
"perpetual peace." An analysis of M. Doyle's recent conception of
"liberal democratic peace" shows the flaws in his justification of the
tendency of liberal states to be war-prone toward nonliberal states.
Alternatively, the development of Kant's ideas in the theories of
"discourse ethics" (K. O. Apel and J. Habermas) and "cosmopolitan
democracy" confirms the relevance of Kant's cosmopolitan ideal to
current discussions about peace and human rights. The analysis also
affirms that the true solution to the problems of securing peace and
protecting human rights can only be achieved by peaceful means,
based on international law with the United Nations as its legitimate
political representation.

I

Introduction

THE PROBLEM OF WAR AND PEACE is of primary importance in our time,
especially after the devastating wars of the 20th century. In a nuclear

*Edward Demenchonok has worked as a senior researcher at the Institute of Phi-
losophy of the Russian Academy of Sciences, Moscow, and is currently a Professor of
Foreign Languages and Philosophy at Fort Valley State University in Georgia. He is a
vice president of the International Society for Universal Dialogue. His numerous books
and articles are in the fields of the philosophy of culture, social philosophy, and ethics.
American Journal of Economics and Sociology, Vol. 66, No. 1 (January, 2007).

age, war threatens the future of humankind. There is also a growing concern about the violation of human rights in the world, primarily in underdeveloped countries with authoritarian regimes. These two problems of paramount importance—securing peace and the global enforcement of human rights—are at the center of current academic debates regarding the status of international law and the role of the United Nations as its political representative.

In the broad spectrum of these debates among philosophers and political theorists, one can identify two main currents: one represented by "democratic peace" and "just war" theories, and the other by the movement toward cosmopolitanism. Both share the normative goals of peace and democratization, but they differ in their views on peace and democracy as well as on the best means for achieving these goals. To support their respective positions, the advocates of these views often appeal to Immanuel Kant's political philosophy, especially his philosophical essay "Toward Perpetual Peace."

In what follows, I shall explore these two currents of thought and their complex relation to Kant's philosophy. First, I will analyze the theories of "democratic peace," in particular Michael Doyle's influential conception of "liberal peace." I will then examine the development of Kant's cosmopolitan ideas in the theories of "discourse ethics" (Karl-Otto Apel, Jürgen Habermas) and "cosmopolitan democracy" (David Held and Patrick Hayden, among others). My analysis will confirm the ongoing relevance of Kant's political philosophy to current discussions about the future of peace and human rights. It will also affirm that the only lasting solution to the problems of securing peace and protecting human rights globally can be achieved, not by force or unilateral actions, but only by peaceful means, based on the rule of international law and the United Nations as its legitimate political representative.

II

"Democratic Peace": A Paradoxical Alternative to Perpetual Peace

THE THEORY OF "democratic peace" represents the specific view that peace and human rights depend on the global "spread of democracy" by Western states. This concept first emerged in the context of liberal international theories in the early 1980s and was perhaps best articulated in the theory of "liberal peace" by Michael Doyle. During the last decade, however, the ideas of "democratic peace" and "just war" (Jean Elshtain, Michael Ignatieff, among others) were adopted and transformed by neoconservative theorists and incorporated into their foreign policy doctrines. Thus the idea of "spreading democracy" throughout the world not only became common rhetoric in the speeches of U.S. political leaders but was also used as a guideline in implementing American foreign policy.

At first glance, the concept of "democratic peace" appears attractive in that it combines two great political ideals: democracy and peace. On closer inspection, however, its core idea of promoting "global peace through the spread of democracy" by the force of a superpower raises some serious questions and doubts. Many critics point to a glaring discrepancy between its declared goals (democracy and peace) and its means of implementing these goals (economic coercion and military force), and they argue that its political implementation is not conducive to solving the global problems of war and human rights. Some have even suggested that "democratic peace" functions only as an ideological justification for a policy of global domination by the world's only superpower.

The advocates of "democratic peace" typically try to support their position by appealing to the empirical generalization that democracies, as opposed to dictatorships, are usually peaceful in their dealings with one another.[1] They also appeal to the authority of Immanuel Kant to support their claims. Their interpretation of Kant results in an attempt to reduce his "perpetual peace" philosophy to the "democratic peace" ideology of forcibly spreading democracy on a global scale.

Michael Doyle is one of the leading scholars in political philosophy to contribute to the theory of "democratic peace" by developing his own "liberal peace" version. His two-part article "Kant, Liberal Legacies, and Foreign Affairs," first published in 1983, was a seminal work that shaped the conceptual framework for the later development of this theory. Doyle argues that "a separate peace exists among liberal states," which remain in a "state of war" with nonliberal states, and by the steady expansion of the "liberal zone of peace," a world peace gradually will be established.[2]

The problem of war and peace is divided in Doyle's theory into the "state of peace" in the liberal zone and the "state of war" in the rest of the world. This division supposedly derives from the different domestic policies concerning human rights in liberal and nonliberal societies. Consequently: "Differences in international behavior then reflect these differences."[3] This view takes the rights of individuals to be basic and justifies a state policy that promotes these rights, not only domestically, but also internationally. The concept of "liberal peace" thus sets the parameters for Doyle's approach to the legacy of liberal thought. To justify his theory, he appeals to Kant's political philosophy.

Kant, in his philosophical essay "Toward Perpetual Peace" (1775), envisioned a lawful state in which "enlightened people" have control over decisions regarding war and have joined with other states in a peaceful federation. He also envisioned a gradual shift from an international to a cosmopolitan order. Kant indicates, in a concise form, the main causes of war and their solutions. He formulates six preliminary articles that he thinks are necessary to build mutual confidence. Further, the state of peace must be "formally instituted," and this requirement is formulated in a set of three definitive articles. The first definitive article requires that the civil constitution of each state be republican. Unlike a despotic (i.e., nonrepublican) form of government in which war can be easily declared without sufficient reason by the ruler, the republican constitution grants the citizens right of control over the major political decisions that affect them, such as war and peace. This gives a "favorable prospect" for perpetual peace because the citizenry would prefer to avoid suffering the calamities of war. Civil law, however, does not end the violent state of nature, since an internally peaceful state can be bellicose to other states. This cause of war, according to the second definite article, shall be removed by the right of nations based on "a federation of free states" (*foedus pacificum*).[4] The third definite article affirms the idea of a cosmopolitan right that will transform the political and international right into "a universal right of humanity." Kant believed that, by fulfilling these basic conditions, humanity could potentially advance toward a state of perpetual peace.

Approaching Kant's work from his own theoretical perspective, Doyle finds arguments regarding the relatively peaceful relations of liberal states with one another, but he has difficulties explaining why they are "unusually war-prone in their relations with non-Liberal states."[5] In Kant's first definite article, Doyle finds a valuable insight for his explanation of how the republican constitution and laws, principles of freedom, and representative government (with checks and balances and separation of power) provide favorable conditions for the liberal state to be more "cautious" regarding war and more peace-prone. But are the presence of liberal principles and republican institutions enough to ensure that a liberal state will be peaceful in its dealings with other states? Will republican constitutional and institutional safeguards always be strong enough to protect the citizens from the abuse of power and militaristic ambitions of politicians?

Kant's political philosophy appeals to the interactive nature of international relations, and Doyle largely adopts Kant's methodological approach concerning the systemic interrelations of states. However, Doyle also limits it by the assumption that "peace holds only in the interaction between Liberals" but not in relations between liberal and nonliberal states.[6] This assumption is reflected in his interpretation of Kant's second definitive article. Doyle's emphasis on "liberal republic" as the meaning of "state," and his substitution of "pacific federation of Liberal republics" for Kant's "federation of free states," changes the meaning of Kant's "federation," narrowing it to a separate alliance limited to exclusively liberal republics, and excluding nonliberal states.[7] "Liberal peace" is thus limited to a zone of liberal states, which are in a perpetual "state of war" with other states (labeled as nonliberal). It is hard to see how this could count as a true peace in Kantian terms.[8]

Kant first set his hopes for perpetual peace on "enlightened nations" gradually becoming republics that would seek peace and form peaceful alliances. But his idea of *foedus pacificum* is not limited to republican states and does not exclude the other states seeking peaceful alliances. As Kant's formulation of the second definitive article states: "The Right of Nations shall be based on a Federation of Free States."[9] In this formulation, as well as in his further explanation of this article, he refers to "states" and "nations" in a general sense, and not just to "republics." He speaks of "civilized people, each united within itself as a state,"[10] and he encourages them to submit to lawful peaceful alliances, in which the concept of international right will couple with a free federation. A peaceful federation, securing the freedom of each state, is viewed as inclusive, not exclusive: "For even if one of the parties were able to influence the others physically and yet itself remained in a state of nature, there would be a risk of war, which is precisely the aim of the above articles to prevent."[11]

III

Perpetual War for Liberal Peace?

IN THE "LIBERAL PEACE" THEORY, the differences in form of government between liberal and nonliberal states become an absolutely insurmountable barrier between the state of peace and the state of war. Doyle's argument is focused on the difference between liberal and nonliberal states with regard to the claim of publicity and human rights. Indeed, liberal states have more opportunities in such respect. But this advantage is viewed as a pretext for "a presumption of enmity," assuming that the nonliberal states are "not just" but "aggressive."

Respect for human rights is obviously important, but in Doyle's theory, it is viewed as an absolute criterion for determining relations of war and peace between liberal and nonliberal states. Nonliberal states are viewed as lacking legitimacy and having no real sovereignty, and as such, they "do not acquire the right to be free from foreign intervention."[12] Instead of searching for ways of promoting enforcement of human rights in the existing diverse (and imperfect) world, nonliberal states are viewed on Doyle's theory as "outlaw" states and excluded from international dialogue and cooperation, at least until such time as they become liberal states. Paradoxically, however, the concept of peace among states is held hostage (in Doyle's theory) to the requirement for nonliberal states to meet the human rights criteria by becoming liberal states—a goal that can only be achieved by a long-range process of socioeconomic development of these societies under conditions of peace. The state of war by itself thus remains an obstacle to this development, aggravating underdevelopment and providing an excuse for authoritarian regimes to keep people under coercive control and to repress democratic reform movements. By contrast, peaceful coexistence and cooperation would provide favorable conditions for the socioeconomic and political advancement of the societies, thus paving the way for their democratic development.

In commenting on Kant's three definite articles, Doyle indicates the sources of each of them: republican representation, international respect for individual rights, and transnational interdependence. As he writes:

> Immanuel Kant's 1795 essay "Perpetual Peace" offers a coherent explanation of important regularities in world politics: the tendencies of Liberal states simultaneously to be peace-prone in their relations with one another and unusually war-prone in their relations with non-Liberal states.[13]

Doyle presents these sources as "three necessary and together sufficient causes of the two regularities."[14] The role of these three sources as factors contributing to peace between liberal states is clear enough; but what is unclear is why they should be the "necessary" causes of "unusually war-prone" relations of liberal states toward nonliberal states, represented (in Doyle's theory) as an empirical "regularity" in global politics. Doyle claims that "Liberal republics see themselves as threatened by aggression from nonrepublics that are not constrained by representation."[15] This assumes, somewhat uncritically, that representative (republican) government always constrains aggressiveness and that nonrepresentative (nonrepublican) government does not. But Doyle goes further and insists that liberal republics may legitimately feel threatened by nonliberal ones, and thus may be legitimately "war-prone" toward them, even "irrespective of [any] actual threats to national security in relations between Liberal and non-Liberal societies."[16] What is the ground for such bellicosity? Doyle's answer is simply that the foreign policy goals of liberal states are designed to promote democracy overseas, even by force:

> And even though wars often cost more than the economic return they generate, Liberal republics are prepared to protect and promote— sometimes forcibly—democracy, private property, and the rights of individuals overseas in nonrepublics that, because they do not authentically represent the right of individuals, have incomplete right to noninterference.[17]

He admits: "These wars may liberate oppressed individuals overseas; [but] they also can generate enormous suffering."[18] Still, Doyle thinks that the price in suffering is worth paying since, in his view, the only way toward world peace is through spreading democracy, sometimes forcibly, and through the global expansion of the liberal zone: "the occasion for wars with non-Liberals would disappear as non-Liberal regimes disappeared."[19] Many critics, however, see this as a recipe for "perpetual war" rather than "perpetual peace."

Yet Doyle insists that this theory, which promotes war in the name of democracy and peace, is perfectly compatible with Kant, thus portraying Kant as an adherent of "liberal peace." As Doyle writes:

> Kant's own position is ambiguous. He regards most of these wars as unjust and warns liberals of their susceptibility to them. At the same time, Kant argues that each nation "can and ought to" demand that its neighboring nations enter into the pacific union of liberal states—that is, become republican.[20]

Here, Kant is portrayed not as a consistent principled champion of peace but rather as "ambiguous," as making an exception for (and morally justifying) the forcible "republicanization" of other states.

However, the passages from Kant's "Toward Perpetual Peace" to which Doyle refers show that Kant was unequivocally consistent in his condemnation of war. The first reference is from Kant's explanation of the third definite article on cosmopolitan right, in which he condemns colonial wars and points out the "*inhospitable* conduct of the civilized states" and "the injustice they display in *visiting* foreign countries" and actually conquering them. As an example, Kant mentions the colonization of India, to which "foreign troops were brought in under the pretext of merely setting up trading posts."[21] The second reference is from Kant's second definite article about the rights of nations based on the federation of free states:

> Each nation, for the sake of its own security, can and ought to demand of the others that they should enter along with it into a constitution, similar to the civil one, within which the rights of each could be secured. This would mean establishing a *federation of peoples.*[22]

Here, Kant writes about the moral obligation of states to seek their security and peace through lawful alliances with their neighbors. Kant's "ought" refers to the moral obligation of each nation to seek peaceful alliances with other states and, therefore, to be open and inclusive. The purpose of this is the collective security of the members of the federation, not forcing them all to become republican states. Contrary to Doyle's claim, there is no "ambiguity" in these passages; Kant is consistent in condemning war and championing peace. Kant also mentions the *rights of peace*, which include "the right to form *alliances* or confederate leagues of several states for the purpose of communal defense against any possible attacks from internal or external sources." But he emphasizes the difference of these alliances from expansionist military-political blocs, insisting that "these [alliances] must never become leagues for promoting aggression and internal expansion."[23]

According to Doyle's interpretation, "the Kantian peace has two tracks."[24] The first track is transnational and is related to commerce, cultural and other transnational ties, the role of global civil society in politics, and a commitment to human rights. "The second Kantian track is the international track of war."[25] As Doyle explains, human beings have been driven into forming liberal republics by the pressures of war. The "positive outcome" of war is that the pressure of war creates incentives for authoritarian rulers to grant popular participation, to cede representation and republican institutions. But he also notes that "the Kantian logic of war may find itself supplemented by a nuclear logic of destruction."[26] While the two tracks use different means—"the transnational track creates incentives for conflict as well as cooperation; the international track of war obviously presupposes war in the first place"—both tracks help engender liberal regimes and expand pacific union.[27] According to Doyle's optimistic calculations, all the states will become republican by the year 2050.[28] However, there is no guarantee, in Doyle's theory, that the forcible spread of democracy might not trigger a quite different scenario, one that Doyle even mentions in his earlier articles regarding "educative wars" in a nuclear age: "Long before the nations completed their process of graduation into republicanism, a nuclear wasteland might well have reduced them to barbarism."[29]

It seems clear that many of Doyle's ideas of "liberal peace" and "spreading democracy" are at odds with both the letter and spirit of Kant's work. For example, Kant's fifth preliminary article of perpetual peace explicitly requires that: "No state shall forcibly interfere in the constitution and government of another state."[30] Moreover, Kant's goal of lasting peace is perfectly consistent with peaceful legal means for achieving it. In the conclusion to the section on "Cosmopolitan Right" in "The Theory of Right," Kant says the following:

> Now, moral-practical reason within us pronounces the following irresistible veto: *There shall be no war*, either between individual human beings in the state of nature, or between separate states. . . . For war is not the way in which anyone should pursue his rights.[31]

It is only under peaceful conditions that the security and property of "people living together as neighbors under a single constitution can be guaranteed by *law*."[32] Kant also warns against misguided attempts "to put it [perpetual peace] into practice overnight by revolution," that is, by forcibly changing a constitution. Instead, he suggests that gradual reforms are "the only means for continually approaching the supreme political good—perpetual peace."[33]

According to Doyle's interpretation, "Kant assumed that republics formed an endpoint of political evolution: 'the highest task nature has set mankind.'"[34] Thus, the politico-economical "processes of nature" and its purposive plan are driving mankind toward "liberal peace." Doyle even claims to see a confirmation of the objective "regularities" of "democratic peace" in world politics, and he thinks this implies a justification for "spreading democracy," even if it requires sacrifices and causes "enormous suffering." However, it seems clear that the goals of "liberal peace" and the means for attaining it are far removed from Kant's concept of "perpetual peace." For Kant, a cosmopolitan order of law and peace is no mere utopia, but a feasible long-range project for humanity. He even saw signs of the possibility of its realization—for example, in the "spirit of commerce" of his day, in the peaceful character of republics, and in the function of the political public sphere—all of which he articulated as an "intention of nature." Kant's teleological philosophy of history has been rightly criticized (along with the 19th-century "meta-narratives" of Hegel and others), and while it clearly stands in need of modification, it nonetheless continues to possess a normative relevance. As Karl-Otto Apel writes: "Once we rethink teleology in terms of opportunities to realize the cosmopolitan order of law and peace in history, it is also possible to reevaluate Kant's assessment of the positive means that help realize these goals."[35]

In summary, the theory of "liberal democratic peace," with its idea of liberal states expanding, even forcibly, their "zone" of control and peace, seems to be pointing more toward a "world republic" or "world hegemony" rather than toward a Kantian "federation of free states." Overall, it represents an alternative to the Kantian path of world peace through peaceful federation and cosmopolitan law and, as such, it is hard to see how the "democratic peace" project could guaranty either a robust, worldwide democracy or a universal and just peace.

IV

From an International to a Cosmopolitan Order

IN CONTRAST TO "democratic peace" theories, there exists another trend that approaches the problems of global peace and human rights from a broader, more cosmopolitan perspective. This trend is represented by "discourse ethicists," such as Karl-Otto Apel and Jürgen Habermas, and by adherents of "cosmopolitan democracy," such as David Held, Martha Nussbaum, Kenneth Baynes, James Bohman, Amartya Sen, Stephen Anthony Appiah, and Patrick Hayden, among others. Amid the diversity of voices in the new cosmopolitan movement, one can identify two main tendencies: one emphasizes identification with humanity as a whole and "world-citizenship," and the other emphasizes ethics and the protection of the cultural diversity of nations and minority groups. Yet for all of these cosmopolitan philosophers, Kant serves as a source of inspiration in the search for solutions to today's problems. And while most of them believe that Kant's theory needs modification, they all insist it continues to possess normative relevance.

Many of these philosophers view the contemporary period as a transitional phase from an international to a cosmopolitan order. They endorse the development of international law and institutions such as the United Nations, as well as transnational democratic movements, as vehicles for the realization of this cosmopolitan order. From this perspective they explore the problems of peace and human rights protection as well as other important issues concerning international law, national sovereignty, and the problem of nonliberal societies.

"Democratic peace" theory has a serious lacuna in its treatment of international law: international law is narrowly interpreted in this theory as merely a "guarantee of respect" or "international respect for individual rights" (cf. Doyle's comments on Kant's second definite article). This narrows the meaning of international law in two important respects. First, it underestimates the role of international law as an instrument for preventing war and securing peace. The factors of mutual confidence among states, mentioned by Doyle (representative governments, shared values, publicity and transparency of foreign policy, and commercial ties) are certainly helpful, but they are no substitute for the legal mechanisms—international law and institutions—that secure peaceful relations. For the last half-century, international law and the United Nations as its political representative have served as a basis for the collective security of all nations. Second, this interpretation seems to equate the universal "principles of law" with the legislative autonomy of a democratic state. The "liberal peace" theory, which views the republican state as exclusive and juxtaposes a liberal "zone" of law and peace to nonliberal states, assumes that international law is solely the product and realm of the republican states. But can a democratic state or group of states by themselves legislate international law?

Western liberal democracies, in forging their constitutions and laws, have also contributed to the development of international law. There now exists an internal relationship of sorts between democracy and law. A democratic state can provide the necessary conditions for citizens to freely discuss moral and legal norms, aiming for consensus. The fundamental rights of citizens are grounded in the constitution of a democratic state. But is the legislative role of democracy in the constitution of positive law (by the sovereignty of a people) enough to ground universally valid law, or the validity-claim of "human rights" as international law?

The problem of internal relations and differences between the legislative functions of the democratic state and universal law is addressed by discourse ethics theory, which was developed by Karl-Otto Apel and Jürgen Habermas. According to this theory, there is a close affinity between "discourse ethics" as an ethics of responsibility and a normative theory of democracy. Kant's theory of the categorical imperative is reformulated by discourse ethics into a principle of argumentative universalization, according to which universally valid norms should be acceptable with regard to their expected conse-quences for all affected persons.[36] The transcendental-pragmatic prin-ciple of discourse ethics provides a moral foundation for the positive law of a liberal-democratic state as well as for international law. Universal law secures the rights of human beings as virtual cosmo-politan citizens. Accordingly, any national law can be challenged if it contradicts human rights. In light of this cosmopolitan dimension of international relations, citizens can promote democratically the nec-essary reforms and changes in the policies of their states.[37] As Apel notes, republics and representative democracies have provided "a model of a legal order based on the type of positive rights and constitutions that point toward their development in a cosmopolitan order." But he warns against the idealization of the republican state: "One should not simply equate the model of the republican 'principle of democracy' and its principle of 'national sovereignty' with the global realization of the 'principle of law' postulated by Kant."[38] The various democratic states as self-maintaining systems have their own political interests, which are different from universal "principles of law" (such as human rights) whose moral and legal justification "directs us to a cosmopolitan legal order." The republican constitu-tional state by itself does not guarantee peace: it only "opens up a world-historical opportunity to act on the 'moral duty' to realize a cosmopolitan order of law and peace."[39] Therefore, the realization of these opportunities depends on people and is related to moral duty and co-responsibility.

One can argue that many of the traditional problems in international law stem from a certain dualism in the law's normative orientation. (These problems, in turn, are still reflected in the current UN Charter.) On the one hand, there is a primary orientation in international law toward the preservation of peace by prohibiting the violation of the sovereignty of individual states. (Historically, this follows from the 1648 Treaty of Westphalia that ended the Thirty Years' War.) On the other hand, there is also a concern for human rights and, in the case of their brutal violation, enforcement through a mandate from the UN Security Council (thus limiting the sovereignty of states). In his political philosophy, Kant addressed the tension between these two orientations. Initially, in "Theory and Practice" (1773), Kant thought of an analogy to the civil state among individual human beings: all states should freely submit themselves to the "universal state of all people." But later, in "Toward Perpetual Peace," he made an important step in developing his cosmopolitan ideal by replacing the "world republic" with a "federation of free states." In a world state, each person's rights would be limited to the rights of citizens of a state, but there would be no cosmopolitan rights of a world citizen. Instead, Kant proposed a pacific league of nations (*foedus pacificum*), and he called for a basic shift from an international to a cosmopolitan order. Cosmopolitan law unifies peoples globally, beyond their nation-states, thus yielding strong pacifying effects.

An important issue in thinking about cosmopolitanism is national sovereignty. A number of philosophers have discussed Kant's principle of the internal sovereignty of nations as a condition of global order. These philosophers question the unqualified principle of internal sovereignty as a part of existing international law. Some consider the "sovereignty of states" an obstacle to accountability and legal enforcement of human rights on a global scale. They emphasize instead the necessity for executive, legislative, and judicial components to world organizations transcending the nation-states. Still others see the universalism of cosmopolitan law as overly unifying in contrast to the sociocultural diversity of existing societies.

Jürgen Habermas, for one, states that the challenge posed by the wars of the 20th century and by globalization has given new impetus to Kant's idea of a cosmopolitan order. He indicates the "contradictory character" of Kant's concept of federation and asserts that such a "union of peoples" needs to be not merely a moral but also a legal arrangement. Habermas considers the regulation in the Charter of the United Nations (Article 2) as ambiguous, both limiting and guaranteeing the sovereignty of individual states. His position seems to be that the autonomy of citizens should not be mediated by the sovereignty of states: "The point of cosmopolitan law is, rather, that it goes over the heads of the collective subjects of international law to give legal status to the individual subjects and justifies their unmediated membership in the association of free and equal world citizens."[40] He views the future world order as "the postnational constellation."[41] He also believes that a properly reformed United Nations could implement and enforce this legal status for human rights, and he makes some suggestions for such reforms.

Habermas characterizes the contemporary world situation as "a period of transition from international to cosmopolitan law," but at the same time, he also sees some indications of a regression to nationalism and chauvinistic ethnocentrism. He expresses concern about the recent tendency toward "superpower unilateralism" in the international arena via U.S. policies that promote the "spread of democracy," even by military force. He analyzes the challenge created by the recent war in Iraq to international law, to the role of the United Nations, and to a future world order. He points out that the U.S. invasion was in violation of international law in that neither of the two preconditions for a legally permissible use of military force existed: the war was neither a case of self-defense against an imminent Iraqi attack, nor was there an appropriate Security Council resolution according to Chapter VII of the UN Charter.[42] Habermas also questions whether the "regime change" in Iraq and the proclaimed goal of "spreading democracy" can justify American unilateralism. As he observes, with the UN Charter there are no more "just and unjust wars," only legal or illegal ones under international law: "A war in violation of international law remains illegal even if it leads to normatively desirable outcomes."[43]

Habermas emphasizes that humanitarian interventions must be strictly regulated by the UN Charter requirements. Because innocent lives are at risk, the required force "must be so finely regulated that the declared motives of a world-police action will lose the odour of pretext, and as such, be capable of winning worldwide acceptance."[44] He further shows the contradictions of the unilateral imposition of democracy and human rights by military force. Not only is the achievement of this proclaimed goal by military means problematic, the use of such means has already shown negative consequences by undermining an international order based on international law and institutions. The military implementation of a politics of hegemonic unilateralism (presented under the guise of a global civilizing force) has side effects that are in conflict with its own normative criteria and mission of ameliorating the world. The increased militarization of life abroad, as well as domestically, has led to the curtailment of fundamental law as well as to the infringement of the civil liberties of U.S. citizens.

Habermas is highly sceptical about the central claim made by liberal internationalists that "wars that make the world better need no *further* justification."[45] His criticism strikes at the core of the "democratic peace" doctrine in both its neoliberal and neoconservative versions. Habermas points out the danger inherent in the moralization and ideologization of international relations, which can lead to a growing fundamentalism. His basic thesis is that "justice between nations" cannot be achieved through moralizing, but only through the legalization of international relations.

What is in dispute here is not the normative goals of democratization and justice between nations but the means to achieve these goals. Habermas critically analyzes the neoconservatives' attempts to justify unilateralism and to offer up their own alternative to the domestication of state power through international law and the policies of the United Nations. For them, "international law is finished as a *medium* for the resolution of conflicts between states, and for the advancement of democracy and human rights."[46] They make the "revolutionary" claim that "if the regime of international law fails, then the hegemonic imposition of a global liberal order is justified, even by means that are hostile to international law."[47] Their vision of a U.S. global political order "has definitely broken with the reformist program of UN human rights policies." Moreover, this vision of goals "is shattering the civil limits that the UN Charter—with good reason—had placed on their realization."[48] Habermas expresses grave concern that "[t]he Bush administration, with moralistic phrases *ad acta*, has laid aside the 220-year-old Kantian project for the *legalizing* of international relations."[49]

Habermas distinguishes between universally valid law, such as international law, and pseudo-universalism with its pretensions to universalize one's own values (which is nothing more than ethnocentrism). He argues for an "egalitarian universalism" that, he thinks, is imminent in law and in its procedures and that promotes multilateral

will-formation in interstate relations. Moreover, the idea of equal
treatment, related to the law of peoples as of states and to the
vocabulary of human rights, can serve opposition and liberation
movements as the standard for an ideological critique of the abuse of
"spreading democracy" by hegemonic power. Habermas further differentiates between the pseudo-universal "imperial claim" that the
political culture of a particular state is an example for the rest of the
world, and "the universal validity claim" that commits Western democracies to the procedure of democratic self-determination and human
rights. As he writes: "It is precisely the universalistic core of democracy
and human rights that forbids their unilateral realization at gunpoint."[50]

In examining the UN core mission of maintaining peace and the
global enforcement of human rights, Habermas emphasizes its paramount importance for today's world. He calls for "a confirmation and
transformation of international law and its institutions, in particular the
UN," for promotion of a cosmopolitan order, and for a new approach
to the distribution of state authority "that refers back to the Kantian
tradition."[51] As he concludes: "There is no sensible alternative to the
ongoing development of international law into a cosmopolitan order
that offers an equal and reciprocal hearing for the voices of all those
affected."[52]

V

Cosmopolitan Democracy and the Human Right to Peace

MANY AUTHORS SEE THE NEED for regulatory instruments at the supranational level and for global government. However, they mostly agree
that this should not involve the simple transference of sovereignty to
the supranational level; and they try to find a balance between the
local and the global. Some of them introduce the concept of democracy into Kant's cosmopolitanism. David Held, Kenneth Baynes, James
Bohman, Daniele Archibugi, and Patrick Hayden, among others, refer
to Kant in sketching "the cosmopolitan model of democracy."

Cosmopolitan democracy offers an alternative to liberal internationalism. While both address the themes of peace and human rights, they
differ significantly in their approach to these themes. Liberal international theories, including that of "democratic peace," have tended to

dominate discourse in the post–Cold War world. However, they are limited in their approach by the existing framework of international order (which they do not seek to change) and by the economic status quo and U.S. hegemony (which they generally support). Cosmopolitanism, by contrast, provides a fundamentally different normative focus to international political theory by placing the individual human being at the center of global politics. Cosmopolitan theorists are critical of the democratic deficit in the current international order, and they have striven to develop a cosmopolitan democracy model for global governance. Their guiding principles are: moral universalism, which is rooted in Kant's philosophy and that promotes the idea that every human being is qualified for equal membership in the universal human community; the "juridification" of basic rights as the process of democratic legitimation; and the development of transnational institutions as the basis for juridical norms and principles of cosmopolitan justice.[53]

Cosmopolitanism expands the ideas of human rights and peace into the concepts of "human security" and the "human right to peace." In response to the limitations of the traditional view of security, cosmopolitanism provides the basis for a more expansive concept of "human security," defined as the protection and welfare of the individual human being. The "human security" approach deals with all forms of violence, and its goal is the preservation of human well-being. Its concern is not just for the citizens of a particular state, but for all of the citizens of the world.[54] It calls for shifts from power struggles and militarism toward dialogue and multilateral efforts aimed at eliminating war and providing conditions for peaceful and dignified human life.

Human rights, given their universal and cosmopolitan character, provide a normative basis to advance claims to human security. From the vantage point of human rights (and most importantly the right to peace) it is possible to discuss the most serious consequences of war and other violent threats to human existence.[55] The guarantee of the protection of the right to peace is understood holistically. This approach helps researchers in developing the comprehensive concept of peace, which means not merely absence of fighting, but a condition of liberty and security in the absence of aggression itself.[56] The comprehensive concept of peace includes "the capabilities approach," which deals with those "central human capabilities" without which our life would not be human.[57] It also deals with the quality and conditions of existence itself and includes the capabilities to survive and live a healthy life, to enjoy a decent standard of living, and to exercise civil and political freedoms.[58]

The cosmopolitan perspective "regards war as *generally illegitimate* and requires strong justification for particular instances of warfare as genuinely *humanitarian exceptions* to an otherwise comprehensive interdiction of the use of military force."[59] It emphasizes that such exceptions for "human security crises" should only be recognized as legitimate by a UN Security Council resolution and not simply for the purpose of furthering "national interests." Hayden, for one, notices the emergence of regressive tendencies, such as "military and rights-violating behavior already witnessed in the 'war on terrorism,' which challenge the egalitarian and humanitarian principles of cosmopolitanism."[60] The cosmopolitan concept of human security and the right to peace de-legitimizes war and organized violence as means for politics. It offers an alternative to the traditional security dilemma and to the "democratic peace" and "just war" theories by stressing the emergence of global security structures guided by the humanitarian norms of just and lasting peace. As such, the principles of cosmopolitanism serve as a basis for developing a system of global governance and global civil society.

The basic steps in approximating Kant's cosmopolitan ideal, including the project of a "federation of free states," were marked by the development of international law and institutions, including the League of Nations in 1919 after World War I and later the foundation of the United Nations in 1945 after World War II. The United Nations was created as a worldwide organization in scope and membership, open to the participation of every state that agreed on its principles and fulfilled the obligations assumed by them in accordance with the UN Charter. It is tolerant of differences in forms of government and constitutions. The United Nations faced great perils during the Cold War, and now it is challenged by the "democratic peace" and "just war" project of a hegemonic "world state." Today's United Nations is far from being an ideal implementation of Kant's *foedus pacificum*. Its many failures in protecting human rights show that a satisfactory global order of law has not yet been realized. Nevertheless, it serves as an important mechanism for preventing war through cooperation among the major powers in the transitional stage from an international to a cosmopolitan order. Many philosophers view the current United Nations as being in the process of growth and improvement through reforms; and as Apel observes, a properly reformed United Nations could, on Kantian terms, "be entirely suitable for making possible the next phase in approximating the ideal order of peace and law founded on a federation of free peoples."[61] The strengthening of international cooperation and the joint efforts of all nations in finding the solutions to war and other global problems could break the vicious circle of violence and pave the way toward the more peaceful development of humanity on the planet.

Notes

1. A critique of the "democratic peace" theory from different perspectives is expressed in many publications. Among the recent ones are: Kozhemiakin, Alexander V. (1998). *Expanding the Zone of Peace? Democratization and International Security*. New York: St. Martin's Press; Gilbert, Alan. (1999). *Must Global Politics Constrain Democracy? Great Power Realism, Democratic Peace, and Democratic Internationalism*. Princeton, NJ: Princeton University Press; Gowa, Joanne. (1999). *Ballots and Bullets: The Elusive Democratic Peace*. Princeton, NJ: Princeton University Press; Linden, Harry van der. (2001). "Beyond the Liberal Peace Project: Toward Peace with Justice." *Journal of Social Philosophy* 32(3): 419–430; Ivie, Robert L. (2005). *Democracy and America's War on Terror*. Tuscaloosa, AL: University of Alabama Press.

2. Doyle (1997: 284, 252).

3. Ibid., 211.

4. Kant (1991: 102, 104).

5. Doyle (1997: 284).

6. Ibid., 252.

7. Doyle (1997: 257).

8. In contrast to the "liberal peace" dichotomy, various scholars have made efforts to theoretically express and articulate the diversity of today's world. One of the most influential efforts comes from John Rawls and his theory of "the law of peoples," which distinguishes five different types of society. Rawls interprets Kant's idea of *foedus pacificum* as the idea of a social contract extending to the Society of Peoples. His theory retains both the

Kantian pluralism of states and a concept of international justice, and it extends the liberal political ideas of right and justice in two steps. The first step is to liberal societies, and the second to "nonliberal though decent peoples" that meet certain conditions of respecting human rights and do not have aggressive aims, thus being acceptable as members in good standing in a Society of Peoples. See Rawls, John. (1999). *The Law of Peoples.* Cambridge, Harvard University Press, 6, 62–64. However, Rawls's theory lacks a philosophical foundation. His development of "the Law of Peoples" out of a liberal idea of justice is an attempt to universalize his conception of "justice as fairness." His parallels between domestic and international relations, between relations of free and equal citizens within a democratic state and of "free and equal peoples in the Society of Peoples" imply that the subjects of a just relationship are no longer persons as cosmopolitan citizens but "peoples," i.e., sovereign states. As J. Habermas commented on Rawls's *The Law of Peoples,* this book "has been justly criticized because he relaxes the strong principles of justice . . . and places the guardianship of these weakened principles in the hands of individual democratic states" (Habermas, 2004).

9. Kant (1991: 102).
10. Ibid., 103.
11. Ibid., 99.
12. Doyle (1996: 31–32).
13. Doyle (1997: 284).
14. Ibid., 284; Doyle (2005: 463–466).
15. Doyle (1997: 308).
16. Doyle (1997: 284).
17. Ibid., 308.
18. Ibid., 308.
19. Ibid., 257n.
20. Ibid., 282.
21. Kant (1991: 106).
22. Ibid., 102.
23. Kant, MM (1991: 170).
24. Doyle (1997: 475).
25. Ibid., 476.
26. Doyle (1996: 54–55).
27. Doyle (1997: 481).
28. Ibid., 481.
29. Doyle (1996: 55).
30. Kant (1991: 96).
31. Ibid., 174.
32. Ibid., 174.
33. Ibid., 175.
34. Doyle (1996: 55).

35. Apel (1997: 100).
36. Apel (1996: 165).
37. Apel (1999: 2001).
38. Apel (1997: 101).
39. Ibid., 101.
40. Habermas (1997: 128).
41. Habermas (2001).
42. Habermas (2003: 365).
43. Ibid., 364.
44. Habermas (2004).
45. Habermas (2003: 367).
46. Habermas (2004).
47. Habermas (2003: 365).
48. Ibid.
49. Habermas (2004).
50. Habermas (2003: 369).
51. Habermas and Derrida (2005).
52. Habermas (2003: 370).
53. Hayden (2005: 34).
54. Falk (2003).
55. Shue (1996).
56. Walzer (1997: 51).
57. See Nussbaum (1999: 41–42, 2002: 69).
58. Sen (1999: 6–11).
59. Hayden (2005: 90).
60. Ibid., 155.
61. Apel (1997: 80).

References

Apel, Karl-Otto. (1996). *Selected Essays*, vol. 2, ed. Eduardo Mendieta. Amherst, NY: Humanity Books.
———. (1997). "Kant's 'Toward Perpetual Peace' as Historical Prognosis from the Point of View of Moral Duty." In *Perpetual Peace: Essays on Kant's Cosmopolitan Ideal*, eds. James Bohman and Matthias Lutz-Bachmann. Cambridge: MIT Press.
———. (1999). "The Problem of Justice in a Multicultural Society." In *Questioning Ethics, Contemporary Debates in Philosophy*, eds. Richard Kearney and Mark Dooley. New York: Routledge.
———. (2001). "On the Relationship Between Ethics, International Law and Politico-Military Strategy of Our Time: A Philosophical Retrospective on the Kosovo Conflict." *European Journal of Social Theory* 4(1): 29–39.

Doyle, Michael W. (1996). "Kant, Liberal Legacies, and Foreign Affairs." In *Debating the Democratic Peace*, eds. Michael E. Brown, Sean M. Lynn-Jones, and Steven Miller. Cambridge: MIT Press.

———. (1997). *Ways of War and Peace, Realism, Liberalism, and Socialism.* New York: W.W. Norton.

———. (2005). "Three Pillars of the Liberal Peace." *American Political Science Review* 99(3): 463–466.

Falk, Richard. (2003). *The Great Terror War.* New York: Olive Branch Press.

Habermas, Jürgen. (1997). "Kant's Idea of Perpetual Peace, with the Benefit of Two Hundred Years' Hindsight." In *Perpetual Peace: Essays on Kant's Cosmopolitan Ideal*, eds. James Bohman and Matthias Lutz-Bachman. Cambridge: MIT Press.

———. (2001). *The Postnational Constellation: Political Essays.* Cambridge: MIT Press.

———. (2003). "Interpreting the Fall of a Monument." *Constellations* 10(3): 364–370.

———. (2004). "America and the World: A Conversation with Jürgen Habermas," an interview with Eduardo Mendieta. *Logos: A Journal of Modern Society & Culture* 3(3) (Summer), http://www.logosjournal.com/habermas_america.pdf.

Habermas, Jürgen, and Jacques Derrida. (2005). "February 15, or What Binds Europeans Together: A Plea for a Common Foreign Policy, Beginning in the Core of Europe." In *Old Europe, New Europe, Core Europe: Transatlantic Relations After the Iraq War*, eds. Daniel Levy, Max Pensky, and John Torpey. New York: Verso. This article originally appeared in the *Frankfurter Allgemine Zeitung*, May 31, 2003.

Hayden, Patrick. (2005). *Cosmopolitan Global Politics.* Burlington, VT: Ashgate.

Kant, Immanuel. (1991). "Perpetual Peace: A Philosophical Sketch." In *Kant's Political Writings*, 2nd ed., ed. Hans Reiss. Cambridge: Cambridge University Press.

———. (1991). "The Metaphysics of Morals." In *Kant's Political Writings*, 2nd ed., ed. Hans Reiss. Cambridge: Cambridge University Press. ["MM" in text]

Nussbaum, Martha. (1999). *Sex and Social Justice.* Oxford: Oxford University Press.

———. (2002). *Women and Human Development: The Capabilities Approach.* Oxford: Oxford University Press.

Sen, Amartya. (1999). *Commodities and Capabilities.* New Delhi: Oxford University Press.

Shue, Henry. (1996). *Basic Rights, Subsistence, Affluence, and U.S. Foreign Policy*, 2nd ed. Princeton, NJ: Princeton University Press.

Walzer, M. (1997). *Just and Unjust Wars*, 3rd ed. New York: Basic Books.

2
Discourse Ethics, Democracy, and International Law

Toward a Globalization of Practical Reason

By Karl-Otto Apel*

ABSTRACT. This paper deals with the foundational "architectonics" (Kantian) at the ground of the internal relation between the three concepts raised in the title. First, I provide a short introduction into the ultimate foundation of practical philosophy by the *transcendental-pragmatic conception of discourse ethics*. Then, I discuss the foundational relation between *discourse ethics, positive law,* and *democracy* as a *constitutional state of law*. Finally, I explore the foundational relation between human rights as part of universal law, the democratic state of law, and international law or *jus gentium*. By taking issue with Kant, Habermas, and Rawls, I try to show that a rational foundation of ethics, as well as a rational approach to the traditional problems of international law, is only possible through a critical transformation of Kant's approach via a *transcendental-pragmatic* conception of *discourse ethics*.

I

Introduction: In View of a Foundational "Architectonics" of Practical Philosophy

In what follows, I want to make an "architectonical" comment on the internal relationship among the three topics that I have raised for discussion: *discourse ethics, democracy,* and *international law.* My

---

*Prof. Dr. Karl-Otto Apel is Professor Emeritus at the Johann Wolfgang Goethe University in Frankfurt, Germany, and one of Europe's leading moral and social theorists. His many books include *Towards a Transformation of Philosophy* (1980), *Towards a Transcendental Semiotics* (1993), *Ethics and the Theory of Rationality* (1996), and *The Response of Discourse Ethics* (2001).

American Journal of Economics and Sociology, Vol. 66, No. 1 (January, 2007).

comment is to be "architectonical" in the Kantian sense, concerning the place of the three topics within a transcendental foundation of practical philosophy.

In what follows, I will first give a roughly sketched account of the transcendental-pragmatic foundation of *discourse ethics* as a basic precondition of practical philosophy; second, I will comment on the relationship between *discourse ethics* and *positive law*. In both parts of my discussion, I shall also give an argument dealing with Habermas's understanding of "architectonics" as outlined in his book *Between Facts and Norms*.[1] Finally, I will make some remarks on the foundational relationship between *human rights* and *democracy*, on the one hand, and the actual problems of *international law* (*jus gentium*), on the other. In this last part of my essay, I shall also give an argument against the late John Rawls's conception of the *law of peoples*.[2]

II

On the Transcendental-Pragmatic Foundation of Discourse Ethics

I SHOULD FIRST SAY that I am well aware that any talk of "transcendental," especially in connection with "foundation," sounds outmoded today. It is often equated with a *metaphysical fundamentalism* or *foundationalism* and, as such, it could be seen as offering an obsolete paradigm of philosophy.

In this vein, Richard Rorty and also my friend Jürgen Habermas propagate "de-transcendentalization" as a methodological precondition of any modern, topical philosophy. Now, I admit that Kant could not avoid entangling or reentangling himself in metaphysical foundationalism. The problem is already present in his theoretical philosophy, especially in his supposition that "things-in-themselves" are unknowable, but it is just as much present in his practical philosophy, especially in his making the foundation of practical philosophy rest on the supposition that there are two realms or "worlds" (one of unconditioned "perfect virtue" and the other of empirically conditioned "human law") whose citizens are simply human beings. But these metaphysical features of Kant's philosophy, I think, contradict the spirit of his critical distinction between the "transcendental" (i.e., the conditions of the possibility of empirical validity) and the "transcendent" (i.e., what could only be conceived from God's point of view). And I have come to the conviction that Kant's metaphysical suppositions can be avoided by a *transformation of classical transcendentalism.*[3] Let me elaborate.

The Kantian distinction between unknowable "things-in-themselves" and mere "appearances" can be replaced, I propose, by the Peircean distinction between the "real" as the "knowable" (in the long run) and what cannot, as yet, be "known." Also, the supposition that both Descartes and Kant share of the "I think" (the "*cogito*"), which, as Husserl recognized, implies a "transcendental solipsism," can be replaced by the transcendental supposition of "I argue" as a member of a discourse community. The "I argue" implies the use of language and intersubjective communication. It follows, then, that we can also transform Kant's foundation of *practical philosophy.* For example, in the case of the transcendent "kingdom of ends," namely, a community of reciprocal relations among purely reasonable beings (which Kant needed in order to ground the validity of his "categorical imperative"), we can now say that this is just a *metaphysical anticipation of the transcendental* presupposition of an *ideal communication community.* This presupposition, in turn, is necessarily connected with any serious argument that, by virtue of its universal claim to validity, must implicitly postulate universal acceptability.

I am suggesting with this presupposition that the ideal communication community is also the nonmetaphysical but transcendental-pragmatic basis of *discourse ethics,* as I have tried to show since around 1970.[4] I want to add that, in my opinion, there is no other possibility of grounding normative ethics on what Kant called the (nonempirical) "fact of reason." And this means that we should avoid any derivation of moral norms from empirical facts or from "transcendent" (metaphysical) suppositions. The meaning of Kant's "fact of reason," I suggest, can be explicated as follows.

It belongs to the "self-consistency of reason" (Kant's *Selbsteinstimmigkeit der Vernunft*) that we cannot dispute, on pain of committing self-contradiction in our argument, that in serious argumentation we have already necessarily acknowledged certain *fundamental norms of discourse ethics:* namely, that we are all partners of an unlimited discourse community, having equal rights and, I emphasize, also equal co-responsibility for solving all communal problems. In this way, the fundamental norms require us to actively seek solutions for all moral problems as well, but only in accordance with the procedural rules of a serious discourse, that is to say, without open or concealed strategic use of language and, of course, without the intervention of violence. In the case of moral problems, we have also acknowledged that, along with the procedural rules of discourse, we should justify norms of action in accordance with a *principle of universalization*—a principle that, on the level of discourse ethics, roughly corresponds to Kant's first formulation of the "categorical imperative." It states that valid norms that have to be universally followed should be acceptable with regard to their expectable consequences by all affected persons.

Jürgen Habermas, who has also formulated this principle, recently declared that it is not yet an "imperative" of discourse ethics, but only a "rule of argumentation" for "practical discourses."[5] As I understand it, this means that for Habermas the *principle of discourse ethics* (or, rather, of "moral philosophy"[6]) cannot be grounded immediately by recourse to the "discourse principle," but only on the level of application of the practical discourse, that is, together and equiprimordially with law.[7] Thus, the "discourse principle" that makes up the normative basis of "discourse theory" (and no longer of "discourse ethics"![8]) is "morally neutral" according to the recent position of Habermas, since only the applicative differentiation of practical discourse constitutes the norms of morals and of law.

According to my *foundational architectonics*, however, I would partly confirm and partly contradict this Habermasian approach. First, I should insist that the *discourse principle* is not "morally neutral" and that the *universalization principle*, which immediately follows from the discourse principle, is not only a rule of argumentation but a moral imperative as well. For without these two principles that are transcendentally implied in the conditions of serious argumentation, the ethical conditions of the application of discourse to the empirical-life world would not be grounded; and thus, the very obligation of settling concrete moral problems by practical discourses, which Habermas acknowledges as a basic feature of practical discourse, would also remain ungrounded. And without this grounding, the application of the moral norms would lack the validity derived from the universalization principle. This would mean that any practical discussions that are not connected a priori with the ethical co-responsibility of those who in the real-life world argue for the solution of communal problems could not hope to succeed by recourse to practical discourse. Rather, lacking the principles of universality and discourse ethics, such "problem solving" could violate basic morality and (by the strategic use of language) even lead to violence. Hence, I conclude from this disagreement with Habermas that the entire point of establishing and defending the foundation of discourse ethics would be lost.

On the other hand, it is also true that the responsible application of discourse ethics and its universalization principle raises a special problem that does not seem to arise for Kantian ethics. Since the *application* of discourse ethics depends on the possibility of real discourses with all affected persons in order to take into account all interests (including value preferences) of the affected persons, it is obviously dependent on the cooperation of those persons (or, in the case of those who cannot speak for themselves, their advocates). From this condition it follows that a *responsible application* of discourse ethics is situated, as it were, between two polar opposites.

At the one pole, there is the situation that is counterfactually anticipated in every serious discourse: the situation of an *ideal communication community*. Only in this case, we can, or rather could, directly apply the norms that follow from the *universalization principle*. But the other pole is constituted by the possibility of a complete refusal of communicative cooperation by our virtual partners in the life-world; they might prefer strategic negotiations or open conflict, even war, to practical discourses. In reality, the application situation for discourse ethics may be located somewhere between the two poles. This means that even in the numerous public dialogues and conferences of our day about human moral problems in the broadest sense, we are more or less confronted with a willingness to practical discourses, open or concealed forms of bargaining, and even forms of open or concealed conflict.

This situation of a responsible application of discourse ethics, in my opinion, constitutes the need for a supplementation of the procedural norms of discourse ethics that are grounded in the counterfactual anticipation of an ideal communication community. Here, there are two possibilities, both of which have been realized in the course of history. Either (1) the actors of good will (who also risk responsibility) are compelled to connect their willingness to consensual communication with recourse to *strategic-counterstrategic actions,* as for example in the extreme case of military self-defense. (This possibility I have tried to elaborate elsewhere as *part B* of discourse ethics.[9]) Or (2) there is the possibility, also developed in the course of history, of relying on the institutionalization of a system of law, that is, of *legal norms* that can be enforced by sanctions. These norms are needed because they can supplement the motivational force of moral norms and unburden the benevolent but responsible moral actors from strategic counteractions in cases of conflict.[10]

Now, at this point, I can agree to Habermas's postulate of a supplementary constitution of positive law (and, that is, of the constitutional state of law) along with the purely discursive constitution of moral norms. But again, I would insist that the *normative constitution of positive law* systematically presupposes the prior constitution of ideal moral norms; for only ideal moral norms can be grounded through "domination-free discourses," whereas the norms of positive law, which are not only based on moral but also on pragmatic reasons, must be grounded by the authority of a state that can enforce them. Here again, I am making a discourse-ethical argument that there is a normative priority to the discursive foundation of morality as it applies to the law. This foundation makes it clear that positive law must not contradict morality as long as it is an institution of justice.

My argument, however, does not yet provide a normative account for the necessary difference between the norms of morality and positive law. This difference, as I have already suggested, follows from the fact that positive law, which is legally defined and enforced by the authority of a constitutional state, must be a response to the challenge of the real situation of a responsible application of moral norms. It must be a normative answer to the fact that dialogical cooperation, which from the viewpoint of discourse ethics is an indispensable requirement for the constitution and application of moral norms, cannot be guaranteed in the real-life world.

A special answer to this situation of applying morality is in fact given by the norms of law, insofar as they are different from moral norms, that is, by their being authorized primarily by the coercive (compulsory) power of the state. But I would argue that even this dependence on force, along with the pragmatic reasons of adopting and passing the norms of law, must be ultimately justified by the *transcendental-pragmatic foundation of discourse ethics*. Why is this needed?

In my view, the authority of a constitutional state to adopt and pass legal norms that, being enforced only by it, are not based on domination-free procedures, must itself be justified by the moral co-responsibility of the human discourse community. And since in the real world the foundation and particular function of the discursive community must be incorporated and instituted by an individual community, we are led in this way to the legislative function of a democratic state.

III

Democracy, Positive Law, and Human Rights

IN THE PRECEDING SECTION, I have suggested that the legislative function of democracy is internally related to the foundation of positive law and that this internal relation can itself be grounded by the *transcendental-pragmatic foundation of discourse ethics*, namely, by recourse to the rational process of legitimating norms by building consensus within an ideal discourse community. Just such a process provides validity for these norms. But more importantly, this rational process is already presupposed by anyone who is engaged in serious argumentation. Further, the fact that there is some internal connection between democracy and discourse ethics is widely recognized in our day. In many cases this acknowledgment even seems to make it easier, especially for Anglo-American philosophers, to understand discourse ethics, since it apparently helps them to ignore or overlook the transcendental-pragmatic foundation of discourse ethics.[11] But in my view, it is precisely this situation, in which the transcendental-pragmatic foundation is ignored, that constitutes a crucial problem for any clear understanding of the internal relationship between democracy and law. This problem becomes apparent when anyone tries to understand the validity-claim and function of human rights—i.e., the claim that while specific norms are created for an individual community, they must also function according to a universalized agreement on basic human rights in order to be valid—only on the precondition of this internal connection between positive law and democracy. Let me elucidate this problem by reformulating it as a question.

Should it be possible to ground the validity-claim of "human rights" only by recourse to the legislative function of a democracy with regard to positive law, especially with regard to the fundamental rights of citizens that are grounded in the constitution of a democratic state? In other words: Is no external normative intervention conceivable with regard to the conception of human rights, as it is brought about by the constitution of positive law through the people's sovereignty in an ideal democratic state?

Jürgen Habermas has given an affirmative answer to this question in his book *Between Facts and Norms* (*Faktizität und Geltung*). Here, he separated for the first time the *discourse-theoretical foundation* of law from that of morality; and he identified the former's foundation ultimately with that of the legislative function of a democracy, since in a democracy, the authors of the legislative function are identical with the recipients of that function.[12]

John Rawls has agreed, in effect, with Habermas's conception in this respect, especially with his thesis of the "political autonomy" for the grounding of human rights.[13] This is all the more remarkable since Rawls, after all, continues the tradition of "political liberalism," a tradition that in its classic formulation conceived of human rights as some external authority that could intervene in the positive law of states in order to protect private rights.

Of course, Rawls, once he presented the new foundation of his "theory of justice" as purely political and thus independent of metaphysics,[14] had to refuse any external foundation of human rights as political rights, for instance, by recourse to a metaphysics of natural law. Thus he arrived at a partial agreement with Habermas who, in his political philosophy of law, wants to overcome the antagonism between liberalism and communitarianism by a strictly "proceduralistic" foundation for the constitution of positive law that appeals to the nature of the democratic state.[15]

I believe, however, that even if we abandon the metaphysical foundation of "human rights" by recourse to natural law and suppose, along with Habermas, that they have their destination as basic elements of positive law (for instance, as "basic rights" of constitutional states), there are still strong reasons why "human rights"—as the paradigms of universally valid law—must have a unique status above all positive law as well as a capacity for external intervention (even in the political autonomy of a democracy that is grounded by the people's sovereignty).

The first reason for this is constituted by the fact that there is a *plurality of sovereign democratic states* (from which, it might be claimed, human rights are constituted by shared agreement). Habermas has accounted for this argument, but he reduces its difficulty to a Rousseau-inspired understanding of the ethno-ethical aspect of the concept of "people's sovereignty." Therefore, Habermas calls for the elimination of the ethno-ethical dimension from the conception of the political autonomy of a democracy with regard to justifying its authority for constituting legal norms. It should be replaced, for instance, by a conception similar to "constitutional patriotism." But I think that this Habermasian proposal deals only with one aspect of the fact that there is a plurality of democratic states. The other aspect is constituted by the fact, detected at the time of Bodin and Richelieu, that sovereign states, being independent *systems of self-maintenance,* are basic subjects of a *"raison d'état."* In our day, this means that, notwithstanding the pretended openness of the constitutional norms of all democracies to the universal validity-claims of international law, there are always special normative reservations of the particular states due to the different imperatives of their "raison d'état." One could cite the resistance of the United States to the institution of an international court of justice, or the legislative differences concerning the law of asylum seekers or immigrants within the European democracies, as good illustrations of this point.

These different conceptions, which are based on different political discourses according to the autonomy of different sovereign states, could never be only an expression of the universal idea of "human rights" because they are necessarily also an expression of the interests of particular systems of self-maintenance. But does this not mean that a perfect political order of law, which would represent the idea of human rights, could and should be realized by a "world-state," or at least by a federation of republics that would regulate the international relations in accordance with a convention on human rights?

Kant, in his essay of 1784 entitled "The Idea of a Universal History from a Cosmopolitan Point of View," has touched upon this problem. He states in the seventh thesis of his essay that the "problem of establishing a perfect civil constitution is dependent on the problem of a lawful external relation between states and cannot be solved without the solution of the latter problem."[16] Thereby he indeed draws a radical conclusion from the fact of the plurality of states. Ten years later, in his philosophical project "On Perpetual Peace," Kant in fact considered a solution to the problem in terms of a cosmopolitan system of law.[17]

But Kant's solution was in a sense *aporetic*, as we must recognize today after having twice tried to realize the Kantian proposal (first in the failed League of Nations, and then in the United Nations). On the one hand, Kant considers it plausible that states, like individual persons, must try to surmount the "state of nature" (the *bellum omnium contra omnes* in Hobbes' sense) by subjecting themselves to the legal force (and coercive power) of a "World republic" or "state of peoples" (*civitas gentium*) that eventually would comprise all peoples of the earth.[18] But on the other hand, such a "world state," according to Kant, would contradict the very idea of a "law of peoples" (*Völkerrecht, jus gentium*), which proceeds from the autonomy of all peoples.[19] Hence, the idea of a "single state of peoples" would undermine such a solution to the problem from the very point of view of the idea of the "law of peoples."[20] In fact, Kant also considered the idea of one world state as constituting a real danger to human freedom, namely, the danger that such a state might eventually become a "soulless despotism."

In this situation Kant can only conceive of one remaining solution: the idea of one "world republic" has to be replaced, he suggests, by "the negative surrogate" of a "league of nations" (*Völkerbund*), which as a "federation of free states" would constitute a *"foedus pacificum"* that could perhaps provide a basis for a growing state of peace in the world.[21] During the 20th century we have tried out this project, first by the Geneva League of Nations and then later by the foundation of the United Nations Organization (UNO), which still exists today.

However, the basic dilemma that was touched upon by Kant still confronts us in the form of the political controversy, or even conflict, between the "unilateralists" and "plurilateralists" in connection with the Iraq War. The first party to the conflict can point to the many occasions—for example, Sudan, Rwanda, Uganda, and the Congo— where the UNO was not willing or not able to intervene in longstanding ethnic wars. For examples of successful and relatively rapid pacification of conflict situations, however, one can point to the crises in Bosnia, Kosovo, and Macedonia, where the effective power of NATO through its military interventions (not always sanctioned by a UNO mandate) could quickly provide at least a state of peace. But in these latter cases, the agreement between the effective power of NATO, on the one hand, and the legal authority of the United Nations, on the other, was not seriously called into question, whereas this is precisely what happened in the case of the Iraq War.

Here, for the first time, the potential conflict between the two apparent solutions to the problem of establishing an international order of law has become manifest. Likewise, the imminent danger for the freedom and the very conception of international law has become visible as well. For it was the technological and military superpower of the United States, the only current candidate for a world hegemony, that completely ignored the moral and legal authority of international law that is represented by the United Nations. Indeed, it disregarded all acknowledged rules of international law by high-handedly opening a preemptive war.

I think that this key experience of recent global politics has shown that the idea of law, in the sense of the universal conception of human rights, cannot be adequately realized either by particular democratic states or by a world-state as despotic superpower. Although each form of positive law must be authorized and enforced with the aid of state power, the *universal conception of law* cannot be reduced to any legislative autonomy of a state; it must keep a distance from all state functions while at the same time using them for its realization.

This does not mean that the universal conception of law, for example, of human rights, must be based on a so-called metaphysics of natural law; but it does mean that it must be based ultimately on the *transcendental-pragmatic* foundation of morality, that is, on the fundamental norms of an *ideal communication community* that we always already have acknowledged in every serious discourse. Thus, we have simultaneously ascertained the *transcendental basis of the idea of a democracy* and a regulative principle for possible distantiation and critique of every factual democratic state. For every democratic state is a particular institution and, as such, it is subject to the functional constraints of a power system. But the primordial discourse of humanity is a meta-institution: it may and should very well become the concern of a global reasoning public, but it cannot be definitely represented by the single sovereign states or by a world-state or hegemonic superpower.

Therefore, I think that the present conflict between unilateralists and plurilateralists with regard to settling questions of global peace and security must itself be settled by an institution that is open to the meta-institution of global discourse, and this can only be a federation of nations like the UNO. It must certainly be continually strengthened by reforms, but it must never be dominated by a single power system.

IV

Democracy and the "Law of Peoples"

IN THE PRECEDING DISCUSSION on the relationship between law and the democratic state, we touched upon the problem of the foundation of international law (or, as it was previously called, *jus gentium*, or in German, *Völkerrecht*). And it seems clear that by pleading for a furthering of the role of the United Nations in dealing with world problems, I have also pleaded for a further elaboration of international law. For the UNO, I think, must be primarily considered as a political representation of international law.

The problem of the internal relation and difference between universal law and the legislative function of the democratic state, which we have dealt with in the previous section, has for a long time found a certain equivalent in the history of international law, namely, in the tension between, on the one hand, its orientation toward "human rights" and hence a cosmopolitan law of single citizens (in German, *Weltbürgerrecht*) and, on the other hand, its orientation toward the sovereignty of the single states.

Thus in the peace treaties at the end of the Thirty Years' War, the "sovereignty" orientation became predominant, largely because of the priority of preserving international peace. But after 1945, the "human rights" orientation gained new ground. Finally, at the occasion of the Kosovo conflict,[22] both orientations stood against each other, at least at the beginning. Russia and China defended the sovereignty of Serbia and, in the Security Council of the United Nations, they blocked any resolution in favor of the Albanians by their veto; but then NATO intervened in defense of the human rights of the Albanians without a mandate from the UNO. Later, this illegal intervention was legitimized by the United Nations—roughly speaking, by appeal to the priority of protecting human rights against the danger of genocide. Thus the authority of the United Nations as the political representation of international law was saved—in accordance, I think, with the moral foundation of universally valid law. (As already noted, this cannot be said with regard to the intervention of the United States in Iraq.)

Based on the above observations of the historical situation of international law, what can be said, from the vantage point of the application of discourse ethics, about the *systematic foundation of international law?* Recently, the late John Rawls, after having twice outlined a foundation of the philosophy of justice (first a moral one and later a purely political one[23]), finally presented an architectonical overview (or survey) of the problems of international law under the title of *The Law of Peoples*. (This overview first appeared in essay form and later in a book of the same title.[24]) In what follows, I will comment on Rawls's conception of the "law of peoples" from the point of view of my own architectonical approach.

First, I should like to express my appreciation for Rawls's attempt at globalizing the problem of political justice by taking into account the dimension of foreign politics. He thereby surpassed, I would say, the usual naiveté of the Western equation of the problems of political justice with those of a domestic theory of democracy. He rightly states that: "Every society must have a conception of how it is related to other societies and of how it is to conduct itself toward them . . . [I]t must formulate certain ideals and principles for guiding its politics toward other peoples."[25] By his step toward international law, Rawls also tries to invalidate the objection or at least suspicion of "historicism," to which his original conception of "justice" in the "western democratic tradition" had exposed itself. (Richard Rorty, as is well known, even offered an affirmative interpretation of Rawls's historicism in his "notorious" essay, "The Priority of Democracy to Philosophy."[26] Rawls himself did not accept Rorty's historistic and culture-centric interpretation, but explicitly claimed that his conception of justice is "*universalistic* insofar as it is possible to *extend* it appropriately toward a *reasonable* conception of justice for the relation between all nations."[27])

In his classic work *A Theory of Justice*, Rawls had not, however, given a philosophical (ultimate) foundation for his basic conception of "justice as fairness," which he nevertheless presupposed in his construction of the "original position" (especially for the restrictive conditions he imposed on it). And in his later philosophy, especially in his book *Political Liberalism*, Rawls explicitly denied the possibility of a "nonmetaphysical" (and hence not cultural-dependent) foundation of justice.[28] Instead, in his first essay on "The Law of Peoples," he proposes the following conception of a quasi-empirical method of universalization by extension:

[A] constructivist view . . . do[es] not begin from *universal first principles* having authority in all cases. [It is] *universal* in its reach once it is *extended* to give principles for all politically relevant subjects, including a *law of peoples for the most comprehensive subject, the political society of peoples.* Its authority rests on the principles and conceptions of practical reason, but always on these as *suitably adjusted to apply to different subjects as they arise in sequence.*[29]

In what follows, Rawls explains this conception in more detail:

[C]onstructivism assumes . . . that there are other forms of *unity* than that defined by completely general first principles forming a consistent scheme. *Unity* may also be given by an appropriate *sequence of cases* and by supposing that the parties in an original position . . . are to proceed through the sequence with the understanding that *the principles for the subject of each later agreement are to be subordinate to those of subjects of all earlier agreements, or else coordinated with and adjusted to them by certain-priority rules.*[30]

How does this conception of universalization by extension work in Rawls's construction of the "Law of Peoples"?

I think that already in Rawls's organization of the subject matter, the lack of a universal first principle (which I would derive from the implicit morality of the discourse principle of an ideal communication community) shows some problematic consequences. Certainly, in his book version, Rawls proposes the following differentiation of the subject matter. His uppermost distinction is that between ideal and nonideal theories. Now, it is primarily noteworthy that under the head of "ideal theories," he subsumes not only "liberal-democratic peoples," but also "non-liberal-democratic peoples," for example, "respectable hierarchic peoples," especially those with "consultation hierarchies." Under the head of "non-ideal theories," Rawls subsumes the cases of "outlaw peoples" and of "burdened peoples," who because of "unfavourable circumstances"—such as poverty—cannot develop institutions of a well-ordered society.

Now, from an empirico-pragmatical perspective, Rawls no doubt has good reasons for accepting "respectable hierarchic peoples" in a global society that can acknowledge, and be acknowledged by, roughly the same "international law of peoples." His main reason for this is provided by a conception of tolerance with regard to the "fact of pluralism" that itself is derived from the situation within the framework of a liberal-democratic society. And his main pragmatic criterion, on the level of the "law of peoples," consists in the supposed fact that the "respectable hierarchic" peoples, in contradistinction to the "outlaw peoples," are nonaggressive with regard to other peoples and, therefore, must not be the object of sanctions because their institutions are different from Western ones.

This is certainly plausible, especially in the present world situation. (Rawls himself, in his 1999 book, takes the fictive example of an Islamic society called Kazanistan.) But what about the case in which a non-liberal-democratic people is aggressive not against other peoples but only against its own members, say, by suppressing "human rights"?

This case in fact constitutes the crucial problem for Rawls's conception of the law of peoples, and his treatment of it is not quite coherent, either in the first essay or even in the later book version. In order to understand Rawls's difficulties with the problem of balancing the concern of defending "human rights" with the concern of international toleration, I think it is necessary to return once more to his methodological approach.

Since Rawls cannot take recourse to a transcendental approach that would provide a moral foundation for "human rights," and thus for the law of a liberal-democratic state as well as for international law, he is compelled to find another, more restricted means of extending his early "theory of justice." This theory that, according to Rawls, was constructed for "a hypothetically closed and self-sufficient liberal democratic society," had to be extended in such a way "as to cover a society's relations with other societies to yield a *reasonable law of peoples.*"[31]

His answer to this problem is a conception of analogy between the just relationship of "free and equal citizens" in a liberal democracy and the just relationship of free and equal peoples on the level of international law. Thus the subjects of a just relationship are no longer persons as citizens but as "peoples." This step, I think, is deeply problematic, since by its logical structure it does not lead in the direction of a law of "cosmopolitan citizens" (*Weltbürgerrecht*), but rather in the direction of a law of sovereign states, as it was developed in the modern era in tension with the concern for "human rights." But this is precisely what Rawls wants to avoid, especially in his book version, where he distances himself from the whole European tradition of sovereignty and the *raison d'état* that was developed since Bodin and the Thirty Years' War. Rawls wants to overcome this tradition and the pertinent doctrine of the *jus ad bellum* in favor of "human rights." For this reason, he even prefers the term "law of peoples" to the possible alternative term "international law of constitutional states." (By contrast, Habermas in *Between Facts and Norms* wants to eliminate the ethno-ethical dimension from Rousseau's conception of "people's sovereignty" in order to keep open the universalistic dimension of democratic legislation against the danger of nationalism.[32])

But Rawls, as far as I can tell, cannot make his tendency for strengthening the case of human rights compatible with the logical structure of his conceptual analogy (i.e., the analogy between the just relationship of "free and equal citizens" in a liberal democracy and the just relationship of "free and equal peoples" on the level of international law). Instead, the internal contradiction between the two conceptions becomes visible in many places. For example, in his earlier essay version of "The Law of Peoples," Rawls expresses the intuition that the "system of law" that is valid in a "non-liberal-democratic" society must "meet the essentials of legitimacy in the eyes of its own people."[33] But this intuition, insofar as it is plausible as a universalistic human right of citizens in all states, obviously does not follow from the conception of analogy. It rather takes recourse, even on the level of the law of peoples, to the more foundational level of the votes of single citizens. Taken seriously, it would be a piece of a "cosmopolitan law of citizens" rather than an element of a law of "free and equal peoples."

In fact, all Rawlsian descriptions of the law of "hierarchical peoples"—especially his characterization of "respectable hierarchies of consultations" that must replace parliamentary representation[34]— cannot show that, after all, human rights as political rights of free and equal citizens in shaping and criticizing all public institutions could be ensured. Rights of political participation can at best be indirectly produced by a corporate system of group representation, as Rawls shows.

Thus it turns out, I suggest, that the internal relationship between universal law (including human rights) and democracy, although it is not one of identity (as I have tried to show in the preceding case against Habermas), is indeed strong enough to exclude all known alternatives. It is interesting to see that Rawls, in his later account in the book *The Law of Peoples*, eventually must confirm this. For he admits in some places that "respectable hierarchical peoples" are not "completely just,"[35] and that by tolerating them "within the limits of certain conditions, we could hope, in the long run, to open up for these peoples a development towards the status of 'liberal democracies.' "[36]

I agree to *this* assessment, and add that it corresponds indeed to the perspective we would take from the vantage point of a transcendental-pragmatic foundation of discourse ethics, and thereby of the foundational architectonics of the different dimensions of practical reason. I suggest that, indeed, Rawls's architectonics of his overview of the "law of peoples" had to be changed in the following way.

The conception of analogy, which is suggested by Rawls's method of universalization by extension, has to be avoided or at least severely restricted, since it is a misleading residue of the modern notion of *jus gentium.* Instead, the foundational part of international law has to be provided by a cosmopolitan law of citizens. (This, I suggest, is neither equivalent to the positive law of a "world-state" nor to that of single sovereign states, but it has to be incorporated for the time being by the law of a community of nations.)

I accept Rawls's organization of the subject matter of international law by the distinction between ideal and nonideal parts, but I would not subsume "hierarchical peoples" under the heading of the ideal part, although for pragmatic reasons of foreign politics the Rawlsian distinction between "respectable" and "nonrespectable peoples" may indeed be more important than the distinction between democracies and nondemocracies. But this latter distinction, which corresponds to a political "human rights" orientation of international law, comes closer to the (transcendental-pragmatic) foundation of universally valid law by the morality of an ideal discourse community.

In any event, our treatment of ideal and nonideal situations of international relations must ultimately (i.e., beyond the provisory limits of positive international law) be a matter of a discourse ethics of co-responsibility.[37] It has its foundation in the principle that the probable consequences of our actions must be acceptable to all possible members of a possible communication community, that is, ideally even for the single members of an "outlaw society" in Rawls's sense. But it is also a matter of an ethics of responsibility for consequences that we must make a distinction between ideal and nonideal conditions of communication and cooperation in our political interaction. This must be the last basis for our distinction between different types of "peoples" or "societies" on the level of international law.

Notes

1. Cf. Jürgen Habermas, *Faktizität und Geltung. Beiträge zur Diskurstheorie des Rechts und des demokratischen Rechtsstaats* (Frankfurt am Main: Suhrkamp, 1992).

2. Cf. John Rawls, "The Law of Peoples," in *On Human Rights: The Oxford Amnesty Lectures*, ed. Steven Shute and Susan Hurley (New York: Basic Books, 1993). See also John Rawls, *The Law of Peoples* (Cambridge: Harvard University Press, 1999).

3. Cf. Karl-Otto Apel, "Intersubjektivität, Sprache und Selbstreflexion: Ein neues Paradigma der Transzendentalphilosophie?" in *Anknüpfen an Kant. Konzeptionen der Transzendentalphilosophie*, ed. W. Kuhlmann (Würzburg: Königshausen & Neumann, 2001), 63–78. See also Karl-Otto Apel, "Transzendentalpragmatische Reflexion: die Hauptperspektive einer aktuellen Kant-Transformation," forthcoming.

4. Cf. Karl-Otto Apel, "Das Apriori der Kommunikationsgemeinschaft und die Grundlagen der Ethik," in *Transformation der Philosophie*, vol. II (Frankfurt am Main: Suhrkamp, 1973), 358–436. Translated into English as "The *apriori* of the Communication Community and the Foundations of Ethics," in *Towards a Transformation of Philosophy* (London: Routledge & Kegan Paul, 1980); reprinted by Marquette University Press (Milwaukee, WI: 1998), 225–360. See also Karl-Otto Apel, *Diskurs und Verantwortung* (Frankfurt am Main: Suhrkamp, 1988), and *Auseinandersetzungen. In Erprobung des transzendentalpragmatischen Ansatzes* (Frankfurt am Main: Suhrkamp, 1998).

5. See Jürgen Habermas, "Zur Architektonik der Diskursdifferenzierung," in *Reflexion und Verantwortung*, ed. D. Böhler, M. Kettner, and G. Skirbekk (Frankfurt am Main: Suhrkamp, 2003), 44–64.

6. Cf. Habermas, *Faktizität und Geltung*, loc. cit., and Karl-Otto Apel, "Auflösung der Diskursethik? Zur Architektonik der Diskursdifferenzierung in Habermas' *Faktizität und Geltung*," in Apel, *Auseinandersetzungen*, loc. cit., 727–838.

7. Ibid. (Apel), 105ff and 138ff. Cf. also Karl-Otto Apel, "Regarding the Relationship of Morality, Law and Democracy in Habermas's *Philosophy of Law* (1992) from a Transcendental-Pragmatical Point of View," in *Habermas and Pragmatism*, eds. M. Abulafia et al. (London: Routledge, 2000), 17–30.

8. Ibid.

9. See Apel, *Diskurs und Verantwortung*, loc. cit., 103ff.; see also Karl-Otto Apel, *The Response of Discourse Ethics* (Leuven: Peeters, 2001), 77ff.

10. See Karl-Otto Apel, "Diskursethik vor der Problematik von Recht und Politik," in *Zur Anwendung der Diskursethik in Politik, Recht und Wissenschaft*, eds. K.-O. Apel and M. Kettner (Frankfurt am Main: Suhrkamp, 1992); see also Apel, *The Response of Discourse Ethics*, 95–115.

11. Cf. my argument with Michael Walzer in Karl-Otto Apel, "Globalisierung und das Problem der Begründung einer universalen Ethik," in *Ein Ethos für eine Welt*, eds. K.-J. Kuschel, A. Pinzano, and M. Zillinger (Frankfurt am Main: Campus, 1999), 48–75, 60ff; translated into English as "Globalization and the Need for Universal Ethics," in *European Journal of Social Theory* 3(2) (2000): 137–150.

12. Cf. Habermas, *Faktizität und Geltung*, loc. cit; cf. also "Zur Architektonik der Diskursdifferenzierung," loc. cit., 45ff.

13. See John Rawls, "Reply to Habermas," *Journal of Philosophy* 92, 132–180, III and IV.

14. Cf. John Rawls, "Justice as Fairness: Political, not Metaphysical," *Philosophy and Public Affairs*, 14(3) (1985): 225.

15. Cf. Jürgen Habermas, "Drei normative Modelle der Demokratie," in *Die Einbeziehung des Anderen* (Frankfurt am Main: Suhrkamp, 1996), 277–292.

16. Immanuel Kant, "Idee zu einer allgemeinen Geschichte in weltbürgerlicher Absicht," in *Akademie-Textausgabe*, VIII, 7. Satz, 24.

17. Immanuel Kant, "Zum ewigen Frieden," loc. cit., 341–386.

18. Ibid., 357.

19. Ibid., 354.

20. Ibid., 357.

21. Ibid., 354 and 357.

22. Cf. Karl-Otto Apel, "On the Relationship Between Ethics, International Law and Politico-Military Strategy in Our Time: A Philosophical Retrospective on the Kosovo Conflict," *European Journal of Social Theory* 4(1) (2001): 29–40.

23. Cf. John Rawls, *A Theory of Justice* (Cambridge: Harvard University Press, 1971); cf. also "Justice as Fairness: Political not Metaphysical," loc. cit.

24. Cf. Rawls, "The Law of Peoples," loc. cit. (1993), and *The Law of Peoples*, loc. cit. (1999).

25. Rawls, "The Law of Peoples" (1993), 44.

26. Cf. Richard Rorty, "The Priority of Democracy to Philosophy," in *Objectivity, Relativism and Truth* (Cambridge: Cambridge University Press, 1991), 175–196. For a critical comment, see Apel, *Diskurs und Verantwortung*, loc. cit., 403ff.

27. Rawls, loc. cit. 44 (emphasis by K.-O. Apel).

28. Rawls, loc. cit. 46.

29. Rawls, loc. cit. 45f. (emphasis by K.-O. Apel).

30. Cf. Rawls loc. cit. 44 (emphasis by K.-O. Apel).

31. Cf. Rawls, *The Law of Peoples* (1999), loc. cit., §2 (emphasis by K.-O. Apel).

32. Cf. Habermas, *Faktizität und Geltung*, loc. cit., 131ff.

33. Rawls, "The Law of Peoples" (1993), 79.

34. Ibid.

35. Cf. Rawls, *The Law of Peoples* (1999), loc. cit., §8.

36. Ibid., 75, 95, 101.

37. Cf. Apel, *The Response of Discourse Ethics*, loc. cit.; cf. Karl-Otto Apel, "Diskursethik als Ethik der Mit-Verantwortung vor den Sachzwängen der Politik, des Rechts und der Marktwirtschaft," in *Prinzip*

Mitverantwortung, eds. K.-O. Apel and H. Burckhart (Würzburg: Königshausen & Neumann, 2001).

References

Apel, K-O. (1980). "Das Apriori der Kommunikationsgemeinschaft und die Grundlagen der Ethik." In *Transformation der Philosophie*. Bd. II. Frankfurt am Main: Suhrkamp Verlag, 1973. Trans. as "The *A Priori* of the Communication Community and the Foundation of Ethics." In *Towards a Transformation of Philosophy*, pp. 225–360. London: Routledge & Kegan Paul.

——. (1988). *Diskurs und Verantwortung*. Frankfurt am Main: Suhrkamp Verlag.

——. (1992). "Diskursethik vor der Problematik von Recht und Politik." In *Zur Anwendung der Diskursethik in Politik, Recht und Wissenschaft*. Frankfurt am Main: Suhrkamp Verlag.

——. (1998). "Auflösung der Diskursethik? Zur Architektonik der Diskursdifferenzierung in Habermas' *Faktizität und Geltung*." In *Auseinandersetzungen*, pp. 727–838. Frankfurt am Main: Suhrkamp Verlag.

——. (1999). "Globalisierung und das Problem der Begründung einer Universalen Ethik." In *Ein Ethos für eine Welt*. Frankfurt am Main: Campus Verlag. Trans. as "Globalization and the Need for Universal Ethics." *European Journal of Social Theory* 3(2) (2000): 137–150.

——. (2000). "Regarding the Relationship of Morality, Law and Democracy in Habermas's *Philosophy of Law* (1992) from a Transcendental-Pragmatic Point of View." In *Habermas and Pragmatism*, pp. 17–30. London: Routledge.

——. (2001). "Intersubjektivität, Sprache und Selbstreflexion." In *Anknüpfen an Kant*, pp. 63–78. Würzburg: Königshausen u. Neumann.

——. (2001). "On the Relationship Between Ethics, International Law and Politico-Military Strategy in Our Time: A Philosophical Retrospective on the Kosovo Conflict." *European Journal of Social Theory* 4(1): 29–40.

——. (2001). *The Response of Discourse Ethics*. Leuven: Peeters.

Habermas, J. (1992). *Faktizität und Geltung*. Frankfurt am Main: Surkamp Verlag.

——. (1996). "Drei normative Modelle der Demokratie." In *Die Einbeziehung der Anderen*, pp. 227–292. Frankfurt am Main: Suhrkamp Verlag.

Kant, I. (1795). "Zum ewigen Frieden." In *Kants Werke*, pp. 341–386. Bd. VIII.

——. ([1784] 1980). "Idee zu einer allgemeinen Geschichte in weltbürglicher Absicht." In *Kants Werke: Akademie Textausgabe*, pp. 15–32. Bd. VIII. Berlin: Walter de Gruyter & Co.

Rawls, J. (1971). *A Theory of Justice*. Cambridge: Harvard University Press.

——. (1985). "Justice as Fairness: Political, not Metaphysical." *Philosophy and Public Affairs* 14(3): 223–251.

——. (1993). "The Law of Peoples." In *On Human Rights*, pp. 41–82. New York: Basic Books.

——. (1995). "Reply to Habermas." *Journal of Philosophy* 92: 132–180.

——. (1999). *The Law of Peoples.* Cambridge: Harvard University Press.

Rorty, R. (1991). "The Priority of Democracy to Philosophy." In *Objectivity, Relativism and Truth*, pp. 175–196. Cambridge: Cambridge University Press.

3
Rethinking Global Justice from the Perspective of All Living Nature and What Difference it Makes

By James P. Sterba*

ABSTRACT. I begin this chapter with an account of what is deserved in human ethics, an ethics that assumes without argument that only humans, or rational agents, count morally. I then take up the question of whether nonhuman living beings are also deserving, and I answer it in the affirmative. Having established that all individual living beings, as well as ecosystems, are deserving, I go on to establish what it is that they deserve and then compare the requirements of global justice when only humans are taken into account with the requirements of global justice when all living beings are taken into account. I argue that the more adequate global justice that takes into account all living beings imposes some additional obligations on us that are absent from a less defensible human-centered global justice, but not as many as one might initially think.

I

Introduction

JUSTICE REQUIRES giving what is deserved. That in turn requires figuring out both what is deserved and who it is that deserves it.

*James P. Sterba is Professor of Philosophy at, and a Founding Faculty Fellow of, the Joan B. Kroc Institute for International Peace Studies at the University of Notre Dame. He has published 24 books, most recently the award-winning *Justice for Here and Now* (Cambridge: Cambridge University Press, 1998) and *Three Challenges to Ethics: Environmentalism, Feminism, and Multiculturalism* (Oxford: Oxford University Press, 2000). He is a past president of Concerned Philosophers for Peace, the North American Society for Social Philosophy, and the International Association for Philosophy of Law and Social Philosophy (American Section).

American Journal of Economics and Sociology, Vol. 66, No. 1 (January, 2007).

Here, priority should be given to who it is that is deserving rather than what it is that is deserved. This is because the more there are who are deserving, other things being equal, the fewer good things each of them can deserve. Political philosophers have long recognized this priority when they are trying to determine what the human members of a particular society or state deserve; they have acknowledged that this question cannot be conclusively resolved without taking into account distant peoples and future generations as also deserving. Unfortunately, most political philosophers tend to stop there; they do not take the next logical step of asking whether nonhuman living beings are also deserving. In this chapter, I begin with an account of what is deserved in human ethics, an ethics that assumes without argument that only humans, or rational agents, count morally. I then take up the question of whether nonhuman living beings are also deserving and answer it in the affirmative. Having established that all individual living beings, as well as ecosystems, are deserving, I go on to establish what it is that they deserve and then compare the requirements of global justice when only humans are taken into account with the requirements of global justice when all living beings are taken into account.

Needless to say, in human ethics, there is considerable disagreement over what it is that people deserve. For libertarian justice, what people deserve is determined by an ideal of liberty. For welfare liberal justice, it is determined by an ideal of fairness. For socialist justice, it is determined by an ideal of equality. For communitarian justice, it is determined by an ideal of the common good. And for feminist justice, it is determined by an ideal of a gender-free society. Now, I have argued elsewhere that when these five conceptions of justice are correctly interpreted, they all can be seen to support the same basic practical requirements.[1] Since I cannot in this paper lay out my entire practical reconciliation argument, what I propose to do is to focus on the most contentious part of that argument, where I attempt to show that libertarians should endorse a right to a basic needs minimum that extends to both the distant peoples and future generations before arguing that all living beings are deserving as well.

II

Liberty and Welfare

LET US BEGIN by interpreting the ideal of liberty as a negative ideal in the manner favored by libertarians.[2] So understood, liberty is the absence of interference by other people from doing what one wants or is able to do. Libertarians go on to characterize their political ideal as requiring that each person should have the greatest amount of liberty commensurate with the same liberty for all.[3] Interpreting their ideal in this way, libertarians claim to derive a number of more specific requirements, in particular, a right to life, a right to freedom of speech, press, and assembly, and a right to property.

Here, it is important to observe that the libertarian's right to life is not a right to receive from others the goods and resources necessary for preserving one's life; it is simply a right not to be killed unjustly. Correspondingly, the libertarian's right to property is not a right to receive from others the goods and resources necessary for one's welfare, but rather a right to acquire goods and resources either by initial acquisition or by voluntary agreement.

While libertarians would allow that it would be nice of the rich to share their surplus resources with the poor, they nevertheless deny that government has a duty to provide for such needs. Some good things, such as the providing of welfare to the poor, are requirements of charity rather than justice, libertarians claim. Accordingly, failure to make such provisions is neither blameworthy nor punishable. As a consequence, such acts of charity should not be coercively required. For this reason, libertarians are opposed to coercively supported welfare programs.

Now in order to see why libertarians are mistaken about what their ideal requires, consider a typical conflict situation between the rich and the poor. In this conflict situation, the rich, of course, have more than enough resources to satisfy their basic needs.[4] By contrast, the poor lack the resources to meet their most basic needs even though they have tried all the means available to them that libertarians regard as legitimate for acquiring such resources. Under circumstances like these, libertarians usually maintain that the rich should have the liberty to use their resources to satisfy their luxury needs if they so wish.

Libertarians recognize that this liberty might well be enjoyed at the expense of the satisfaction of the most basic needs of the poor; they just think that liberty always has priority over other political ideals, and since they assume that the liberty of the poor is not at stake in such conflict situations, it is easy for them to conclude that the rich should not be required to sacrifice their liberty so that the basic needs of the poor may be met.

Of course, libertarians would allow that it would be nice of the rich to share their surplus resources with the poor. However, according to libertarians, such acts of charity are not required because the liberty of the poor is not thought to be at stake in such conflict situations.

In fact, the liberty of the poor is at stake in such conflict situations. What is at stake is the liberty of the poor not to be interfered with in taking from the surplus possessions of the rich what is necessary to satisfy their basic needs.

Now, when the conflict between the rich and the poor is viewed as a conflict of liberties, we can either say that the rich should have the liberty not to be interfered with in using their surplus resources for luxury purposes, or we can say that the poor should have the liberty not to be interfered with in taking from the rich what they require to meet their basic needs. If we choose one liberty, we must reject the other. What needs to be determined, therefore, is which liberty is morally preferable: the liberty of the rich or the liberty of the poor.

The "Ought" Implies "Can" Principle

I submit that the liberty of the poor, which is the liberty not to be interfered with in taking from the surplus resources of others what is required to meet one's basic needs, is morally preferable to the liberty of the rich, which is the liberty not to be interfered with in using one's surplus resources for luxury purposes. To see that this is the case, we need only appeal to the "ought" implies "can" principle, a principle common to all moral and political perspectives. According to this principle, people are not morally required to do what they lack the power to do or what would involve so great a sacrifice that it would be unreasonable to ask and/or, in cases of severe conflict of interest, unreasonable to require them to abide by.

Now applying the "ought" implies "can" principle to the case at hand, it seems clear that the poor have it within their power willingly to relinquish such an important liberty as the liberty not to be interfered with in taking from the rich what they require to meet their basic needs. Nevertheless, it would be unreasonable in this context to ask or require them to make so great a sacrifice. In the extreme case, it would involve asking or requiring the poor to sit back and starve to death. Of course, the poor may have no real alternative to relinquishing this liberty. To do anything else may involve worse consequences for themselves and their loved ones and may invite a painful death. Accordingly, we may expect that the poor would acquiesce, albeit unwillingly, to a political system that denied them the right to welfare supported by such a liberty, at the same time that we recognize that such a system imposed an unreasonable sacrifice upon the poor—a sacrifice that we could not morally blame the poor for trying to evade.[5] Analogously, we might expect that a woman whose life was threatened would submit to a rapist's demands at the same time that we recognize the utter unreasonableness of those demands.

By contrast, it would not be unreasonable to ask and require the rich in this context to sacrifice the liberty to meet some of their luxury needs so that the poor can have the liberty to meet their basic needs.[6] Naturally, we might expect that the rich, for reasons of self-interest and past contribution, might be disinclined to make such a sacrifice. We might even suppose that the past contribution of the rich provides a good reason for not sacrificing their liberty to use their surplus for luxury purposes. Yet, unlike the poor, the rich could not claim that relinquishing such a liberty involved so great a sacrifice that it would be unreasonable to ask and require them to make it; unlike the poor, the rich could be morally blameworthy for failing to make such a sacrifice.

Consequently, if we assume that however else we specify the requirements of morality, they cannot violate the "ought" implies "can" principle, it follows that, despite what libertarians claim, the right to liberty endorsed by them actually favors the liberty of the poor over the liberty of the rich, and thus provides the basis for a right to welfare on libertarian premises.

III

Distant Peoples and Future Generations

Now for libertarians, fundamental rights are universal rights, that is, rights possessed by all people, not just those who live in certain places or at certain times. Given then the universal character of the libertarian right to welfare that we have just established, we need to determine what its implications are for distant peoples and future generations. Put briefly, I argue that when a libertarian ideal of liberty is correctly interpreted, it leads to a universal right to welfare and, further, that the recognition of this universal right to welfare leads to considerable equality in the shares of goods and resources over place and time.[7]

IV

The Moral Deservingness of All Living Beings

Most political philosophers, as I have indicated, are committed to anthropocentrism; they just assume without argument that all or only human beings, or all or only rational agents, are deserving or count morally. In order to show that this view is mistaken, I will need a really good argument that nonhuman living beings are deserving or count morally. A really good argument, by definition, must be a non-question-begging argument. So what I will need is a non-question-begging argument that nonhuman living beings are deserving or count morally. Is there such an argument?

Consider. We clearly have the capacity of entertaining and acting upon both anthropocentric reasons that take only the interests of humans into account and nonanthropocentric reasons that also take the interests of nonhuman living beings into account. Given that capacity, the question we are seeking to answer is what sort of reasons it would be rational for us to accept.

In this regard, there are two kinds of cases that must be considered. First, there are cases in which there is a conflict between the relevant anthropocentric and nonanthropocentric reasons. Second, there are cases in which there is no such conflict.

It seems obvious that where there is no conflict and both reasons are conclusive reasons of their kind, both reasons should be acted upon. In such contexts, we should do what is favored both by anthropocentrism and by nonanthropocentrism.

Now when we turn to rationally assess the relevant reasons in conflict cases, three solutions are possible. First, we could say that anthropocentric reasons always have priority over conflicting nonanthropocentric ones. Second, we could say just the opposite, that nonanthropocentric ones always have priority over conflicting anthropocentric reasons. Third, we could say that some kind of compromise is rationally required. In this compromise, sometimes anthropocentric reasons would have priority over nonanthropocentric reasons, and sometimes nonanthropocentric reasons would have priority over anthropocentric reasons.

Once the conflict is described in this manner, the third solution can be seen to be the one that is rationally required. This is because the first and second solutions give exclusive priority to one class of relevant reasons over the other, and only a question-begging justification can be given for such an exclusive priority. Only by employing the third solution, sometimes giving priority to anthropocentric reasons and sometimes giving priority to nonanthropocentric reasons, can we avoid a question-begging resolution. What we need, therefore, are conflict resolution principles that specify these priorities.

V

Conflict Resolution Principles

BUT HOW ARE THESE PRIORITIES to be specified? Now surely, even if we hold that all living beings should count morally, we can justify a preference for humans on grounds of preservation. Accordingly, we have:

1. **A principle of human preservation:** Actions that are necessary for meeting one's basic needs or the basic needs of other human beings are permissible even when they require aggressing against the basic needs of individual animals and plants, or even of whole species or ecosystems.[8]

Nevertheless, preference for humans can still go beyond bounds, and the bounds that are required are captured by the following:

2. A principle of disproportionality: Actions that meet nonbasic or luxury needs of humans are prohibited when they aggress against the basic needs of individual animals and plants or even of whole species or ecosystems.

This principle is strictly analogous to the principle in human ethics that similarly prohibits meeting some people's nonbasic or luxury needs by aggressing against the basic needs of other people. Without a doubt, the adoption of such a principle with respect to nonhumans would significantly change the way we live our lives. Such a principle is required, however, if there is to be any substance to the claim that the members of all species count morally. We can no more consistently claim that the members of all species count morally and yet aggress against the basic needs of animals or plants whenever this serves our own nonbasic or luxury needs then we can consistently claim that all humans count morally and then aggress against the basic needs of other human beings whenever this serves our nonbasic or luxury needs. Consequently, if saying that species count morally is to mean anything, it must be the case that the basic needs of the members of nonhuman species are protected against aggressive actions that only serve to meet the nonbasic needs of humans, as required by the principle of disproportionality. Another way to put the central claim here is to hold that counting morally rules out domination, where domination means aggressing against the basic needs of some for the sake of satisfying the nonbasic needs of others.

Nevertheless, in order to avoid imposing an unacceptable sacrifice on the members of our own species, we can also justify a preference for humans on grounds of defense. Thus, we have:

3. A principle of human defense: Actions that defend oneself and other human beings against harmful aggression are permissible even when they necessitate killing or harming individual animals or plants, or even destroying whole species or ecosystems.

Lastly, we need one more principle to deal with violations of the above three principles. Accordingly, we have:

4. A principle of rectification: Compensation and reparation are required when the other principles have been violated.

Obviously, this principle is somewhat vague, but for those who are willing to abide by the other three principles, it should be possible to remedy that vagueness in practice. Here, too, would-be human guardians of the interests of nonhumans could have a useful role figuring out what is appropriate compensation or reparation for violations of the principle of disproportionality and, even more importantly, designing ways to get that compensation or reparation enacted.

VI

An Objection from a Somewhat Alien Perspective

There remains, however, at least one serious objection to the view that I have been defending. It might be argued that from a somewhat alien perspective my view is not nonanthropocentric enough. Consider the following.

Suppose our planet were invaded by an intelligent and very powerful species of alien that can easily impose their will upon us. Suppose these aliens have studied the life history of our planet and they have come to understand how we have wreaked havoc on our planet, driving many species into extinction, and how we still threaten many other species with extinction. In short, suppose these aliens discover that we are like a cancer on our biosphere.

Suppose further that these aliens are fully aware of the differences between us and the other species on the planet. Suppose they clearly recognize that we more closely resemble them in power and intelligence than any other species on the planet does. Even so, suppose the aliens still choose to protect those very species we threaten. They begin by forcing us to use no more resources than we need for a decent life, and this significantly reduces the threat we pose to many endangered species. However, the aliens want to do more. In order to save more endangered species, they decide to exterminate a certain portion of our human population, reducing our numbers to those we had when we were more in balance with the rest of the biosphere.

Now if this were to happen, would we have moral grounds to object to these actions taken by the aliens? Of course, we could argue that it would be unreasonable for us to do more than restrict ourselves to the resources we need for a decent life, and so we are not morally required to do more. But these aliens need not deny this. They may recognize that the extermination of a certain portion of the human population is not something that humans could reasonably require of each other. What the aliens are claiming, as champions of endangered species, is simply the right to impose a still-greater restriction on humans, recognizing, at the same time, a comparable right of humans to resist that imposition as best they can. Of course, in the imagined case, any resistance by humans would be futile; the aliens are just too powerful.

In so acting, the aliens have placed themselves outside that morality captured by my conflict resolution principles. The moral permissibility to meet one's basic needs and to defend oneself guaranteed by the principles of human preservation and human defense, respectively, is that of strong permissibility. It implies that any would-be guardians of the interests of nonhuman earthly species were morally prohibited from interfering with humans who are taking the necessary actions to preserve and defend themselves, even when this requires that the humans aggress against the basic needs of nonhumans. In our imaginary tale, however, the aliens have rejected this moral prohibition, claiming instead that it is morally permissible for them to ally themselves with the interests of some of the endangered species on our planet. They claim that we cannot morally blame them, or morally object to what they are doing. They say that they have a right to try to impose greater restrictions on our species and that we have a right to resist. And they would be correct. How could we object to the actions of these nonhuman-species-loving aliens?

Likewise, we could not object if similar actions were undertaken by radical Earth Firsters who, so to speak, chose to "go native" and renounced, to some extent, their membership in the human community so as to be able to take stronger steps to protect endangered species. Of course, we might argue that there are other more effective ways for these Earth Firsters to protect endangered species, but if their actions proved to be the most effective at protecting endangered species, what could our objection be? We could oppose them if they go beyond what is morally required, as we could oppose the aliens on those same grounds, but, as in the case of the aliens, we don't seem to have any moral objection against what they are doing. What this would show is that while morality cannot impose requirements that would be unreasonable to accept (i.e., requirements that violated the "ought" implies "can" principle), it can permit (as in this case) actions that it cannot impose, as in lifeboat cases.[9]

Even so, before these radical Earth Firsters could sacrifice the basic needs of fellow humans for the sake of endangered species, they would be first required to use whatever surplus was available to them and to other humans to meet the basic needs of the humans they propose to restrict. Yet clearly, it would be very difficult to have first used up all the surplus available to the whole human population for meeting basic human needs.[10] Under present conditions, this requirement has certainly not been met. So unlike our imaginary aliens who we assumed were able to force us to use no more resources that we needed for a decent life, before they started killing us to further reduce the threat we pose to endangered species, the efforts of radical Earth Firsters would probably never get beyond that first step. All of their efforts would be focused on trying to benefit endangered species by forcing humans to use no more resources than they need for a decent life. Unlike our imaginary aliens, real-life radical Earth Firsters would probably never be able to justifiably get to the second step of taking the lives of fellow humans for the benefit of endangered species.

Accordingly, even though we can envision the perspective of hypothetical aliens and radical Earth Firsters and recognize that it is a morally permissible stance to take, this still doesn't undercut the moral defensibility of the principles of human preservation, disproportionality, human defense, and rectification. These principles still capture the moral requirements we can reasonably require all human beings to accept.[11] In fact, the first step of this somewhat alien perspective requires the enforcement of just those principles. It is only at the second step, simply hypothetically justified in the case of the aliens, and virtually never justifiably realized in the case of real-life radical Earth Firsters, that we have a departure from the principles. Hence, the mere possibility of this somewhat alien moral perspective does not undercut the real-life moral defensibility, on both Kantian and utilitarian grounds, of these conflict resolution principles.

VII

Comparing the Requirements of Global Justice

WE ARE NOW IN A POSITION to compare the requirements of global justice when only humans are taken into account with the requirements of global justice when all living beings are taken into account. When only humans are taken into account, I argued on libertarian grounds that we are only entitled to the goods and resources required to meet our basic needs for a decent life—no more. Otherwise, we would be violating the rights of distant peoples and future generations. Somewhat surprisingly, that is almost the *same conclusion* I arrived at after also taking nonhuman living beings into account. Specifically, the principle of human preservation only permits aggression against nonhuman nature for the sake of what we need for a decent life, and the principle of disproportionality prohibits aggression against nonhuman nature for the sake of nonbasic or luxury needs.

Still, the more inclusive account of global justice does impose some additional obligations. First, in order to avoid unnecessary harm to nonhuman nature, we will have an obligation to meet our basic needs in some ways rather than others. For example, if there were no negative effects on our fellow human beings, it would be permissible for us to meet our basic needs through the consumption of meat and dairy products provided by factory farming, but we can't do this once the interests of particularly farm animals are appropriately taken into account. Second, we will have additional obligations to help nonhuman living beings based on restitution. For example, where we humans have endangered nonhuman species by aggressing against them for the sake of our luxury needs, we would have an obligation to try to restore those species to a flourishing condition. Third, we have an obligation to control our population to a greater extent under a more inclusive global justice than we would under a human-centered global justice. Of course, even in a human-centered global justice, we would need restrictions on population growth. While existing people are not required to sacrifice their basic needs for the sake of future generations, they are required to do what they can to restrict the membership of future generations so that those generations will be able to meet their basic needs.[12]

But what does this entail? We could limit human reproduction to the legitimate exercise of the basic human need to procreate, which would be roughly one child per family. It is unclear whether such a restrictive population policy would be necessary for respecting the rights of future generations. But suppose it is. At some point, it would be possible to abandon such a policy because the welfare rights of future generations were no longer threatened. Even at that point, however, nonhuman species could still be threatened by the size of the human population. So a global justice that took all living beings into account would want to continue this restrictive population policy. Nevertheless, at some point even a more inclusive global justice would favor relaxing this restrictive population policy in favor of one that served the long-term survivability of the human species, consistent with maintaining humans within their environmental niche, where, unlike today, they would be in balance with the rest of the biotic community. Yet this is just to endorse a goal of a more inclusive global justice without saying much about how to reach it. Others will have to do better.

Summing up, I have argued that in a human-centered global justice, even the libertarian ideal of liberty supports a right to welfare that extends to both distant people and future generations, and that this right would lead us to provide each individual with the goods and resources that are required for a decent life, but no more. I also argued that in a more inclusive global justice that took all living beings into account, the principles of human preservation, disproportionality, human defense, and restitution specify the non-question-begging resolution of our conflicts with nonhuman living beings, and these principles require that we also restrict ourselves to using the goods and resources we need for a decent life, but no more. Yet I also argued that this more inclusive global justice imposes additional obligations on us, obligations that are absent from a less defensible human-centered global justice. These additional obligations require that we meet our basic needs in certain ways but not others, that we attempt to restore species that we have endangered, and that we accept an even more restrictive population policy. As far as theories of justice go, this is about as demanding as you get.

VIII

Epilogue

DIFFERENT VERSIONS OF THIS CHAPTER have been presented to a variety of audiences. Invariably, at some point in the question period, someone asks: How do I distinguish basic from nonbasic needs? Usually, the questioner does not realize how widespread the use of this distinction is. While the distinction is surely important for environmental ethics, as its use in this chapter attests, it is also used widely in moral and political philosophy generally. For example, the defense of a right to welfare depends on this distinction. So it would really be impossible to do much moral, political, or environmental philosophy without a distinction between basic and nonbasic needs.

Typically, I respond to the question, as I do in the text, by pointing out that the fact that although not every need can be clearly classified as either basic or nonbasic—as similarly holds for a whole range of dichotomous concepts like moral/immoral, legal/illegal, living/nonliving, human/nonhuman—this should not immobilize us from acting, at least with respect to clear cases. This puts our use of the distinction in a still broader context, suggesting that if we cannot use the basic/nonbasic distinction in moral, political, and environmental philosophy, the widespread use of other dichotomous concepts is likewise threatened. It also suggests how our inability to clearly classify every conceivable need as basic or nonbasic should not keep us from using such a distinction, at least with respect to clear cases.

There is also a further point to be made here. If we begin to respond to clear cases, for example, and if we stop aggressing against the clear basic needs of nonhuman nature for the sake of clear luxury needs of humans, then we will be in even better position to know what to do in the less clear cases. This is because sincerely attempting to live out one's practical moral commitments helps one to interpret them better, just as failing to live them out makes interpreting them all the more difficult. Consequently, we have every reason to act on the conflict resolution principles that I have defended in this chapter, at least with respect to clear cases.

Let me conclude by indicating what I think is the weakest link in the arguments of this chapter. It is the one concerning human reproduction. Some such argument is needed because if the human population were to maintain its present size, or continue to increase, then even limiting human consumption to basic needs will still drive many nonhuman species into extinction. A policy of one child per family is, at best, only a temporary solution. The real question is how to fashion a policy that favors the long-term survival of the human species and a return of humans to their environmental niche. Here I have only endorsed the goal without saying much about how to reach it. I hope others will be able to do better.

Notes

1. See James P. Sterba, *How to Make People Just* (Lanham, MD: Rowman and Littlefield, 1988) and also *Justice for Here and Now* (New York: Cambridge, 1998).

2. Ibid.

3. See John Hospers, "The Libertarian Manifesto," in James P. Sterba, *Morality in Practice*, 7th ed. (Belmont, CA: Wadsworth, 2003).

4. Basic needs, if not satisfied, lead to significant lacks or deficiencies with respect to a standard of mental and physical well-being, Thus, a person's needs for food, shelter, medical care, protection, companionship, and self-development are, at least in part, needs of this sort. For a discussion of basic needs, see my *How to Make People Just*, 45–48.

5. See James P. Sterba, "Is There a Rationale for Punishment?" *Philosophical Topics* 18(1) (1990): 105–125.

6. By "the liberty of the rich to meet their luxury needs" I continue to mean the liberty of the rich not to be interfered with when using their surplus possessions for luxury purposes. Similarly, by "the liberty of the poor to meet their basic needs" I continue to mean the liberty of the poor not to be interfered with when taking what they require to meet their basic needs from the surplus possessions of the rich.

7. For the argument, see *Justice for Here and Now*, Ch. 3.

8. For the purposes of this paper, I will follow the convention of excluding humans from the denotation of "animals."

9. The direct analogy is to a lifeboat case in which you are trying to secure a lifeboat for one person from someone else who has an equal claim to it.

10. This is what I think presently holds with regard to the means for protecting endangered species in the Royal Chitwan National Park in Nepal.

11. It is also possible to reformulate these principles in a more linguistically species-neutral way so that they do not make direct reference to the

human species. See James P. Sterba, "A Biocentrist Fights Back," *Environmental Ethics* 20(4) (1998): 361–376.

12. James P. Sterba, "The Welfare Rights of Distant Peoples and Future Generations: Moral Side-Constraints on Social Policy," *Social Theory and Practice* 7(2) (1981): 99–124.

References

Hospers, John. (2003). "The Libertarian Manifesto." In *Moraility in Practice*, 7th ed., ed. James P. Sterba. Belmont, CA: Wadsworth.

Sterba, James P. (1981). "The Welfare Rights of Distant Peoples and Future Generations: Moral Side-Constraints on Social Policy." *Social Theory and Practice* 7(2): 99–124.

———. (1988). *How to Make People Just.* Lanham: Rowman and Littlefield.

———. (1990). "Is There a Rationale for Punishment?" *Philosophical Topics* 18(1): 105–125.

———. (1998a). "A Biocentrist Fights Back." *Environmental Ethics* 20(4): 361–376.

———. (1998b). *Justice for Here and Now.* New York: Cambridge University Press.

4

Human Rights, Global Justice, and Disaggregated States

John Rawls, Onora O'Neill, and Anne-Marie Slaughter

By Alyssa R. Bernstein*

ABSTRACT. Human rights are urgently important rights that all individual persons may validly claim and that all governments are obligated to respect. According to some philosophers, no government can plausibly claim legitimate authority unless its legal and political system ascribes such rights, and no society can plausibly claim to be just unless it has a legitimate government. John Rawls presents his own version of this conception in the context of his account of the moral basis of a just global system of public law, which he calls the Law of Peoples. According to some of his critics, including Onora O'Neill, not only is the Law of Peoples statist, but also it relies on a false view of the state. O'Neill has developed a new conception of an ideally just global order in which states have fewer, and corporations more, powers and obligations to secure human rights, in contrast to Rawls's conception. Her conception is consistent with Anne-Marie Slaughter's account of the transformation of state sovereignty due to globalization.

*Alyssa R. Bernstein is Assistant Professor of Philosophy at Ohio University and a past Fellow of the Carr Center for Human Rights Policy at Harvard University. As a doctoral student in Harvard's Philosophy Department she worked with Rawls while writing her dissertation, "Human Rights Reconceived: A Defense of Rawls's Law of Peoples." She has written mainly on Rawls, Kant, political philosophy, and philosophy of law. Bernstein presented an earlier version of this paper at the July 2005 conference of ISUD (the International Society for Universal Dialogue) in Helsinki, Finland, and thanks the audience and fellow panelists for their comments and criticisms. For helpful comments on a written draft, she thanks Nathaniel Goldberg, Daniel Shannon, and Steve Hicks. Research and conference-travel expenses for this paper and its ancestors were funded partly by the Carr Center for Human Rights Policy at Harvard University's Kennedy School of Government and partly by Ohio University's Institute for Applied and Professional Ethics.

American Journal of Economics and Sociology, Vol. 66, No. 1 (January, 2007).

However, contrary to initial appearances, it is not the case that O'Neill's and Slaughter's views taken together require significant modification of Rawls's conception of human rights. There is no fundamental conflict between Rawls's conception of human rights and Slaughter's account of state transformation. And O'Neill's criticisms of Rawls's view are unwarranted.

I

Introduction

ACCORDING TO A CURRENTLY INFLUENTIAL philosophical conception, human rights are best understood as a set of urgently important rights that all individual persons may validly claim and that all governments are obligated to respect because no government can plausibly claim legitimate authority unless its legal and political system ascribes such rights, and no society can plausibly claim to be just unless it has a legitimate government. This conception is endorsed (explicitly or tacitly) by a number of contemporary philosophers,[1] but few have developed systematic justifications of it other than John Rawls. He presents his own version of this conception in *The Law of Peoples* (1999).[2] According to some of his critics, it relies on a false view of the state. I will argue to the contrary.

Over the past half-century, since the *Universal Declaration of Human Rights* (*UDHR*) was issued, the capacities and functions of state governments have changed as international organizations (both governmental and nongovernmental) have proliferated and become increasingly powerful. Over the past dozen years, accelerating globalization has generated much scholarly and public discussion, and many have argued that the international institutions created after World War II must be reformed or reinvented in order to take account of new political realities. These include, according to Anne-Marie Slaughter,[3] "two major shifts: from national to global and from government to governance."[4] Furthermore, a third important shift is now occurring, she argues: states are becoming "disaggregated" as transnational government networks become increasingly important for world order in the 21st century. More than ever before, officials of domestic governments are engaging in activities beyond the boundaries of their states, due to increased capacities as well as increased needs for doing so. As a consequence, the long-dominant concept of the unitary state is giving way to the concept of the disaggregated state as the structures of domestic government become more international.[5]

In the new order Slaughter sees emerging, and advocates, it will not be "up to 'the state' to uphold human rights."[6] Instead, it will be up to transgovernmental networks consisting of officials of particular branches of different state governments, as well as "broader policy networks, including international organizations, NGOs, corporations, and other interested actors."[7] The members of these networks would be the bearers of the obligations created by treaties and other international agreements.

How, if at all, does the emergence of such a world order bear on the above-described philosophical conception of human rights? Does it render it obsolete, either entirely or partially? Or should we instead conclude that what requires modification is not this conception of human rights but this new world order? In what follows I will argue that the emergence of this new world order does not render this conception of human rights obsolete but instead requires that it be further developed.

Among the reasons for the transformation of state sovereignty in this era of globalization is the increasing power of large transnational corporations. Thus the question arises: If states are losing power to corporations, are states also losing some of their responsibilities and rights, and are corporations acquiring some or all of these, including responsibilities to respect, uphold, and secure human rights? Can corporations acquire and fulfill such responsibilities? If so, does justice require that they do so?

Neither Rawls nor Slaughter address the questions that I have raised in the preceding two paragraphs. One prominent contemporary philosopher who does is Onora O'Neill.[8] She argues that corporations and other nongovernmental organizations can help secure human rights and promote justice, and should be encouraged, expected, and better enabled to do so when and where states are unable. She also criticizes Rawls's conception of global justice on the ground that it is "statist," by which she means that it assumes falsely that states alone are the "primary agents of justice" carrying responsibility for either fulfilling or delegating to others all obligations of justice.

O'Neill has developed a new conception of an ideally just global order in which states have fewer, and corporations more, powers and obligations to secure human rights, in contrast to Rawls's conception. Her conception is consistent with Slaughter's account of the transformation of state sovereignty. But contrary to initial appearances, it is not the case that O'Neill's and Slaughter's views taken together require significant modification of Rawls's conception of human rights; so I will argue.

I will begin with an account of Rawls's conception of human rights and global justice, after which I will briefly consider how Slaughter's account of the transformation of state sovereignty bears on it. Next I will take up O'Neill's views on these topics. As I hope to show, her rejection of Rawls's view on the ground that it is statist is unwarranted. Moreover, there appears to be no fundamental conflict between Rawls's conception of human rights and Slaughter's account of state transformation. Insofar as Slaughter's account is representative of a "liberal" political theory (which sees states as complex entities undergoing retreat or transformation), as contrasted to a "realist" theory of international relations (which sees states as unitary, coherent actors that remain powerful),[9] the arguments I offer will, if cogent, provide some support for the broader conclusion that globalization is not rendering obsolete conceptions of human rights such as that developed by Rawls.

II

Rawls

The Law of Peoples (*LP*) outlines a conception of the moral basis of a just system of international law. It proposes a set of principles to be included in the foundation charter of a Society of Peoples (the nucleus of a law-governed international community that can develop into a fully just global order), as well as a list of basic human rights by reference to which these principles are to be interpreted. Moreover, it presents arguments justifying this list and those principles, as well as several theses about human rights.

Rawls views basic human rights as urgently important rights of all individual persons, which are grounded in principles of justice that apply to all governments and legal systems. These principles set constraints on the use of political power in making and implementing foreign as well as domestic policy. In order to determine the set of these basic human rights, one would have to determine which principles of justice apply to all governments. Rawls undertakes this task in *LP*.

Taking a bottom-up or "at-least" approach, Rawls starts from the idea that a just society has at least a legitimate government, which must be understood as at least a system of law such that the people governed are not merely forced but instead obligated to obey it. In this way, as I will further explain below, Rawls develops an argument aiming to show that at least a proper subset of the basic rights of the citizens of a fully just liberal democratic society are universal and internationally enforceable basic human rights: that all individuals are entitled to claim them, that all governments are obligated to respect and secure them, and that the international community may and should enforce them worldwide (via appropriate procedures and measures) for moral reasons that are independent of facts about whether states have explicitly committed themselves to respect and secure these rights.[10] Rawls aims to show this by means of arguments that no government would have good moral reason to reject, arguments that they cannot reject while reasonably claiming legitimacy

In developing his conception of a fully just liberal democratic society, which he calls Justice as Fairness (JF),[11] Rawls analyzes the idea of fair social cooperation among individual human beings who are members of the same society, all free citizens of equal political status. He argues for two fully general, fundamental principles of societal justice,[12] which are to guide and constrain the citizens of a democratic society (i.e., one characterized by popular sovereignty) in using the coercive powers of their government domestically. These two principles are to constitute its foundation charter.

Analogously, in *LP* Rawls argues for certain fully general, fundamental principles of fair social cooperation among legitimately governed states,[13] which are to guide and constrain the international uses of their coercive powers. These principles spell out some of the logical implications of an abstract idea of social cooperation among states aiming to establish a just and stable system of global public law. The principles are to be included in the foundation charter of such a legal order.

In order to determine whether the set of internationally enforceable basic human rights contains the same elements as the set of the basic rights of the citizens of a fully just liberal democratic society, Rawls takes a top-down approach. He starts from JF and asks whether *all* of the basic rights of such a society's citizens, that is, the rights specified by JF's two principles of justice, should count as basic human rights. His answer is no, not all of them: internationally enforceable basic human rights are at most a proper subset of those citizens' rights.[14]

In the next three sections I will further explain, first, the rationale behind Rawls's list of basic human rights; second, the idea of public reason and its role in the top-down argument; and third, the criteria of decency and their role in the bottom-up argument. Then I will explain Rawls's idea of the basic structure, its role in *LP*, and its implications regarding corporations.

A. *Human Rights and* The Law of Peoples

In *LP*, Rawls argues that certain long-standing principles of international conduct (i.e., that states are to observe a duty of nonintervention, and that states have the right of self-defense but no right to instigate war for reasons other than self-defense) have rightly been revised in recent years[15] to allow for intervention in cases of "grave violations of human rights."[16] He further modifies these principles by substituting the term "peoples" for the term "states"; thus, he puts the normative idea of a well-ordered society under a legitimate government (a type of moral ideal to which he refers using "peoples" as a technical term) in place of the idea standardly used in political science (particularly in realist international-relations theory), according to which a state is a rational, self-interested collective agent that mainly aims to acquire and retain military, economic, and diplomatic power over other states. He imagines the governments of peoples setting up a system of international public law, and argues that only peoples that satisfy criteria of decency, including honoring certain basic human rights, are entitled to the rights traditionally ascribed to all states.

Rawls presents his proposed list of internationally enforceable basic human rights as merely an incomplete, abstract sketch.[17] Its function is mainly to indicate that the list of basic human rights appropriate for a Law of Peoples would largely agree with classic bills of rights, but that not all of the rights listed in the *UDHR* should be classified as permissibly enforced internationally on moral grounds independent of official commitments to secure them.

In *LP*, Rawls argues that if the concept of basic human rights is supposed to get employed by political leaders and policymakers in their practical reasoning about using coercive force internationally, then the philosopher must keep that in mind when developing an interpretation of the concept.[18] The interpretation must specify which rights are to count as belonging to the category of internationally enforceable basic human rights. Therefore, Rawls argues, it should meet the requirements of public reason. The idea of public reason, which I explain in the next section, shapes *LP*'s conception of basic human rights. For in *LP* Rawls argues that a global legal order must recognize the basic moral equality of every individual human person by securing for everyone all of the basic human rights that can be adequately justified as such rights by public reason.

B. *Public Reason, Political Liberalism, Reciprocity, and Reasonableness*

According to Rawls, a conception of justice should establish a shared basis for public justifications, which are attempts to convince others by using public reason, that is, by reasoning in ways appropriate to fundamental political questions, relying only on beliefs and political values that it is reasonable for others also to acknowledge. In a well-ordered society effectively regulated by a publicly recognized and generally accepted political conception of justice, each citizen "cooperates, politically and socially, with the rest on terms all can endorse as just." When citizens disagree about the justice of policies, institutions, rules, and principles, they must offer each other justifications of their political judgments. A public justification offers valid argument proceeding from premises that all of the disagreeing parties (assumed to be free, equal, and fully capable of the relevant kinds of reasoning) "may reasonably be expected to share and freely endorse."[19]

Rawls first presented his idea of public reason by describing JF as a form of political liberalism that "tries to articulate a family of highly significant (moral) values that characteristically apply to the political and social institutions of the basic structure" and that "gives an account of these values in the light of certain special features of the political relationship as distinct from other relationships, associational, familial, and personal." One distinctive feature of the political relationship is the fact that whenever political power is used by a government, it is always coercive. In a constitutional democratic regime, political power "is regarded as the power of free and equal citizens as a collective body." Moreover, constitutional democratic societies are always characterized by "the fact of reasonable pluralism," that is, the fact that diverse reasonable comprehensive doctrines arise in conditions of freedom. Taking note of these facts, Rawls considers what kind of conception of justice, supported by what reasons and values, should guide citizens in exercising political power over each other. He concludes that the conception must be a "political conception of justice,"[20] one based on and expressing values that each citizen can endorse.[21]

Political liberalism uses the idea of public justification in order to bracket intractable religious and philosophical controversies, that is, to set them aside so that it may be possible to reduce the divisiveness of political conflicts. It avoids either rejecting or presupposing as true any particular comprehensive doctrine,[22] aiming thereby to "preserve the conditions of effective and democratic social cooperation on a footing of mutual respect between citizens regarded as free and equal." In order to achieve this aim, it uses ideas implicit in the political culture to develop a public basis of justification that all citizens can endorse from within their own comprehensive doctrines. If this attempt succeeds, it yields a political conception of justice that can form the core of an "overlapping consensus of reasonable doctrines," and citizens holding them will be able to affirm it after reasoned reflection upon their considered convictions about justice.[23]

A conception of justice applicable to the basic structure of a system of social cooperation is reasonable if and only if its principles satisfy an appropriate criterion of reciprocity. Terms of cooperation may be regarded as fair if and only if those proposing them have good reason to regard them as acceptable to all of the participants, who are thought of as equals acting freely and not subject to domination, manipulation, or the pressures generated by an inferior social, economic, or political position. If the system of social cooperation to which a conception of justice is to apply is a single society, then a reasonable conception of justice for it is one that meets the criterion of reciprocity for equal citizens acting freely. If the system of social cooperation is a Society of Peoples, then a reasonable conception of justice is one that meets the criterion of reciprocity for equal peoples acting freely.

Some of the differing moral doctrines, and their associated conceptions of justice and governmental legitimacy, that may arise over time in conditions of freedom can coexist within a single constitutional democracy (whether as part of the overlapping consensus supporting a political liberal conception of justice, or as among views that do not threaten it). Others cannot. Among the latter are nonliberal doctrines. Some of these cannot, but others can, govern societies that can be members in good standing of a Society of Peoples. Nonliberal societies of this latter kind are reasonable as regards relations between peoples, although less than reasonable as regards their domestic structure of political and economic institutions.

A well-ordered liberal society[24] is a fully reasonable society: its basic structure is ordered in accordance with a conception of justice that meets the liberal criterion of reciprocity. A nonliberal society is not a fully reasonable society in this technical sense. A nonliberal society may be a well-ordered society, that is, its basic structure may be ordered according to the requirements of a conception of justice; however, this conception does not meet the liberal criterion of reciprocity. Therefore, every nonliberal society, whether well-ordered or not, is to some degree unjust, according to Rawls.

There is, however, a significant moral difference between those nonliberal societies that are well ordered in accordance with some conception of justice, and those that are not. There is also a significant moral difference between those nonliberal societies that are well ordered in accordance with a conception of justice that requires that the society's basic structure of political and legal institutions provide for the good of all members by recognizing and securing their basic human rights, and those that are well ordered in accord with a conception of justice that does not require this. And liberal political philosophers need to take due account of these moral differences when developing the principles to guide states in using force internationally.

These considerations constitute the basis of Rawls's "top-down" argument. I will now sketch his "bottom-up" argument. Then I will consider whether the transformation of state sovereignty and the increasing power of corporations require any modification of Rawls's conception of human rights.

C. The Criteria of Decency

The moral ideas that play the principal roles in the bottom-up argument are the idea of justice (understood in abstraction from any particular substantive conception of distributive justice, including JF) and a version of the idea of a well-ordered society more abstract than the one that figures in JF. Rawls conceives a Society of Peoples as a system of social cooperation among well-ordered societies following a Law of Peoples. An implication of this idea is that each participating society must be both capable of acting as an agent and capable of constraining its own actions and aims according to moral requirements. Among the factors determining whether a society has these capacities and will reliably so act is its governing ideology or set of values, whether religious or secular, including its conception of its own fundamental interests as a society.

Rawls argues that participating societies must satisfy his first criterion of decency,[25] which states a requirement of nonagressiveness vis-à-vis other societies, as well as his second criterion,[26] which comprises three conditions of governmental legitimacy. One of these conditions requires respect for the basic human rights that he lists. Rawls's justification of his second criterion of decency may be summarized as follows.[27] A system of laws must meet certain conditions if it is to be viable. However, if those to whom the laws are applied are to have *bona fide* moral duties and obligations to obey them, the legal system must meet not only the conditions of viability but also a further condition: the officials of the government must be trying in good faith to govern justly and to ensure that the laws accord with their conception of justice and its idea of the common good of the society.

Furthermore, argues Rawls, a society's political and legal system can be regarded as morally defensible, and the society as well ordered, only if it is ordered in accordance with a conception of justice that understands the common good of the society as requiring that the fundamental interests (as it understands them) of everyone in the society be secured. Thus Rawls regards a society as well ordered only if the political and legal system is structured so as to ensure that everyone's fundamental interests (as it understands them) are secured. In addition, the governing conception of justice must understand the fundamental interests of those to whom the laws are applied in a way that is consistent with recognizing them not only as human beings but also as moral persons, for their being moral persons is entailed by the very idea of a political and legal system ordered in accordance with a conception of justice that imposes *bona fide* moral duties and obligations upon them.

Rawls holds that any society meeting the criteria of decency would have a moral character entitling it to respectful treatment by other states. He hypothesizes that at least some decent yet nonliberal democratic societies might be both able and willing to participate in establishing and maintaining a just and stable system of global public law. If the hypothesis is true, then the principles of *LP* and its list of basic human rights must meet the condition of endorsability by such societies, that is, the criterion of reciprocity applicable to a Society of Peoples. Therefore, the list of basic human rights will be shorter than the list of the basic rights of the citizens of a fully just liberal democratic society.

D. The Basic Structure and Corporations

In the preceding three sections I have provided an overview of Rawls's conception of human rights. I will soon consider its implications with regard to the increasing power of corporations and the transformation of state sovereignty. In order to do so, I must first explain the idea of the basic structure of a well-ordered society. This idea plays a central role both in JF and in *LP*.

In JF,[28] Rawls assumes that the main political and social institutions of a society fit together into one system of social cooperation, assign basic rights and duties, and regulate the division of advantages that arises from social cooperation over time. These institutions include the constitution, the legally recognized forms of property, and the structure of the economy. Collectively, they form "the background social framework within which the activities of associations and individuals take place."[29]

JF takes the basic structure of a well-ordered society as the primary subject of political justice.[30] Among the main reasons for doing so is that "the effects of the basic structure on citizens' aims, aspirations, and character, as well as on their opportunities and their ability to take advantage of them, are pervasive and present from the beginning of life."[31] JF's two principles each apply to one of the two principal aspects of the basic structure: (1) the constitutional regime, and (2) the background economic and social institutions. The first principle of justice, which applies to the constitution, specifies and secures citizens' equal basic liberties; the second limits economic and social inequalities. Rawls assigns lexical priority to the first principle. The second is always to be applied within a setting of background institutions that satisfy the requirements of the first.[32]

It is important to note that the principles of JF constrain or limit, without uniquely determining, the principles suitable for local justice, that is, the principles to be followed directly by associations and institutions within the basic structure: "Firms and labor unions, churches, universities, and the family are bound by constraints arising from the principles of justice. . . ." These constraints "arise indirectly from just background institutions within which associations and groups exist, and by which the conduct of their members is restricted."[33]

Analogously to JF, *LP* takes the basic structure of a Society of Peoples as its primary subject.[34] The number of *LP*'s principles and the fact that Rawls does not specify priority relations among them may seem to ruin the parallelism. However, the principles together are analogous to JF's first principle of justice in that they "define the basic equality of all peoples" that honor human rights.[35] Together they have priority over the further guidelines and standards to be formulated: guidelines for "setting up cooperative organizations" and "standards of fairness for trade."[36] Thus, according to Rawls's version of political liberalism, principles of justice structuring governmental institutions and international relations are to set constraints applying to all non-governmental organizations, including corporations, in both their domestic and their transnational activities. The basic structure of a system of social cooperation, whether among individuals or among societies, must secure the basic human rights.

III

Slaughter

I HAVE ARGUED THAT Rawls's conception of human rights requires all systems of social cooperation to secure the basic human rights. Now I will consider the relation between this conception of human rights and Slaughter's account of state disaggregation. The process Slaughter describes is, she says, not the disappearance of state governments but their transformation as new international forms of governance emerge.[37] I will argue that the emergence of new forms of governance does not undermine Rawls's conception of human rights, although it requires further development of his conception of global justice.

Slaughter explains that governmental officials ranging from judges, cabinet ministers, and legislators to regulators and police have been creating cross-border networks with their counterparts in other countries in order to cope with globalization-generated problems relating to travel, markets, terrorism, and looming environmental disasters. She argues that these networks are an increasingly important and valuable form of global governance. It is clear, she thinks, that "we need more government on a global and regional scale," yet a world government with centralized decision-making authority and coercive power is undesirable.[38] She notes that governmental networks can perform many of the functions of a world government without that form. Therefore, she contends, we should wake up to their strengths, take fuller advantage of such networks, and provide them with the necessary support, in part by recognizing them formally in international law.[39] In the world she envisions, states would remain "crucial actors,"[40] though relating to each other in more diverse ways: the officials in the different branches and institutions of government "would participate in many different types of networks, creating links across national borders and between national and supranational institutions."[41] These government networks would work alongside, within, and in some cases in place of traditional international organizations.[42]

The "structural core" of such a world order would be "a set of horizontal networks among national government officials in their respective issue areas, ranging from central banking through anti-trust regulation and environmental protection to law enforcement and human rights protection."[43] Vertical networks are created when states delegate some particular aspect of their governing authority to a supranational organization.[44] Although "it is impossible to grant supranational officials genuine coercive power" in the absence of a world government, domestic government officials may exercise their coercive powers to implement supranational rules and decisions.[45] But "a core principle" of the world order Slaughter favors is "the importance of keeping global governance functions primarily in the hands of domestic government officials."[46]

Slaughter offers descriptions of current governmental networks, an analysis of our current world order, and predictions about the future of its ongoing processes of transformation. She does not discuss Rawls's conception of human rights. However, it seems clear that insofar as her account is descriptive or empirical, it does not conflict with *LP*, for two reasons: (1) *LP* is not a descriptive account but a normative conception, and (2) *LP* does not require governmental institutions to have any particular form, but only to satisfy the appropriate requirements of justice. Appropriate requirements include at least those that apply to all states. Changes in the forms of government do not reduce the requirements of justice; instead, the latter set moral constraints determining the permissible forms.

Whether governmental institutions of the form(s) Slaughter describes can satisfy the requirements of justice is an open question. Slaughter contends that an order of disaggregated states could better secure justice and human rights, especially once informal governmental networks become recognized and formalized in international law. But whether this is true is partly an empirical question: its answer depends not only on what exactly she means by "human rights" and "justice" but also on how the formalized governmental networks would actually function.

Slaughter also proposes a set of global norms to constrain the operation of governmental networks, and suggests that they be part of a "global transgovernmental constitution." The principles she proposes[47] appear consistent with, although not entailed by, Rawls's principles. However, she does not develop their contents or justifications to any great extent; indeed, she says that "the content of these specific principles is less important in many ways than the simple fact that there be principles—benchmarks against which accountability can be measured." What is most important is that governmental networks should be understood as a form of government, and held "to the same standards and subject to the same strictures that we hold all government."[48] A Rawlsian can agree, with the caveat that these standards and strictures be based on and constrained by *LP*, in particular its list of basic human rights, suitably interpreted.

IV

O'Neill and Rawls

I HAVE ARGUED THAT there is no fundamental conflict between Rawls's conception of human rights and Slaughter's account of state disaggregation. But O'Neill's conception of an ideally just global order does conflict with Rawls's. I will now examine this conflict.

O'Neill objects to "modern liberalism" on the grounds that it focuses solely on rights, downplays the importance of imperfect duties, and "marginalizes the entire tradition of the virtues."[49] Moreover, she classifies Rawls as a "welfare liberal" and objects to welfare liberalism, as she characterizes it, because she regards it as based on the view that there are no obligations other than those of justice. Furthermore, she objects to Rawls's conception of global justice and human rights on the ground that it is statist.

O'Neill's characterizations of modern liberalism and welfare liberalism, however, do not correctly apply to Rawls's version of liberalism.[50] And as I will now argue, O'Neill misinterprets *LP*. I will focus on her contention that *LP* is statist, since one of my main aims presently is to determine whether O'Neill has developed a conception of an ideally just global order that conflicts with Rawls's regarding states' and corporations' obligations and powers to secure human rights. O'Neill presents her contention that *LP* is statist in two recent articles that focus mainly on the urgency of finding new ways to secure rights and promote justice for the members of societies in which political and legal institutions are dysfunctional.

O'Neill argues against regarding transnational companies or corporations (TNCs) as without obligations to actively undertake to promote justice where state institutions are failing to do so. She rebuts the contention that TNCs' obligations of justice extend only as far as compliance with laws, as well as the contention that TNCs are not capable of actively promoting justice by going beyond compliance with laws, even in dysfunctional states where the laws are not properly enforced. Furthermore, she suggests that since many "obligations of justice require exemptions from certain standard ethical requirements," we "could accept" such exemptions for TNCs or other nongovernmental organizations that take on justice-promoting tasks within weak or failing states, if these exemptions are not status related but task related.[51]

O'Neill does not deny that state institutions are important, indeed crucial, for securing justice. She notes that "even in cases where certain nonstate agents have acquired selected state-like capabilities . . . they do not enjoy the range of capabilities held by states that succeed in being primary agents of justice."[52] But she argues that although TNCs may be "ill constructed to substitute for the full range of contributions that states can (but often fail to) make to justice," still "there are many contributions that they can make, especially when states are weak."[53] Corporations can and should use their power "to support and strengthen reasonably just states."[54] For what "those in weak states need is a process of institution building by which justiciable rights are increasingly secured"; if state institutions can be strengthened and greater political justice be secured, this "in turn may deliver economic justice."[55] Her concern is that reform may take a very long time, and that in the meantime lives are being lost or are lived in miserable conditions.

Many, if not all, of O'Neill's views on these topics are compatible with Rawls's. However, apparently she does not see this; she dismissively labels Rawls's view "statist." Given that she herself evidently sees reasons to regard states as essential components of a just global order, and expresses some skepticism about global governance through powerful global institutions,[56] it is somewhat surprising that she denounces statism—until we understand precisely what she means by it. But once we understand this, we see that she has misinterpreted Rawls's view.

O'Neill asserts that Rawls's theory of justice links principles of justice of universal scope "to a substantially statist view of agents of justice."[57] A statist view, according to her, assumes that states alone have "the will and the capabilities to discharge, delegate, or assign all obligations of justice"; that is, statist views assume that states alone are what O'Neill terms "primary agents of justice."[58] But Rawls nowhere says, and indeed his view is incompatible with the idea that, actual states have such authority over all obligations of justice. Yet O'Neill evidently takes him to hold this view. This seems clear from the specific arguments she makes, which I will now examine.

"Up to a point," O'Neill says, "statist approaches to anchoring the obligations of justice may, it seems, be on the right track."[59] The problem with them, she says, is that they allocate these obligations "in ways that may not work."[60] Specifically, there are three reasons why it is a mistake to regard states as "the sole agents of justice," or as "always appropriate primary agents of justice": (1) many states are unjust; (2) many states are incapable of securing justice for their citizens or members; and (3) "even states with some capacities to secure rights . . . often find that processes of globalization require them to make their borders more porous, thereby weakening state power and allowing powerful agents and agencies of other sorts to become more active within their borders. For example, weak states often cannot do much to control the activities of transnational corporations or of international crime within their borders, and may not succeed in regulating legitimate business either."[61]

Rawls, too, pays particular attention to weak and rogue states or, in his terms, "burdened societies" and "outlaw states." Far from regarding their governments as the proper agents to determine and assign, as well as discharge or delegate, all obligations of justice, Rawls undertakes to determine the contents of the principles of justice that should guide well-ordered societies in identifying and dealing with such states (whether by using force in self-defense, undertaking humanitarian intervention, or providing various forms of assistance).[62] In doing so he is guided by the conviction that justice is the first or highest virtue of social institutions, and that whenever we employ political power, whether as citizens or as officials of government, whether domestically or internationally, morality requires us to guide our conduct by appropriate principles of justice.[63]

Nor does Rawls deny that we also have duties of justice in our various nonpolitical roles in life, and simply as human beings. He merely restricts the focus of his inquiry to questions about political power and the principles of justice pertaining to its uses. His subject matter is political and legal institutions. This restricted focus should not be taken to show that Rawls denies that principles of justice apply to nonpolitical institutions, associations, or practices. Indeed, he says explicitly: "While the principles of justice as fairness impose limits on these social arrangements within the basic structure, the basic structure and the associations and social forms within it are each governed by distinct principles in view of their different aims and purposes and their peculiar nature and special requirements."[64]

O'Neill is of course right that actual states should not be assumed to be adequately securing justice when they lack either the capabilities or the will to do so. But Rawls is not guilty of this error. She is also right that states should not be thought of as having monopolies on obligations to secure justice. But Rawls is not guilty of this error, either. He does think of governments as complex political and legal institutions with the distinctive role of employing power for the public good in accord with appropriate principles of justice, but apparently so does O'Neill. So where, if at all, does her view clash with his? She does discuss a topic he does not address—namely, whether corporations can and should undertake actively to promote justice in failed states. But merely taking up a further question does not by itself amount to contradicting the answers to questions previously addressed. Nor does her view about corporations as agents of justice necessarily conflict with his views. However, she has merely sketched, not developed in detail, her suggestion to exempt corporations from certain standard ethical requirements so that they may carry out certain justice-promoting tasks in failed states. If this can be done without placing impediments in the way of reforming and rebuilding the institutions of government to meet the standards of Rawls's criteria of decency, then a Rawlsian may have no objection. However, he or she may well prefer Slaughter's quite different approach to such problems. I shall conclude by discussing this approach.

V

Slaughter and Rawls

SLAUGHTER ARGUES IN FAVOR OF governmental networks partly on the ground that they "could provide multilateral support for domestic government institutions in failed, weak, or transitional states."[65] If the full range of influential political agents, scholars, and commentators sought actively to create and use governmental networks as instruments of global governance, and if their participants more fully embraced the international and global aspects of their roles, these networks could "improve the governing performance of both actual and potential members" as well as improve compliance with international rules.[66] If membership in governmental networks had clear value in the form of status as well as services, then the networks could develop a disciplinary system involving suspension of membership for "severe and demonstrable infractions."[67] This would permit targeting specific government institutions for either reform or reinforcement. Such targeting, applying pressure to some of a state's institutions while bolstering others, "holds the possibility of helping transitional states stabilize and democratize."[68] Further, in postconflict situations, these networks could help states rebuild their institutions, not only by providing technical assistance and training, but also through ongoing interactions among official counterparts in different state governments upholding professional standards.[69] More generally, governmental networks could "strengthen compliance with international rules and norms, both through vertical enforcement and information networks and by building governance capacity in countries that have the will but not the means to comply."[70]

Slaughter sees corporate and civic actors playing roles in this new order of disaggregated states, since there are "multitudes of nongovernmental actors, who must be engaged in global governance as they are in domestic governance."[71] She proposes that governmental networks be "designated interlocutors" for them, as well as that international organizations, NGOs, corporations, and other interested actors be included in broad policy networks.[72] However, she criticizes the "amorphous 'global policy networks' championed by UN Secretary General Kofi Annan, in which it is never clear who is exercising power on behalf of whom."[73] Noting that "corporate and civic actors . . . may be driven by profits and passions, respectively," she emphasizes that governmental networks would form "the spine" of the broad policy networks she proposes, that is, that these policy networks would have "an accountable core of government officials."[74] Here Slaughter's position apparently diverges from O'Neill's regarding corporations.

Slaughter imagines in detail future possibilities within constraints set by our actual global order, while Rawls leaves up to our imaginations all of the possibilities for further development of institutions and cooperative practices that would be left open (as permitted by justice) to well-ordered states after they had endorsed the Law of Peoples and established the charter of their common legal system. Rawls's project is to develop a political conception of the moral basis of a just system of international law, including a justification of human rights meeting the requirements of public reason. Slaughter's project differs from his, but there appears to be no fundamental conflict between them. Her empirical account of state-disaggregation does not undermine any premises on which Rawls's moral-philosophical arguments rely, and she does not argue against *LP*. O'Neill does argue against *LP*, but her arguments fail. If *LP* is sound and compatible with Slaughter's account of the transformation of states, then we have some reason to doubt that globalization is rendering obsolete conceptions of human rights such as Rawls's, and we have some reason to hope that a just world order is a realistic possibility.

Notes

1. For example, Jack Donnelly, *Universal Human Rights in Theory and Practice*, 2nd ed. (Ithaca, NY: Cornell University Press, 2003).

2. John Rawls, *The Law of Peoples* (Cambridge: Harvard University Press, 1999); henceforth "*LP.*"

3. Dean of Princeton University's Woodrow Wilson School of Public and International Affairs.

4. Anne-Marie Slaughter, *A New World Order* (Princeton, NJ: Princeton University Press, 2004), 12; henceforth "*NWO.*"

5. *NWO*, 12–13.

6. *NWO*, 35.

7. *NWO*, 28–29, 35.

8. Onora O'Neill is the author of a number of articles on Kantian morality as well as on national and global ethical and political issues, and is also the author of the books *Faces of Hunger* (East Melbourne, Victoria: Allen and Unwin, 1986), *Constructions of Reason: Explorations of Kant's Practical Philosophy* (Cambridge: Cambridge University Press, 1989), and *Towards Justice and Virtue* (Cambridge: Cambridge University Press, 1996), henceforth "*FH*," "*CR*," and "*TJV*," respectively.

9. For a helpful overview, see Georg Sorensen, *The Transformation of the State* (New York: Palgrave Macmillan, 2004), Chs. 1 and 10.

10. I do not interpret Rawls as holding that states may legitimately act to enforce rights merely because the rights are justifiable via sound moral and philosophical arguments, even though they are not recognized in positive law.

11. See John Rawls, *A Theory of Justice* (Cambridge: Harvard University Press, [1971] 1999), *Political Liberalism* (New York: Columbia University Press, [1993] 1996), and *Justice as Fairness* (Cambridge: Harvard University Press, 2001); henceforth "*TJ*," "*PL*," and "*JF*," respectively.

12. "(a) Each person has the same indefeasible claim to a fully adequate scheme of equal basic liberties, which scheme is compatible with the same scheme of liberties for all; and (b) Social and economic inequalities are to satisfy two conditions: first, they are to be attached to offices and positions open to all under conditions of fair equality of opportunity; and second, they are to be to the greatest benefit of the least-advantaged members of society (the difference principle)" (*JF*, 42–43).

13. The principles of *LP* are the following:

(1) Peoples are free and independent, and their freedom and independence are to be respected by other peoples.
(2) Peoples are to observe treaties and undertakings.
(3) Peoples are equal and are parties to the agreements that bind them.
(4) Peoples are to observe a duty of non-intervention.
(5) Peoples have the right of self-defense but no right to instigate war for reasons other than self-defense.
(6) Peoples are to honor human rights.

(7) Peoples are to observe certain specified restrictions in the conduct of war.

(8) Peoples have a duty to assist other peoples living under unfavorable conditions that prevent their having a just or decent political and social regime. (*LP*, 37)

14. I develop this argument in "A Human Right to Democracy? Legitimacy and Intervention," in *Rawls's Law of Peoples: A Realistic Utopia?*, eds. Rex Martin and David Reidy (Malden, MA: Blackwell, 2006).

15. To say this is not to say that they have been revised for the right reasons or in precisely the right ways.

16. *LP*, 37.

17. "Among the human rights are the right to life (to the means of subsistence and security); to liberty (to freedom from slavery, serfdom and forced occupation, and to a sufficient measure of liberty of conscience to ensure freedom of religion and thought); to property (personal property); and to formal equality as expressed by the rules of natural justice (that is, that similar cases be treated similarly)" (*LP*, 65, footnotes omitted).

18. Rawls uses the term "conception" to refer to a particular interpretation of a concept (*TJ*, 5, 8–9).

19. All quotations in this paragraph are drawn from *JF*, 27.

20. A conception of domestic societal justice is "political," as Rawls specifies the meaning of this term, if it has the following three features:

(a) It is a moral conception worked out for a specific subject, namely, the basic structure of a democratic society.

(b) Accepting this conception does not presuppose accepting any particular comprehensive doctrine.

(c) A political conception of justice is formulated so far as possible solely in terms of fundamental ideas familiar from, or implicit in, the public political culture of a democratic society. (*JF*, 26–27)

21. All quotations in this paragraph are drawn from *JF*, 40–41.

22. "A conception is fully comprehensive if it covers all recognized values and virtues within one rather precisely articulated system"; by contrast, "a political conception tries to elaborate a reasonable conception for the basic structure alone and involves, so far as possible, no wider commitment to any other doctrine" (*PL*, 13).

23. All quotations in this paragraph are drawn from *JF*, 28–29.

24. Such a society has a constitutional democratic government that answers to and protects the people's fundamental interests as specified in the constitution (*LP*, 23–24).

25. "First, the society does not have aggressive aims, and it recognizes that it must gain its legitimate ends through diplomacy and trade and other ways of peace" (*LP*, 64).

26. "The second criterion has three parts.

(a) The first part is that a decent hierarchical people's system of law, in accordance with its common good idea of justice . . . , secures for all members of the people what have come to be called human rights. . . .

(b) The second part is that a decent people's system of law must be such as to impose *bona fide* moral duties and obligations (distinct from human rights) on all persons within the people's territory. . . .

(c) Finally, the third part of the second criterion is that there must be a sincere and not unreasonable belief on the part of judges and other officials who administer the legal system that the law is indeed guided by a common good idea of justice . . . " (*LP*, 65–66)

27. This justification can be reconstructed from several elliptical passages of *LP* and *PL* in which Rawls refers to works by other authors, including H. L. A. Hart and Philip Soper. I develop this argument in "Justifying Universal Human Rights via Rawlsian Public Reason," forthcoming in *ARSP (Archiv für Rechts und Sozialphilosophie)*.

28. *JF*, section 4.

29. *JF*, 10.

30. *TJ*, section 2; *JF*, section 4.

31. *JF*, 10.

32. *JF*, 42–50.

33. All quotations in this paragraph are drawn from *JF*, 10.

34. *LP*, 3–10, 42 n.52.

35. *LP*, 42.

36. *LP*, 42–43.

37. Sufficient transformation arguably constitutes elimination. However, Slaughter asserts that no such degree of transformation is occurring. Not being an expert in her field(s) I defer to her authority here.

38. *NWO*, 8.

39. *NWO*, 1–4, 8–11, 33–35.

40. *NWO*, 5.

41. *NWO*, 6.

42. *NWO*, 4–6, 10.

43. *NWO*, 19.

44. One example is the European Union's judicial system, which "devolves primary responsibility for enforcing [European Court of Justice] judgments not onto EU 'member-states,' per se, but onto the national judges of those states." Another example is the EU's emerging "vertical administrative network between the antitrust authority of the European Commission and national antitrust regulators that will allow the commission to charge national authorities with implementing EU rules in accordance with their particular national traditions" (All quotations in this paragraph are drawn from *NWO*, 21).

45. *NWO*, 20–21.

46. *NWO*, 20, 262–263.

47. (1) Global Deliberative Equality, (2) Legitimate Difference, (3) Positive Comity, (4) Checks and Balances, and (5) Subsidiarity (*NWO*, 29–30, 244–260).

48. All quotations in this paragraph are drawn from *NWO*, 260.

49. *CR*, 192, 219–223.

50. I support this claim in my dissertation, "Human Rights Reconceived: A Defense of Rawls's Law of Peoples" (Ph.D. diss., Harvard University, 2000).

51. This distinction is unclear, and may not be sustainable in practice, since allowing the exemption changes to some extent the status of the organization, especially if the task continues over a long period of time and the government remains weak. Here arise questions about who is to grant and monitor the exemptions, as well as about how it may be possible to prevent abuse of these powers or privileges.

52. "Agents of Justice," in *Metaphilosophy* 32 (January 2001), 190; henceforth "*AJ*."

53. *AJ*, 193.

54. *AJ*, 194.

55. "Global Justice: Whose Obligations?" in *The Ethics of Assistance*, ed. Deen K. Chatterjee (Cambridge: Cambridge University Press, 2004), 257; henceforth "*GJ*."

56. "I am at least partly sceptical about those attempts to realize cosmopolitan principles through cosmopolitan or global institutions that do not show what is to prevent global governance from degenerating into global tyranny and global injustice. Big may not always be beautiful, and institutional cosmopolitanism may not always be the best route to universal justice" (*AJ*, 181).

57. *GJ*, 243–244.

58. *GJ*, 246.

59. *GJ*, 245.

60. *GJ*, 245–246.

61. *GJ*, 246–247.

62. *LP*, sections 13–16.

63. *TJ*, 3–6.

64. *JF*, 11.

65. *NWO*, 4.

66. *NWO*, 195.

67. *NWO*, 203.

68. *NWO*, 203.

69. *NWO*, 214.

70. *NWO*, 213.

71. *NWO*, 26.

72. *NWO*, 26, 28.

73. *NWO*, 4, 240.
74. *NWO*, 9, 10, 28–29.

References

Bernstein, A. (2006). "A Human Right to Democracy? Legitimacy and Intervention." In *Rawls's Law of Peoples: A Realistic Utopia?*, eds. Rex Martin and David Reidy, pp. 278–298. Malden, MA: Blackwell Press.

Donnelly, J. (2003). *Universal Human Rights in Theory and Practice*, 2nd ed. Ithaca, NY: Cornell University Press.

O'Neill, O. (1986). *Faces of Hunger*. East Melbourne, Victoria: Allen and Unwin.

———. (1989). *Constructions of Reason: Explorations of Kant's Practical Philosophy*. Cambridge: Cambridge University Press.

———. (1996). *Towards Justice and Virtue*. Cambridge: Cambridge University Press.

———. (2001). "Agents of Justice." *Metaphilosophy* 32: 180–195.

———. (2004). "Global Justice: Whose Obligations?" In *The Ethics of Assistance*, ed. Deen K. Chatterjee, pp. 242–259. Cambridge: Cambridge University Press.

Rawls, J. ([1971] 1999). *A Theory of Justice*. Cambridge: Harvard University Press.

———. (1993). *Political Liberalism*. New York: Columbia University Press.

———. (1999). *The Law of Peoples*. Cambridge: Harvard University Press.

———. (2001). *Justice as Fairness*. Cambridge: Harvard University Press.

Slaughter, A. M. (2004). *A New World Order*. Princeton, NJ: Princeton University Press.

Sorensen, G. (2004). *The Transformation of the State*. New York: Palgrave Macmillan.

5
Beyond Intrinsic Value

Undermining the Justification of Ecoterrorism

By CHARLES S. BROWN*

ABSTRACT.   Both Aldo Leopold's "land ethic" and Arne Naess's "deep
ecology" have been criticized as providing intellectual justifications for
both a misanthropic ecofascism and a policy of ecoterrorism for
environmental activists. This chapter argues that each of these two
approaches to providing a ground or framework for an environmental
ethics is subject to the charges of ecofascism or ecoterrorism only to
the extent that each is committed to the notion of "intrinsic value" as
a nonnegotiable moral absolute or, as Kant puts it, "a value beyond all
price." This chapter begins by describing shared value experience
between humans and animals and then points the way to an alternative and pragmatic concept of value that can better guide environmental thinking on matters of law, policy, and activism. This concept
of value emerges from an experiential and epistemic understanding of
the inherent rationality of value experience. A description of value
experience reveals that the lived significance of value experience
exhibits a meaningful and referential structure in which anticipations
of future experience are either satisfied or frustrated in future experience. This meaningful structure of value experience, in which value
experiences point to their own confirmation or disconfirmation, constitutes a self-correcting tendency or a prima facie rationality inherent
in value experience. The result is a pragmatic conception of value that
takes all value intuition and attribution to be intrinsically revisable in
light of future experience. As such, value experience is always subject

*Charles S. Brown is Professor of Philosophy at Emporia State University. He is the
co-editor of *Eco-Phenomenology: Back to the Earth Itself* (SUNY Press, 2003) and author
of many articles on intentionality, value theory, and environmental ethics.

American Journal of Economics and Sociology, Vol. 66, No. 1 (January, 2007).

to negotiation, dialogue, and the weight of future experience. This conception of value undercuts the intellectual, psychological, and moral justification for ecofascism or ecoterrorism.

ACCORDING TO RECENT public declarations by the FBI, animal rights and environmental activists are emerging as a serious domestic terrorist threat in the United States.[1] The FBI estimates that two organizations, the Earth Liberation Front and the Animal Liberation Front, have committed over 600 criminal acts in the United States since 1996, resulting in damages in excess of $43 million. Although no humans have been killed in any known case of environmental activism, the suspicion that environmental activists may be willing to kill innocent human beings to promote their pro-nature political agenda finds some support among environmental philosophers who have suggested that highly respected attempts to ground and articulate an environmental ethics, such as Aldo Leopold's "land ethic" and Arne Naess's "deep ecology," lead to an anti-human ecofascism.[2]

Leopold's moral maxim, "A thing is right when it tends to preserve the integrity, stability, and beauty of the biotic community. It is wrong when it tends otherwise,"[3] would seem to support massive human depopulation by any means necessary. After all, if it is permissible to kill individual deer to preserve the underlying ecosystem, and if humans are plain members and citizens of the ecological community, then it should be permissible to kill individual humans for the good of the whole. According to Tom Regan and others, the requirement that individuals be sacrificed for the good of the whole makes the land ethic into a form of ecofascism.[4] A similar charge may be made against an environmental ethics rooted in deep ecology. In their list of deep ecology's basic principles, Bill Devall and George Sessions state that all life on Earth has intrinsic value, that humans have no right to reduce the richness and diversity of life except to satisfy vital needs, and that the flourishing of nonhuman life requires a decrease in human population.[5] Murray Bookchin, in particular, has drawn the connection between this kind of thinking and that of John Foreman, Earth First! founder, who has welcomed famine as a means of limiting the population, and others who have declared humans to be a plague or a cancer on the planet.[6]

Whatever the merits may be of the charge that deep ecology and the land ethic lead to ecofascism, the connection between ideology and terrorism is more worrisome simply because terrorism does not require the kind of top-down totalitarian governmental structure that any form of fascism does. The possibility of ecofascism is only a dim and distant threat, while ecoterrorism is not only an ever-present possibility but also a steadily emerging temptation to some activists. It is not simply the holism per se of deep ecology and the land ethic that drive these forms of thinking toward Draconian and violent solutions to environmental problems. The problem lies rather in the underlying notion of "intrinsic value." Ethical holism becomes pernicious only when two conditions are met: (1) when the good of the whole is thought to override or trump the intrinsic value of the individual, and (2) when the intrinsic value of the whole is judged to be intrinsic in the strong metaphysical sense of being an atemporal fixed property inherent in the whole—a nonnegotiable moral absolute or, as Kant puts it, "a value beyond all price." As long as value is judged to be a nonnegotiable moral absolute, the possibility and temptation of ecofascism and ecoterrorism exists.

Environmental philosophy needs a pragmatic and nonmetaphysical concept of value that can guide environmental thinking on law, policy, and activism while resisting the temptation of ecofascism and ecoterrorism. In the following pages I hope to develop a notion of value to serve this need, that is, a notion of value not based on a metaphysical interpretation of value as a property of things—God, humans, or nature—but rather as an experiential and epistemic understanding of the inherent rationality of our value experience. This pragmatic understanding of value takes all value intuition and attribution to be intrinsically revisable in the light of future experience. As intrinsically revisable, value experience is always subject to negotiation, dialogue, and the weight of future experience. In this way, value experiences point toward their own confirmation or disconfirmation. This self-correcting tendency of value experience constitutes a prima facie rationality inherent in intentional experience in general and value experience in particular.

The account of value defended here is rooted in a philosophical anthropology that unites a Darwinian conception of moral instincts and a phenomenological conception of moral experience. I offer a phenomenological analysis, that is, a description and interpretation of value experience, to show that value experiences exhibit an intentional structure through which value experience anticipates its own confirmation in future experience and thus contains a measure of rationality.[7] What explicitly renders value experience rational is its revisability in the face of new experience. This will be brought out by describing the inherent intentionality in value experience.

The idea of an evolutionary account of moral sentiments was first developed by Charles Darwin in his *The Descent of Man*, where he gives an account of the naturalistic origin of what he calls humanity's "moral sense."[8] The implications of Darwin's attempt to sketch an evolutionary origin of morality have been developed by natural scientists such as E. O. Wilson, Richard Alexander, and Frans de Waal and philosophers such as J. Baird Callicott. Common to these thinkers is the idea that our so-called moral sentiments of empathy, affection, and sympathy are evolutionarily shaped responses that are selected because they make social groups more efficient, more stable, and more permanent. The claim that morality is made possible by the linguistic conceptualization of inherited social feelings is on the right track but overlooks an important phenomenological fact about moral experience. Moral experience or moral phenomena display an intentional structure not captured by the view of morality as instinct plus language. What is missing from the received view concerning a Darwinian account of morality is a theory of intentionality. Our basic dispositional ways of behaving as humans, our basic possibilities, are, no doubt, prefigured in our genes and in our kinship with other animals. The fundamentals of our moral psychology may start out as gut instinct, but these basic proto-moral sentiments are not just reactions to outside stimuli. They have the quality of being directed to something or are about something. Empathy is not only a feeling with someone or something, but a feeling that has the phenomenal quality of being directed toward some object or state of affairs. Altruism is aimed toward the other. These moral sentiments are experienced by humans not as raw, unstructured feelings but as referring to the other in an attitude of compassion and solidarity. These are psychological/somatological moments directed to an empathetic other and exhibit, as we shall see, a prediscursive intelligibility and a prima facie rationality.

Moral theory and moral philosophy may be a uniquely human activity, but we are not alone in our basic capacity to respond to the world in an attitude of concern. Other social mammals are very much like humans in this respect and share with us, at least in some basic way, a moral or proto-moral openness to the world. Many people believe that dogs are our closest animal companions, and the age-old dog-human relation is, in part, built on our commonalities as well as our differences. I offer the following moral fable to illustrate the moral openness to the world shared by humans and dogs and to locate our moral nature in our animal nature.[9]

Imagine that my canine companion, Lily, and I are playing in my backyard, which is separated from my neighbor's backyard by a large privacy fence. Because of this fence, Lily and I cannot see into the neighbor's yard where another dog lives. Further imagine that one day the dog in the adjacent yard is terribly injured and Lily and I hear the dog's cries and howls but we cannot see him. Lily and I share a common response to the other dog's suffering. We hear and under-stand his pain and suffering in his howls. We both experience a considerable anxiety and an empathetic concern directed toward the injured dog. We both experience a sense of dread over what will happen next. We know something is wrong. We share the immediacy and urgency of the situation. Lily feels she needs to do something, but she doesn't know what. She feels frustration on top of an anguished concern for the dog. I know Lily feels that because I feel it as well. I see her behave very nervously, running to the fence, pawing at it, running back and forth and around in circles; she looks at me and seems to be frightened; she whines and barks. I can hear the agitation and concern in Lily's sounds, and she can hear it in mine.

Skeptics will claim that my interpretations of Lily's experience are mere projections, yet I believe Lily and I share a feeling with a similar intentional structure, a similar cognitive directedness toward the injured dog with similar anticipations. One large difference is that I interpret my anguish at the dog's pain through numerous millennia of linguistic history and the metaphysical categories that dominate those worldviews. But the basic way of experiencing the suffering of the wounded dog is not so different between Lily and myself. We do not have direct access to the dog's pain, but we seem to have something close to, if not identical to, direct access to the dog's suffering, just as we have with humans. Both of us experience a sense of urgency, that something is wrong now, and a sense that something must be done now, as well as the frustration of not knowing what to do. I believe this kind of response is a part of human moral psychology that we share with many mammals and primates.

The Darwinian view of moral instincts that I have just been sketching undermines the traditional anthropocentric view, which holds that humans are the source of all value. Not only do nonhuman species activate my moral sentiments, but other species also share those sentiments. Anthropocentricism may, in some ways, illuminate human dignity, but it also masks a larger and more comprehensive vision of moral experience by establishing a hierarchical conception of moral phenomena and, with it, a logic of domination that is often used to support more particularistic forms of anthropocentricism such as patriarchy, racism, nationalism, classism, and speciesism—each of which appeal to their own conception of intrinsic value as an atemporal metaphysical property. Anthropocentricism encourages us to dismiss any moral sentiments we may experience toward nonhumans as subjective and irrational.

I am always amazed at the stories of scientists who, under the sway of Cartesian dualism, performed vivisections on animals while interpreting their cries and howls not as genuine expressions of suffering and distress but as mere unmeaning mechanical responses. Even Lily knows better that this. Surely, if we look at and listen to such cries and howls not through the distorting lenses of anthropocentric metaphysics but in a spontaneous openness to the world, we are confronted not with mechanically produced sound and motion but with an immediate and natural expression of pain and suffering.

Both Lily and I share an attitude of concern and empathy toward the other's suffering. We share an immediate intuition that something is wrong. This intuition is as much somatic as it is cognitive. We feel, as Hume would say, in our "breast" as much as we project it toward the howling dog. My own human response to the howls of the hurt dog—the somatic anxiety dreadfully directed to the suffering dog, a gut reaction that something is wrong, a vague and diffuse feeling that something should be done (I think I share all this with Lily)—is integrated into my own linguistically based conceptual system and worldview. The prelinguistic intentional comportment of my felt sentiment is conceptualized in ways that Lily's is not. I suspect that Lily's prelinguistic intentional comportments, in this case, an empathic openness to the suffering of others, come and go, and play themselves out quickly. In my own case, the symbolic power of language extends these sentiments by binding them to longer-term projects.

While I think that Lily and I begin at a similar place, a mammalian response to suffering, my own intentional comportment toward the injured dog goes far beyond what I suspect Lily is capable of. Both Lily and I try to get past the fence to access more closely what is happening. The original experience of hearing those howls has been extended into a seeking out of more information—we both look to see what is wrong, we both anticipate and project. These anticipations and projections may be confirmed or disconfirmed in future experience. If we managed to come face to face with the injured dog and I see that the dog is caught in a nonhumane wolf trap, I will search for a way to release the dog. My recognition of the trap as a human artifact opens my experience into new conceptual domains and worlds, and these worlds bleed into my understanding. I don't think Lily would understand the wolf trap. Her projections are more immediate. If we got through the fence and saw the dog was being eaten by a lion, Lily would, I think, understand this. For Lily, all this would unfold into projections of her immediate future. She would run from the lion, anticipating trouble if she stays put, but her power to extend her experience into the future or into other symbolic domains is cut short by her lack of language.

The structure and content of human cognition, moral or otherwise, is distinguished from that of other prelinguistic animals by the temporal range and symbolic worlds that language gives to our immediate sentiments. As our moral instincts are folded into our conceptual systems, they take on new meanings. I can imagine that if I came through the fence and found the dog in an old and carelessly discarded wolf trap, my empathic anxiety of shared suffering would begin to take on air of moral disapproval as the trapped animal opened up the world of animal trapping and that, in turn, opened up the world of human domination of nature. This sense of disapproval is largely cultural and conceptual, but it is made possible and sustained over time by the gut feeling, the moral instinct, that something is wrong. We can hear that in the howls.

Because value experiences are intentional, they bring with them their own procedure for confirmation grounded in the temporal structure of anticipation and either satisfaction or frustration of such anticipation. This anticipatory projection within value experience provides or denies a justification for the sense of that lived experience.[10] If I experience friendship or marriage as good, it is not simply that I enjoy friendship or marriage; it is that I have a sense, even if unarticulated, of how and why each is good. Even if we cannot express it, we know that friendship or marriage extend our sphere of concern while comforting us in ways that help to provide our lives with meaning. To experience friendship or marriage as good is to interpret and impose the sense of good on these relations, but it is also to expect to continue to find goodness in these relations and to have such expectations fulfilled. The very experience of positive values like marriage and friendship is bound up with an implicit understanding of the meaning of marriage and friendship. Our experience of these as good is also subject to the possibility of breakdown, as the final test of value is the test of time.

Experiences of positive value that we call "good" involve knowing what to expect. It is this anticipatory structure that provides an ongoing validation of our experiences of the good. If we initially find friendship and marriage to be bad and fraud to be good, openness to further experience will almost always correct this. That we find value in friendship and disvalue in fraud is not arbitrary. Rarely do our considered judgments about these things disappoint us. Our experience continues to establish friendship and marriage as good in an ever-evolving process of being open to the good. By grounding our values and beliefs in the evolving wisdom of our collective experience, we can avoid the perils of absolutism and relativism. We can avoid dogmatic absolutism by understanding that our experiences and conceptions of the good are always open to revision, and we can avoid relativism by recognizing that our experiences of the good demand their own confirmation in future experiences.

The conditions for the possibility of moral experience are embedded in our animal nature and are greatly expanded by our ability to conceptualize our moral sentiments and intuitions within our linguistic and conceptual worldviews. Even though our moral categories and concepts, rooted in our historically constituted worldviews, allow us the power of abstract moral thinking and moral imagination, we are too often closed off from a genuinely emancipatory moral consciousness because our thinking is too often dominated by the metaphysical categories controlling our thinking. When the openness and temporality of moral experience is reduced to the ahistorical categories of God, humanity, or nature, the open-ended possibilities of experience are eliminated in favor of a finite set of rules governing what can be said or thought about moral experience. The anticipatory structure of value experience demands that our sentiments and evaluative responses to the world be understood as prima facie intuitions about the goodness or badness of the matters at hand. A first glance always requires a second look. Our various understandings of the good are subject to continual assessment in light of subsequent experience, just as we continually reassess our initial understandings of the real and the true. Over our lifetimes and through the centuries the world has unfolded in ways that have rendered our previous understandings of the good as imperfect and parochial.

This analysis of moral phenomena is an experiential and epistemic understanding of the inherent rationality of value experience rather than a metaphysical interpretation of value as a mysterious or mystical property of things. The goods we appreciate for ourselves and for others are never given as absolute but always are provisional and subject to the satisfaction or frustration of future experiences. Here we find the deepest flaw of biocentric approaches to environmental ethics such as the land ethic and deep ecology. To the extent that these and other ecophilosophies understand intrinsic value as an atemporal metaphysical property, biocentricism repeats the pattern of the other centricisms by making its experience and conception of intrinsic value into a metaphysical and moral absolute. Thus, to the extent that biocentric thinking interprets our moral experiences around a nonnegotiable ahistorical metaphysical and moral absolute, the door is still left open to the temptation of ecofascism and ecoterrorism. The logic of domination reenters the picture with the emergence of a moral absolute.

The radical ecological project of unmasking ecodestructive elements in our worldview does not end with the development of new, alternative, and ecofriendly worldviews, but rather with the more radical possibility of shifting power within our worldviews away from the controlling authority of fixed concepts and categories and toward an openness to how the world unfolds. To attempt to think without a radical questioning of the historical and contingent nature of the concepts and categories controlling thought is simply to articulate the combinatorial possibilities of fixed semantic regimes. Rather than give in to a prepackaged way of thinking, we must hold out for a kind of thinking that is open to the world, a kind of thinking that is able to take the world in, to be available to the revelation that the world may offer. Such thinking accepts what the world offers but always takes a second look. Such thinking is characterized by its intrinsic revisability in the face of an always open future.[11]

Moral experience is always a dialectic between our animal sentiments and our historically constructed worldviews. Neither our animal sentiments nor our historically constructed value systems are infallible. We live morally responsible lives only by playing one off against the other. Moral experience is always directed toward a future that is yet to come. The final categories of moral understanding are forever postponed. Without final categories there can be no final answers, and without final answers there can be no final solutions. Final solutions are always based on metaphysical absolutes. Ecological philosophy and environmental ethics will best be served by a notion of value that recognizes the temporality and interrelatedness of all things. By tracing our capacity for moral experience to the becoming of natural selection and the historicity of our worldviews, we can learn to interpret our various intuitions and experiences of value as a prima facie understanding of goodness to be born out in future experience. Such a prima facie understanding of goodness, worth, and value is never absolute and final; it is always provisional and subject to further, but never perfect, confirmation. As such, it would provide a poor means for the justification for fascist or terrorist solutions to environmental or animal rights issues.

The account of value developed here runs counter to the uncritical notion of "intrinsic value" prevalent in mainstream environmental ethics. That notion of intrinsic value—a property inherent in the thing-in-itself—falls out of a tradition interested in providing a metaphysical grounding of value. Such accounts will always be highly speculative and subject to endless challenges. The account developed here focuses on the dynamism and temporality of value experience. This account urges us to understand moral experience as emerging from social relationships—from the face-to-face openness to others structured by compassion and care. Moral philosophy has been too long dominated by an abstract, universalizing rationalism that takes acting from abstract principle as the center of moral phenomena and pushes sentiment and feeling to the margins. The account developed here sees moral phenomena as emerging from relationships, from particular contexts and particular situations.[12] Moral phenomena, in this understanding, is open-ended, in process, and ultimately, although beyond the scope of this paper, in dialogue.

Notes

1. James F. Jarboe, "The Threat of Ecoterrorism." In congressional testimony before the House Resources Committee, Subcommittee on Forests and Forest Health, February 12, 2002. For the full testimony, see http://www.fbi.gov/congress/congress02/jarboe201202.

2. For two insightful essays concerning the possibility and threat of ecofascism, see J. Baird Callicott's "Holistic Environmental Ethics and the Problem of Ecofascism," in *Beyond the Land Ethic: More Essays in Environmental Philosophy* (Albany, NY: State University of New York, 1999) and Michael Zimmerman's "The Threat of Ecofascism," in *Environmental Philosophy from Animal Rights to Radical Ecology*, eds. Zimmerman, Callicott, Warren, Klaver, Clark (Upper Saddle River, NJ: Prentice Hall, 2005).

3. Aldo Leopold, *A Sand County Almanac* (Oxford and New York: Oxford University Press, 1949), 220.

4. Tom Regan, *The Case for Animal Rights* (Berkeley, CA: University of California Press, 1983), 262. Similar criticisms of the land ethic have been made by K. S. Schrader-Frechette in her "Individualism, Holism, and Environmental Ethics," in *Ethics and the Environment* (1966) 1:55–69, and by W.

Aiken in his "Ethical Issues in Agriculture," in *Earthbound: New Introductory Essays in Environmental Ethics*, ed. T. Regan (New York: Random House, 1984), 247–288.

5. Bill Devall and George Sessions, *Deep Ecology: Living as if Nature Mattered* (Salt Lake City, UT: Peregrine Books, 1985), 70.

6. Murray Bookchin, "Social Ecology Versus Deep Ecology." *Socialist Review* 88(3) (1988): 11–29.

7. Charles S. Brown, "The Intrinsic Rationality of Moral Phenomena." *Skepsis* XV/I (2004): 477–494.

8. Charles Darwin, *The Descent of Man: And Selection in Relation to Sex* (New York: Heritage Press, 1972). This is a reprint of the 1874 second edition.

9. An earlier version of this moral fable appeared in my "Ecofascism and the Animal Heritage of Moral Experience," in *Dialogue and Universalism*, 7–8/2005. The focus of that essay was on ecofascism rather than ecoterrorism.

10. Charles S. Brown, "The Real and the Good: Phenomenology and the Possibility of an Axiological Rationality." In *Eco-Phenomenology: Back to the Earth Itself*, eds. Brown and Toadvine (Albany, NY: State University of New York Press, 2003), 3–18.

11. Charles S. Brown, "Respect for Experience as a Way into the Problem of Moral Boundaries," forthcoming, in *Boundary Explorations in Ecological Theory and Practice*, eds. Brown and Toadvine (Albany, NY: State University of New York Press).

12. Val Plumwood, "Nature, Self, and Gender: Feminism, Environmental Philosophy, and the Critique of Rationalism." *Hypathia* 6(1) (Spring 1991): 3–27. Plumwood's criticisms of traditional moral theory are compatible with the account of moral phenomena sketched in this paper.

References

Aiken, W. (1984). "Ethical Issues in Agriculture." In *Earthbound: New Introductory Essays in Environmental Ethics*, ed. T. Regan. New York: Random House.

Bookchin, Murray. (1988). "Social Ecology Versus Deep Ecology." *Socialist Review* 88(3): 11–29.

Brown, Charles S. (2003). "The Real and the Good: Phenomenology and the Possibility of an Axiological Rationality." In *Eco-Phenomenology: Back to the Earth Itself*, eds. C. Brown and T. Toadvine. Albany, NY: State University of New York Press.

——. (2004). "The Intrinsic Rationality of Moral Phenomena." *Skepsis* XV(I): 477–494.

——. (2005). "Ecofascism and the Animal Heritage of Moral Experience." *Dialogue and Universalism* 7–8: 35–48.

———. (Forthcoming). "Respect for Experience as a Way into the Problem of Moral Boundaries." In *Nature's Edge: Boundary Explorations in Ecological Theory and Practice*, eds. C. Brown and T. Toadvine. Albany, NY: State University of New York Press.

Callicott, J. Baird. (1999). "Holistic Environmental Ethics and the Problem of Ecofascism." In *Beyond the Land Ethic: More Essays in Environmental Philosophy*. Albany, NY: State University of New York Press.

Darwin, Charles. (1972). *The Descent of Man: And Selection in Relation to Sex*. New York: Heritage Press.

Devall, Bill, and George, Sessions. (1985). *Deep Ecology: Living as if Nature Mattered*. Salt Lake City, UT: Peregrine Books.

Jarboe, James F. "The Threat of Ecoterrorism." http://www.fbi.gov/congress/congress02/jarboe201202.

Leopold, Aldo. (1949). *A Sand County Almanac*. Oxford: Oxford University Press.

Plumwood, Val. (1991). "Self, and Gender: Feminism, Environmental Philosophy, and the Critique of Rationalism." *Hypathia* 6(1): 3–27.

Regan, Tom. (1983). *The Case for Animal Rights*. Berkeley: University of California Press.

Schrader-Frechette, K. S. (1966). "Individualism, Holism, and Environmental Ethics." *Ethics and the Environment* 1: 55–69.

Zimmerman, Michael. (2005). "The Threat of Ecofascism." In *Environmental Philosophy from Animal Rights to Radical Ecology*, eds. M. Zimmerman, J. B. Callicott, K. Warren, I. Klaver, and J. Clark. Upper Saddle River, NJ: Prentice Hall.

6
Does Kant Have Anything to Teach Us about Environmental Ethics?

By MARC LUCHT*

ABSTRACT. Immanuel Kant's thought typically is represented as hostile to environmental concerns, but his aesthetics offers significant resources for environmental ethics. His account of the disinterestedness of taste raises the possibility of a manner of motivating a noninstrumental and responsive—rather than self-interested and consumerist—attitude toward nature. The aesthetic consciousness thus can help situate us within rather than pit us against the natural world. Kant's thinking about the beautiful and the sublime point to an ambiguous conception of subjectivity, a picture of the subject who experiences itself both as immersed within a meaningful world and as raised above a world to which it is morally superior. Such a conception may orient investigations in environmental philosophy by providing a more realistic view of the relationship between human beings and nature than do either dualistic or monistic theories.

I

Introduction

IMMANUEL KANT'S THOUGHT typically is represented as hostile to many of the concerns motivating the work of environmental ethicists. His sharp distinction between person and thing grounds a position for which only rational beings may be counted as objects of moral worth and the rest of creation in its entirety is reduced to the status of mere instrumentality. Nature's only value is determined on the basis of its capacity to serve human interests and needs, and Kant goes so far as

*Marc Lucht is Assistant Professor of Philosophy at Alvernia College in Reading, PA. Holding a Ph.D. from Emory University, he focuses on phenomenology, environmental philosophy, aesthetics, and ethics, and he has published on Kant, Tolstoy, Santayana, and Nietzsche.

American Journal of Economics and Sociology, Vol. 66, No. 1 (January, 2007).

to tell us that in the absence of human interests, the natural world would be nothing but a "mere wasteland, gratuitous and without a final purpose."[1] Thus his view may be seen as the philosophical consummation of Descartes' program of rendering human beings the "lords and masters of nature" through the achievement of technological control.

Kant goes further than Descartes does, however, by elevating the instrumentality of nature into an ethico-ontological principle. The orders of reason and nature are determined by radically different principles. All objects of experience are determined without exception by a thoroughgoing determinist natural causality; finite rational beings, on the other hand, are obligated to obey the rational laws of freedom. Here, "we find a rule and order altogether different from the order of nature."[2] The laws of nature are the "laws according to which everything happens; those of [freedom] are laws according to which everything ought to happen."[3] Thus reason and nature are divided by a chasm that "cuts off the domain of the concept of nature under one legislation, and the domain of the concept of freedom under the other legislation."[4] This ontological heterogeneity translates into an uncompromising moral distinction between rational human beings and the physical world. Kant claims that a "thing has no worth other than that determined for it by law. [The] lawgiving which determines all worth must therefore have a dignity (i.e., an unconditional and incomparable worth)."[5] Kant thinks that all value is determined ultimately in relation to moral aims, but that the ground of valuing, or reason itself, is beyond all evaluation; since the condition for value is not the subject of evaluation, its worth is incomparable and absolute. Irrational nature, however, contains nothing possessing the capacity to represent its own ends to itself or the capacity to choose its own ends on the basis of that conception; nothing within nature, then, can present itself to us as dignified and deserving of moral concern. As it consists in nothing but a mechanism, nature can make no moral claims upon us, and any significance it possesses is merely relative to the purposes of rational beings. Morally considered, nature is nothing but resource.

If it is too much to say that Kant's position is an invitation to wholesale exploitation of the natural world, it would be equally difficult to abstract from Kant's ethics any form of environmental concern more robust than some sort of injunction to engage in sustainable development. We are obligated by no duties toward any of the nonrational entities belonging to nature; the despoliation of nature must be limited only by our obligations toward other living and future human beings. This interpretation is supported by Kant's remarks about the lack of direct duties toward nonhuman animals. He urges us to refrain from wanton cruelty against animals not because we are bound by any direct duties to them, but because we have duties toward other rational beings. Cruelty to animals may coarsen our sensibilities, dulling our natural sympathetic abhorrence of suffering and thereby rendering us more liable to treat other human beings badly.[6] Animals themselves, however, as irrational, make no moral claims upon us.

Despite his ethics, Kant's aesthetics presents a more nuanced position regarding the appropriate human attitude toward the natural world. In what follows, I shall explore two features of Kant's aesthetics that offer important guidance for understanding the appropriate stance for human beings to take toward nature. First, I shall say a few words about the resources his aesthetics provide for understanding how to *motivate* a concern for nature, and then I shall discuss the way in which Kant's conception of human subjectivity can serve as foundation for a more adequate view of the relationship between human beings and nature than what is found in much of the current work in environmental ethics.

II

Taste and the Noninstrumental Apprehension of Nature

A GREAT DEAL of recent work in environmental philosophy focuses on the attempt to demonstrate that nature has within it nonhuman beings that are intrinsically valuable and even dignified. Hans Jonas, for instance, argues for a "revision of the idea of nature" that will enable the "ought" to be reinserted into the natural world and the discipline of ethics thus to become "part of the philosophy of nature."[7] Phenomenologists such as Erazim Kohák argue that nature incorporates a dimension of value, "not merely as utility but as intrinsic, absolute value ingressing in the order of time. The chipmunk peering out of the stone fence is not reducible simply to the role he plays in the economy of nature. There is not only a utility, but also an integrity, a rightness to his presence."[8] Deep ecologists reject anthropocentric models of ethics and take as axiomatic the notion of biocentric equality, the idea that all entities in the biosphere have an equal right to live, flourish, and pursue their own idiosyncratic ways of attaining self-realization. Thus, for deep ecologists, natural entities are intrinsically valuable and deserving of the same kind of respect that we owe to other human beings.

Yet those thinkers who advocate a conception of nature as intrinsically valuable and argue that human beings therefore are obligated by direct duties toward the natural world face the serious difficulty that most people simply seem not to apprehend or think of nature in a way that motivates a concern for the world for its own sake. Indeed, views such as the biocentrism of deep ecology strike many people as not only dangerously radical but hopelessly romantic. Martin Heidegger, for example, suggests that resistance to the idea that the nonhuman world possesses its own intrinsic significance or moral integrity arises because of a cultural preoccupation with technological ways of thinking. He claims that instrumental rationality has become so prevalent a way of dealing with the world that other modes of approaching nature are increasingly foreign to us. According to Heidegger, even what Edmund Husserl terms the "natural attitude," our unreflective and commonsense way of thinking about and orienting ourselves toward the world, already has its philosophical assumptions. He argues that the modern metaphysical and scientific interpretation concerning the nature of the real as determinate material quantity not only grounds the practice of scientific research but also regulates even ordinary experience and perception of the world.[9] And this interpretation of the nature of being as a manifold of objective facts subject to quantitative representation sets the stage for a more technological kind of thinking. Thus, a being's objectivity allows for the measurability required by the project of acquiring mastery over it. When beings are interpreted as material presence, they become the appropriate material for technological manipulation. For Heidegger, neither "pure" theory nor our more commonsensical understanding of the world is normatively neutral; each already aims at control. As Manfred Frank says, the natural sciences purport to be "value-free but, in truth, provide a form of knowledge intrinsically associated with domination and control."[10]

Heidegger claims that in the modern age, the "earth itself can show itself only as the object of assault."[11] Nature is represented as nothing but raw material available for human use and consumption, and this representation holds "complete dominion over all phenomena that distinguish the age."[12] Even objective properties recede behind function, and nature comes to appear even to ordinary perception as merely "the constant reserve by which man makes secure for himself material, bodily, psychic and spiritual resources."[13] Heidegger thinks that instrumental rationality reaches its apotheosis in the triumph of the market, where all worth is reduced to economic value: with the "technological dominion" that "spreads itself over the earth ever more quickly, ruthlessly, and completely . . . the humanness of man and the thingness of things dissolve into the calculated market value of a market . . . [that] subjects all beings to the trade of a calculation that dominates most tenaciously in those areas where there is no need of numbers."[14]

If Heidegger is correct that instrumental attitudes are so entrenched in modern Western culture that they even affect perception and regulate common sense, then it can only follow that the idea that nature could consist in anything but raw material for human use will seem alien and dangerous. Those thinkers arguing that nature is more than just a "gigantic gasoline station"[15] stand in need of a way to combat such attitudes by encouraging alternate modes of experiencing the world. If people can be prompted to encounter the natural world in a way other than as an array of resources merely awaiting subordination to their material, recreational, and intellectual interests, and if people can be presented with experiential evidence that nature is more than instrumentality, then ideas about its intrinsic worth may well be rendered more plausible.

Kant offers a clue that could help to surmount this practical difficulty. For him, the ability to appreciate nature as beautiful is important, not only insofar as it makes possible sophisticated kinds of pleasure, but also because our aesthetic sensibilities have substantial moral import. In what follows, I attempt to excavate the resources that Kant's account of the pure, disinterested judgment of taste contains for reflection about our attitude toward nature. A broader analysis of the implications of sensibility for morality in general would deal also with Kant's account of intellectual aesthetic judgments, which are tied to particular moral interests. Following Rudolf Makkreel and Henry Allison, I shall assume that the purity of the aesthetic consciousness does not entail that it lacks moral import, and I shall argue that its import bears especially upon our attunement within the natural world.[16] Kant says: "Taste is the ability to judge an object, or a way of representing it, by means of a liking devoid of all interest. The object of such a liking is called beautiful."[17] Our judgment about something's beauty (or lack thereof) is not determined by the possibility of personal gain or sensuous pleasure, nor is it determined by theoretical or even moral interests. In taste, it is the mere representation of an object that prompts a feeling of like or dislike, and that feeling lies at the basis of our judgment that something is beautiful. Thus Kant thinks that when appreciating beauty, my natural attitude in which my own well-being is of paramount concern shifts to an attitude receptive to pure aesthetic considerations. Pure aesthetic judgment requires the suspension of my more typical preoccupation with matters of self-interest and physical pleasure. In the aesthetic consciousness, "we must be able to view the ocean as poets do, merely in terms of what manifests itself to the eye."[18] The representation's pleasure does not relate to the ocean's bearing upon any of my practical endeavors, but is merely contemplative. Aesthetic contemplation is indifferent to the manner in which the judged object's existence might contribute to one's well-being, and we find ourselves enraptured by something independent of its capacity to contribute to the satisfaction of our selfish interests.

In part because of his analysis of the disinterestedness of taste, Kant claims that the feeling of the beautiful in the aesthetic attitude is a "disposition of sensibility that greatly promotes morality . . . [The aesthetic attitude is] the disposition to love something (e.g., beautiful crystal formations, the indescribable beauty of plants) even apart from any intention to use it."[19] Aesthetic consciousness takes no account of the utility of what it contemplates, and Kant therefore thinks that aesthetics can promote morality by habituating us to selfless reflection and conduct, thereby preparing us to treat other (rational) beings not merely as means to our ends, or as our instruments, but as ends in themselves. Yet the aesthetic consciousness involves a non-instrumental way of representing even nonhuman beings. If Kant is correct in his claim that the aesthetic consciousness is a non- or even anti-instrumental attitude involving the consciousness of "love," then the cultivation of aesthetic sensitivity to natural beauty will also have a great deal of bearing upon the way in which we are disposed toward nature.

Heidegger has recognized the manner in which Kant's elaboration of the disinterestedness of the judgment of taste can be deployed to motivate a respectful concern for the natural world. Elucidating the first moment of Kant's judgment of taste in a section of his lectures on Nietzsche entitled "Kant's Doctrine of the Beautiful: Its Misinterpretation by Schopenhauer and Nietzsche," he says:

> To take an interest in something, suggests wanting to have it for oneself as a possession, to have disposition and control over it. When we take an interest in something we put it in the context of what we intend to do with it and what we want of it.[20]

Metaphysical and technological modes of representation objectify with the aim of mastering nature in order "to have disposition and control over" beings. Yet for Kant, such disclosure is exactly what it means to take an interest in something. An object in which we are interested is always placed "in the context of what we intend to do with it," and so represented merely functionally in its capacity to satisfy our goals. When we attend to an object in an interested way, what we attend to is merely its relation to us and our appetites and designs. Heidegger holds that incorporated into the constitution of beings is a natural significance independent of those beings' instrumental relation to human ends, and he thinks that a cultural and philosophical overemphasis on scientific and instrumental rationality has blinded us to that natural significance. He thinks that Kant's notion of "disinterestedness" anticipates his own work, insofar as to "take an interest in something" is precisely to prohibit that being from showing its inherent worth; in an interested attitude, a being is represented only in its relation to the subject's goals. The ubiquity of technological thinking therefore is a kind of violation of natural beings' original integrity, and the earth shows itself only as the "object of assault."

As we have seen, Kant holds that the determining ground of the judgment of taste can never be an interest. The pure aesthetic consciousness is a noninstrumental attitude toward beings, even nonrational beings. Thus Heidegger tells us:

> in order to find something beautiful, we must let what encounters us, purely as it is in itself, come before us in its own stature and worth. We may not take it into account in advance with a view to something else, our goals and intentions . . . We must release what encounters us as such to its way to be.[21]

He interprets Kant's notion of taste as a mode of apprehending a thing such that that thing is disclosed as it is itself, rather than as mere instrumentality. A judgment that something is beautiful, insofar as it is disinterested, reveals the nondistorted being itself "in its *own* stature and worth," in *its own* intrinsic significance, rather than representing that being merely in its relation to *our own* possible employment of it. Heidegger says that "purely to honor what is of worth in its appearance—is for Kant the essence of the beautiful," and he claims that for Kant taste is the "release of what has worth in itself."[22] The "Kantian 'devoid of interest' " characterizing the pure aesthetic consciousness is the "*magnificent discovery*" of the mode of human comportment appropriate for letting a being be what it is.[23] The point here is that Heidegger takes Kant's account of the judgment of taste to be the first preliminary appearance of his own notion of letting beings show themselves from themselves or "letting beings be" (*Gelassenheit*). Heidegger understands Kant's aesthetic judgment to be the apprehension of the thing as it is itself, rather than of the distortion that results from the representation of the thing as a mere instrument.

What this means is that, for Heidegger, Kant provides a way of thinking about how one may reflect upon and comport oneself toward beings, even nonhuman beings, without seeking to appropriate those beings as mere instruments. Disinterested taste is a way of apprehending nature that resists the inclination to assign to nature a merely relative value on the basis of its capacity to satisfy human goals; instead, the aesthetic consciousness involves a love of (at least beautiful) objects for their own sake. In other words, the aesthetic regard of the world is a kind of noncovetous vision, a kind of nonappropriative seeing that does not operate in the service of our drive to order the world according to our purposes. This kind of seeing presupposes the suspension of what Heidegger thinks of as technological representation. My aesthetic vision does not encounter in the surrounding environment a horizon of objects organized and assigned significance according to my projects, for my typical practical engagement in the world has been bracketed. The aesthetic vision, then, is not a vision that seeks to subjugate, but it is a vision that appreciates, a vision that is receptive and responsive. What is more, Kant thinks that taste involves attending merely to what "manifests itself to the eye," thus "we must base our judgment regarding [the object] merely on how we see it. . . . We must not do so on the basis of how we *think* it."[24] The aesthetic apprehension of beings is independent of our more theoretical modes of thinking—and all the biases that orient such thought. If Heidegger is correct in thinking that metaphysical and scientific theories are guided by an agenda of mastery that has infected our commonsense attitudes toward the world by predisposing us toward the appropriation of the instrumentalist stance, then taste as Kant explicates it may give us the resources needed to resist such a technological bias. Taste is an alternative way of apprehending the world, and Kant invites us not only to regard the world from the perspectives of scientific understanding and instrumental rationality but also to adopt an attitude of openness to beings as they appear apart from our knowledge about, and designs upon, them. He suggests that aesthetic apprehension is an encounter with the world independent of theory. Theory, as Heidegger thinks of it, can distort or narrow our view of the world: the world is reduced in theoretical representation to an array of objects merely awaiting their achieving significance by being ordered and mobilized in the service of human endeavor. Kant raises the possibility that aesthetic awareness may help us avoid such simplification.

As I shall suggest in the next section, Kant thinks that aesthetic consciousness is a felt awareness of the intelligibility and significance of natural forms, a kind of awareness closed to reason and science. Here, I am suggesting that Kant gives us reason to think that environmental ethicists should attend to how aesthetic experiences and pure aesthetic judgments put us in touch with nature in a way that our more typical instrumental attitudes cannot.

He also gives us reason to believe that it is important to think about how to relate aesthetic experiences of natural beauty to the aims of conservation and to reflection about the moral dimension of nature. I do not claim that Kant's account of the disinterestedness of taste is anything like the disclosure of an ecological imperative requiring us to respect the nonhuman world. For Kant, a judgment of taste is grounded in feeling, and only reason in its practical employment has the capacity to project authoritative moral prescriptions. Nor am I claiming that Kant himself would endorse the view of a thinker such as Jonas that nonhuman beings might possess intrinsic worth. My claim is more modest but also more foundational. What Kant offers—perhaps against his own intention—is a way of thinking about how to cultivate the very attitude that would dispose one to consider seriously the possibility that natural beings could in fact deserve respect. The disinterestedness of taste is an attunement in which something like an ecological imperative might first speak to us, an attunement that could render us initially receptive to the claim that nonhuman beings may well make upon us. I am suggesting that Kant's inchoate gesture at a noninstrumental attitude toward nature offers resources for thinking about how to encourage an openness that could enable us to suspend routine instrumental attitudes and to hear, for the first time, the call to care about, and respect, beings other than human beings.

III

Aesthetic Consciousness and Subjectivity

MANY PHILOSOPHERS find themselves troubled by the ways in which the Western tradition of dualistic thinking has represented human subjectivity and its relation to the world. Philosophy often distinguishes between human being and world, both metaphysically and morally. The human subject typically is thought of as most importantly a rational being and, as such, different in essence from the natural world, from which it stands apart as a kind of detached, contemplative knower. Many critics, notably romantic thinkers and those working in existentialism, have suggested that such dualistic categories contribute to human alienation and a sense of homelessness, making it difficult for us to consider ourselves a part of nature, and giving us the sense that we have been thrown or abandoned into an indifferent world of which we are not really a part. As we have already seen, this metaphysical disjunction also makes possible a moral distinction: things sharing the kind of essence that human beings possess are dignified and make moral claims upon us, whereas nonrational or at least nonsentient beings possess only relative value as means to some rational being's ends. Dualism sanctions anthropocentrism.

Hence thinkers such as Frank and Heidegger argue that contemporary practices of environmental exploitation were encouraged by a tradition that interprets the relationship between human being and nature in terms of a subject/object schema.[25] Nature has come to be represented as a separate, alien, and purely material expanse that can make no claims upon us, and this separation of human subjectivity from nature and the interpretation of Being as objectivity results in the conceptual and effective reduction of nature to mere resource. Many thinkers concerned with environmental ethics attempt to subvert the distinction grounding current attitudes toward nature by rejecting the idea of subject/object duality and arguing that human beings are wholly integrated in the natural order. Hans Jonas argues that his goal of integrating ethics into the philosophy of nature can be achieved by recognizing the "continuity of mind with organism and of organism with nature."[26] Deep ecologists Bill Devall and George Sessions offer a similar idea. Their notion of biocentric equality is grounded in their resistance to the view that human beings are:

> isolated and fundamentally separate from the rest of Nature, [are] superior to, and in charge of, the rest of creation. . . . Going beyond a narrowly materialist scientific understanding of reality, the spiritual and the material aspects of reality fuse.[27]

As attractive as such views may be, they nevertheless seem to ignore the human rational capacity to disengage from and reflect upon the world in which we typically are involved. Human beings seem to be not merely natural beings, but do in some ways seem unique. As Kant points out, for instance, we not only are capable of behaving in accordance with actual natural laws but intellectually we can transcend the empirical in order to envision what nature is not but ought to be. We can reflect upon and orient ourselves with respect to ideals, the idea of the infinite, and the unconditioned, all of which surpass anything factual. Many human behaviors, such as the production of music and the choice to undergo vasectomies, seem inexplicable in terms of the evolutionary theory employed to understand the behavior of natural organisms. Moreover, when it comes to the motivations driving human conduct, we certainly *experience* ourselves *as if* we were separate from and to a large extent impervious to natural processes: biological evolution now is not just something to which humanity is subject; with the advent of genetic engineering, it is something over which we think we are coming to enjoy free rein. We surround ourselves with devices that insulate us from and obscure from our view the night sky, the weather, the rhythm of the seasons, and the multitudes of living creatures around us; and the artificiality we feel characterizing our urban abodes drives us to seek a "return to nature" when we go on holiday. Our very ordinary language and common sense entrench the distinction between nature and culture. The integration of nature and spirit to which Sessions and Devall aspire is an experience increasingly alien to people living in industrialized societies.

I suggest that Kant offers a compelling characterization of the relation between human subjectivity and the natural world. In his account of the beautiful, he claims that we have reason to think that human subjectivity indeed is immersed within a deeply meaningful world of which it is a responsive part; whereas, in his account of the sublime, he demonstrates a way in which the human subject experiences itself as separate from and transcendent to the world of nature. Kant's aesthetics therefore suggests that there is a fundamental ambiguity characterizing the human relationship with the world. This ambiguity may offer a more satisfactory account of the way in which we actually experience ourselves than does either a strict subject/object dualism or the ideal of total human and natural integration.

Taste, for Kant, is the "ability to judge the beautiful."[28] But pure aesthetic judgments alone do not contribute anything to cognition, and instead are determined by what is merely subjective in the subject, that is, by feeling; they refer to the feeling of pleasure or displeasure in the subject. A judgment about the beauty of an object is not a theoretical statement about some property of the object, but is about how the subject's own capacities are affected by and respond to their encounter with that object. In the consciousness of the beautiful, the representation of the object stimulates the cognitive powers, and we become aware that the mind is enlivened. According to Kant, the sensation of pleasure involved in taste derives from the consciousness of the "imagination in its freedom and the understanding with its lawfulness, as they reciprocally quicken each other," and such that they are stimulated into an indeterminate yet harmonious reflective "free play."[29] Taste rests upon a pleasurable and enlivening sensation of the playful, interactive harmony of the cognitive powers, and this sensation is the "feeling of life's being furthered."[30] When we feel this peculiar kind of pleasure, we call the representation prompting it "beautiful."

What is most important for our present purposes is that the sensation of the cognitive powers quickening in play is a "feeling that allows us to judge the object by the purposiveness that the representation (by which an object is given) has insofar as it furthers the cognitive powers at play."[31] Certain representations stimulate a mental play, the sensation of which is a feeling that the object is purposive for our cognitive powers. What exactly is this purposiveness? A "purpose" is the "object of a concept insofar as we regard this concept as the object's cause."[32] A purpose is something that is brought about in conformity with some concept or plan; it is an object whose structure presupposes as a condition of its possibility a will that brings it about on the basis of, and in conformity with, some conception of what that object is to be—the object is designed. Yet Kant's claim with respect to the judgment of taste is that certain objects exhibit purposiveness even if there are no grounds for thinking that those objects were in fact designed by some will. Natural objects, generated from the mere mechanism of nature, are "deemed beautiful just in case [they exhibit] the form of purposiveness."[33] Some objects strike us as though they were designed. It appears that certain objects' parts were organized by an intellect like our own, since that arrangement appears to be in accord with some concept that *we* have. Thus Kant thinks that we feel aesthetic pleasure when the object is felt as commensurate with the cognitive powers—when it "looks right" to us. Objects we call "beautiful" are those that seem to make sense, those that appear intelligible and meaningful. Nature strikes us as if it is no longer a mere alien mechanism, and it is in response to the apprehension of such objects that we feel ourselves revitalized.

According to Kant, seeing something as beautiful is experiencing that thing as if it were suited for our own cognitive purposes. He says that beautiful forms are like "ciphers" through which nature "speaks to us" in a figurative way.[34] To decipher the significance of a beautiful form is to sense on some level (but not to know) that nature is not merely an indifferent causal system from which we are alienated, but it is to find in some objects a "trace" that nature may be in harmony with the needs of reflective judgment.[35] In the apprehension of the beautiful, nature is felt as not entirely alien or antithetical to our needs and interests; we feel that nature is meaningful and can even relate to our moral ends.

Kant claims that this merely formal purposiveness is "beauty's own characteristic of qualifying" for a linkage with a moral Idea.[36] The apprehension of beauty is the felt consciousness that the order of nature is commensurate with human purposes. Thus he writes as if aesthetics *reveals* a trace of nature's purposiveness to feeling. In the aesthetic consciousness we feel that the principles governing the realms of nature and freedom are not as heterogenous as science and theoretical reason show them to be. The concept of purposiveness "makes the transition" from "lawfulness in terms of nature to the final purpose set by the concept of freedom."[37] Our apprehension of subjective purposiveness in the consciousness of natural beauty is a hint that nature, after all, may not be indifferent to our purposes, and the achievement of our moral aims is felt, though not known, to be possible in the natural world. Awareness of beauty gives evidence to feeling that nature is not mere alien mechanism, and the aesthetic consciousness involves an affective disclosure of the possible harmony of nature with our aims. And this feeling is, in part, the feeling of the enhancement of my life, of my own vital forces: My being is touched by and responsive to the world around me and of which it feels itself a part.

Aesthetics therefore has significant ontological implications. For all of this felt harmony between nature and subject has a foundation and an explanation. As becomes clear in his discussion of the antinomy of taste, Kant thinks that our sense of formal purposiveness is a disclosure of the commensurability of nature and reason because it rests upon a felt insight into the deep kinship or unity of ground out of which arise both human being and nature. He tells us that the deduction of taste leads to three ideas:

> first, the idea of the supersensible in general, not further determined, as the substrate of nature; second, the idea of the same supersensible as the principle of nature's subjective purposiveness for our cognitive power; third, the idea of the same supersensible as the principle of the purposes of freedom and of the harmony of these purposes with nature in the moral sphere.[38]

Kant in the third *Critique* attempts the beginning of a subversion of the sharp division between nature and human being accomplished in the earlier *Critiques*. It is the same supersensible substrate underlying our power of choice in relation to moral laws that is thought to be the hidden substrate underlying phenomenal nature. Thus the aesthetic consciousness is a felt reference to the supersensible substrate underlying both nature and subject. In the aesthetic consciousness, we feel we are much more a part of nature than we appear to be in more detached, disengaged theoretical thinking, which reveals only the heterogeneity of nature and self; we become aware in the involved responsiveness of feeling that there is no final conflict between the moral sense of being human and the sense of the cosmos, that we and nature share a deep connection, and spring from a common root.[39] According to Kant, who is always so sensitive to the finitude of human reason, there are many grounds for believing something besides rational or scientific evidence. Aesthetics helps us to become aware of and reflect upon nature in a new way, as no longer alien or disenchanted, but as a meaningful cosmos in which our aims make sense. In other words, the apprehension of natural beauty amounts to the feeling that there is no sharp bifurcation between subject and object. When the world feels amenable to our minds, our sense of isolation from the world diminishes.

Kant's thinking about the beautiful stands at the capstone of his system, for by showing that we have grounds for hope that there is a continuity between nature and freedom, it provides the required transition between his theoretical and moral works. His account of the beautiful is important for our purposes insofar as it points to certain kinds of experiences in which we are conscious of ourselves as connected with the natural world—and precisely these kinds of experiences are the desideratum of thinkers who claim that more dualistic attitudes make possible the exploitation of nature. The human sense of estrangement from the world is felt because the world seems alien to us, and we think of ourselves as striving against it in order to make a place for ourselves. When the world seems amenable to our needs, however, this sense of duality fades.

What this means, in Kant's view, is that the very same consciousness that offers so much to the refinement and development of human sociability and culture also can orient us within—rather than pitting us against—the natural world. He thinks that taste contributes to culture in several ways. He tells us that the consciousness of the beautiful "contributes to culture, for it teaches us at the same time to be mindful of purposiveness in the feeling of pleasure"; thus in taste we learn that certain pleasures have more than a merely subjective or hedonistic significance and can attune "the spirit to ideas, and so [make] it receptive to more such pleasure and entertainment."[40] In aesthetic experiences we see that certain kinds of pleasure are more than just trivial. Taste enhances our receptivity to moral ideas and, as it involves pleasure, prompts us to seek out and enjoy more opportunities for such attunement. Thus taste reinforces our moral fortitude and orients us within the social world of art and creative life. The aesthetic consciousness also disposes us toward moral feeling and, as we have seen, to the disinterested state of mind required by morality, helping us to cultivate a more noble bearing with regard to other people. What is more, the enlivening of our cognitive powers involved in aesthetic appreciation facilitates social communication.[41] Perhaps most importantly, Kant tells us that when making aesthetic judgments, I expect others to agree with me, and thus in aesthetic reflection, I take account a priori "of everyone else's way of representing [something] in order as it were to compare [my] own judgment with human reason in general and thus escape the illusion that arises from the ease of mistaking subjective and private conditions for objective ones."[42] Taste helps us to "broaden" our thinking, for in this comparing we are encouraged to transcend the particularity of our own idiosyncratic perspective and adopt the "standpoint of others."[43] Thus aesthetic sensibility helps us to resist our narcissistic propensity to retreat into the isolation of our own individual subjectivity by situating us within both the social and natural worlds. In each case, the self-absorption that too often enables us to reduce everything and everyone around us to mere instrumentality is undermined, and we feel as if we are a part of something larger than ourselves. The aesthetic consciousness checks our egocentric presumption that our own point of view is the only one, habituates us to disinterested thinking (thereby subverting our selfishness), facilitates our entry into society, and prompts us to feel that we are responsive parts of a natural world that transcends us. The aesthetic consciousness seems to reduce the antagonism between nature and culture by strengthening the connection I feel with each.

The above account of the way in which, in the consciousness of the beautiful, we experience ourselves as involved parts of a meaningful cosmos is not the whole story of Kant's aesthetics. The account of the dynamically sublime reinforces the human transcendence of the world as disclosed in Kant's ethical thought. In the consciousness of the sublime, we reflect either upon phenomena of immense magnitude or overwhelming power. Here, nature does not appear as if it were designed, but it is "rather in its chaos that nature most arouses our ideas of the sublime, or in its wildest and most ruleless disarray and devastation, provided it displays magnitude and might."[44] Thus the sublime is a case in which nature is felt not as harmonious with our cognitive powers but rather as contrapurposive and violent in its relation to our consciousness. Here I shall focus upon the consciousness of the dynamically sublime, which is a feeling that reinforces the divorce of subject and world by highlighting our rational superiority to nature.

We experience the dynamically sublime when reflecting upon phenomena of immense power, such as tornadoes, volcanoes, and war. Kant says:

> [Though] the irresistibility of nature's might makes us, considered as natural beings, recognize our physical impotence, it reveals in us at the same time an ability to judge ourselves independent of nature, and reveals in us a superiority over nature.[45]

The sublime involves an oscillation between displeasure and pleasure. The displeasure we feel stems from the recognition of our own

physical impotence in the face of nature's power. But this displeasure
gives way to pleasure, for the initial awareness of nature's overwhelming might prompts our subsequent recognition of that within us that
is not natural and remains independent of nature's power. The
sublime is the felt awareness of our rational capacities and hence of
our moral vocation. Kant says that the "feeling of the sublime in nature
is respect for our own vocation." However, by means of a kind of
symbolic substitution or "subreption," "this respect is accorded an
object of nature that, as it were, makes intuitable for us the superiority
of the rational vocation of our cognitive powers over the greatest
power of sensibility."[46] Thus the sublime renders palpable to us our
ability to will independently of nature, including independently of that
which is natural within us, namely, our desires—and not merely
independently of natural determination, but even *against* our own
natural or biological drives. We are elevated above nature insofar as
what is most important within us is not subject to natural causality,
and insofar as we are able to resist nature and overcome its frequently
potent influence on the will. No matter how powerful nature is, either
within us or without, we need not compromise our principles. We are
superior to nature because no matter how strongly we desire some
particular object or course of action, no matter how compelling or
tempting our impulses, no matter how overwhelming a physical force
is directed against us or our lives, we nevertheless have the capacity
to will what is right.[47] Nature can never degrade my moral character,
which stands immune from its most potent force. Our consciousness
of the sublime, then, is a feeling of elevation where we become aware
of our dignity and self-worth.

The consciousness of the dynamically sublime is important morally
for Kant because its reference to our rational autonomy prepares us to
resist our sensuous impulses, and also because it entails an intuitive
disclosure or sensible representation of our rational vocation. In the
third *Critique*, it turns out that morality not only is accessible to reason
but speaks to the entirety of our being. The dynamically sublime is
important for my purposes here, however, because its analysis shows
that aesthetic feelings do not merely situate us within the world, as in
the consciousness of the beautiful, but also can orient us against
or situate us above the world. Kant therefore argues that human

subjectivity finds or experiences or feels itself both within and independent of the natural world. It seems that the human subject is an
essentially ambiguous being.

If Kant is right that human beings are—or at least experience
themselves as—both a part of and yet independent of nature, then
neither the view that the human subject and its culture are radically
other to an alien world nor the view that human beings are just
another organ of an organism-like cosmos is able really to speak to or
capture the taste of our particular kind of being. Views along the lines
of the biocentrism of deep ecology and the holism of ecofeminism will
remain obscure and appear unrealistic to most people. What is more,
if Kant's position is on the right track, then deep ecology's rejection of
the distinction between subject and nature may well result in an
inadequate moral program. If, for instance, deep ecology's rejection of
the distinction between human subject and nonhuman nature leads to
the correlative rejection of the distinction between "ought" and "is,"
then whatever conduct strikes a deep ecologist as "natural" may
appear also as good. Thus many deep ecologists embrace the practices of hunting and carnivory as natural to human beings; yet if we
were to recall that it does not necessarily follow that what *is* the case
also *ought* to be the case, we might subject such practices to a more
critical look. And if Kant is right that human beings are not merely
natural beings, then we are also in a position to see that human beings
in virtue of their rationality may well be faced with the burden of
special responsibilities to entities within the natural world. Indeed, it
is precisely because of our uniqueness that we are able to regard the
world around us with moral concern. Yet Kant's insight that the
human subject does not experience itself as entirely separate from
the world should serve as a check on the pretension that human
beings are radically other than (and hence not beholden to) an
indifferent and mechanical system of pure matter. The *Critique of
Judgment*'s reference to human responsiveness indicates a kind of
openness or felt sensitivity to the vibrancy of the world we inhabit.
The natural world is much more than mere resource, and is much
closer to us than subject/object dualisms allow. Indeed, the aesthetic
consciousness of the beautiful helps me experience myself as a
responsive part of a significant world that I can come to love. Thus

Kant's work provides us with a starting point for coming to grips with the idea that human uniqueness does not sanction wanton disregard of the world around us.

Notes

1. Immanuel Kant, *Critique of Judgment*, trans. Werner S. Pluhar (Indianapolis: Hackett Publishing Co., 1987), 442/331. Hereafter abbreviated as "*CJ*."

2. Immanuel Kant, *Critique of Pure Reason*, trans. Norman Kemp Smith (New York: St. Martin's Press, 1929), A550/B578.

3. Immanuel Kant, *Foundations of the Metaphysics of Morals*, 2nd ed., trans. Lewis White Beck (New York: Macmillan Publishing Co., 1990), 3–4. Hereafter abbreviated as "*FM*."

4. *CJ*, Introduction, 195/35.

5. *FM*, 436/52–53.

6. Immanuel Kant, *The Metaphysics of Morals*, trans. Mary Gregor (New York: Cambridge University Press, 1991), 443/238. Hereafter abbreviated as "*MM*."

7. Hans Jonas, *The Phenomenon of Life: Toward a Philosophical Biology* (New York: Harper & Row, 1966), 282–283.

8. Erazim Kohák, *The Embers and the Stars: A Philosophical Inquiry into the Moral Sense of Nature* (Chicago: University of Chicago Press, 1984), 70–22.

9. Cf. Martin Heidegger, "The Question Concerning Technology," in *The Question Concerning Technology and Other Essays*, trans. William Lovitt (New York: Harper & Row, 1988), 26–27; and Martin Heidegger, "Modern Science, Metaphysics, and Mathematics," in *Basic Writings*, ed. David Krell (New York: Harper & Row, 1988), 268–269.

10. Manfred Frank, "Two Centuries of Philosophical Critique of Reason and its 'Postmodern' Radicalization," in *Reason and its Other*, eds. Dieter Freundlieb and Wayne Hudson (Gordonsville, VA: Berg Publishers, 1993), 71. Hereafter abbreviated as "*TCP*." Cf. also Kohák, x–xi; and Martin Heidegger, "Age of the World Picture," in *The Question Concerning Technology and Other Essays*, trans. William Lovitt (New York: Harper & Row, 1988), 132. Hereafter abbreviated as "*AWP*."

11. Martin Heidegger, "The Word of Nietzsche," in *The Question Concerning Technology and Other Essays*, trans. William Lovitt (New York: Harper & Row, 1988), 100. Hereafter abbreviated as "*WN*."

12. *AWP*,115.

13. *WN*, 107.

14. Martin Heidegger, "What are Poets For?" in *Poetry, Language, Thought*, trans. Albert Hofstadter (New York: Harper & Row, 1989), 114–115.

15. Martin Heidegger, "Memorial Address," in *Discourse on Thinking*, trans. John M. Anderson and E. Hans Freund (New York: Harper & Row, 1966), 50.

16. Cf. Henry Allison, *Kant's Theory of Taste: A Reading of the Critique of Aesthetic Judgment* (New York: Cambridge University Press, 2001), chs. 9 and 10; and Rudolf Makkreel, *Imagination and Interpretation in Kant: The Hermeneutical Import of the* Critique of Judgment (Chicago: University of Chicago Press, 1990), especially ch. 6.

17. *CJ*, 211/53, translation altered.

18. *CJ*, 270/130.

19. *MM*, 443/237.

20. Martin Heidegger, *Nietzsche*, vol. 1, trans. David Farrell Krell (San Francisco: Harper Collins, 1995), 109. Hereafter abbreviated as "*N* I."

21. *N* I,109.

22. Ibid., 111, 109.

23. Ibid.,109, emphasis added.

24. *CJ*, 270/130.

25. Cf. Heidegger, *AWP*, 128; Manfred Frank, "Is Subjectivity a Non-Thing, an Absurdity? On Some Difficulties in Naturalistic Reductions of Self-Consciousness," in *The Modern Subject: Conceptions of the Self in Classical German Philosophy*, ed. Karl Ameriks and Dieter Sturma (Albany, NY: State University of New York Press, 1995),184ff.; and Frank, *TCP*, 71.

26. Jonas, 282.

27. Bill Devall and George Sessions, *Deep Ecology: Living as if Nature Mattered* (Layton, UT: Peregrine Smith Books, 1985), 65.

28. *CJ*, 203/43.

29. Ibid., 287/151.

30. Ibid., 244/98.

31. Ibid., 287/151, translation altered.

32. Ibid., 220/64.

33. Allison, 250.

34. *CJ*, 301/168.

35. Ibid., 300/167.

36. Ibid., 302/169.

37. Ibid., Introduction, 196/36–37.

38. Ibid., 346/218–220, emphasis omitted.

39. See the discussion of the Antinomy of Taste, especially at *CJ*, 346/219–220, *CJ*, 339–340/212–213, and cf. *CJ*, First Introduction, 246–247/436, and *CJ*, Introduction, 176/15.

40. Ibid., 266/126, 326/195.

41. Cf. ibid., sections 18–22 and 306/173.

42. Ibid., 293/160, translation altered.

43. Ibid., 295/161.

44. Ibid., 246/99–100.
45. Ibid., 261–262/120–121.
46. Ibid., 257/114.
47. Ibid., 262/121.

References

Allison, H. (2001). *Kant's Theory of Taste: A Reading of the Critique of Aesthetic Judgment.* New York: Cambridge University Press.

Devall, B., and Sessions, G. (1985). *Deep Ecology: Living as if Nature Mattered.* Layton, UT: Peregrine Smith Books.

Frank, M. (1993). "Two Centuries of Philosophical Critique of Reason and Its 'Postmodern' Radicalization." In *Reason and its Other*, edited by D. Freundlieb and W. Hudson. Gordonsville, VA: Berg Publishers.

——. (1995). "Is Subjectivity a Non-Thing, an Absurdity? On Some Difficulties in Naturalistic Reductions of Self-Consciousness." In *The Modern Subject: Conceptions of the Self in Classical German Philosophy*, edited by K. Ameriks and D. Sturma. Albany, NY: State University of New York Press.

Heidegger, Martin. (1966). "Memorial Address." In *Discourse on Thinking*, trans. J. M. Anderson and E. H. Freund. New York: Harper & Row.

——. (1988). "Age of the World Picture." In *The Question Concerning Technology and Other Essays*, trans. W. Lovitt. New York: Harper & Row.

——. (1988). "Modern Science, Metaphysics, and Mathematics." In *Basic Writings*, ed. D. Krell. New York: Harper & Row.

——. (1988). "The Question Concerning Technology." In *The Question Concerning Technology and Other Essays*, trans. W. Lovitt. New York: Harper & Row.

——. (1988). "The Word of Nietzsche." In *The Question Concerning Technology and Other Essays*, trans. W. Lovitt. New York: Harper & Row.

——. (1989). "What Are Poets For?" In *Poetry, Language, Thought*, trans. A. Hofstadter. New York: Harper & Row.

——. (1995). *Nietzsche*, vol. 1, trans. D. Krell. San Francisco: Harper Collins.

Jonas, H. (1966). *The Phenomenon of Life: Toward a Philosophical Biology.* New York: Harper & Row.

Kant, Immanuel. (1929). *Critique of Pure Reason*, trans. N. Kemp Smith. New York: St. Martin's Press.

——. (1987). *Critique of Judgment*, trans. W. S. Pluhar. Indianapolis, IN: Hackett Publishing.

——. (1990). *Foundations of the Metaphysics of Morals*, 2nd ed., trans. L. W. Beck. New York: Macmillan Publishing.

——. (1991). *The Metaphysics of Morals*, trans. M. Gregor. New York: Cambridge University Press.

Kohák, E. (1984). *The Embers and the Stars: A Philosophical Inquiry into the Moral Sense of Nature.* Chicago: University of Chicago Press.

Makkreel, R. (1990). *Imagination and Interpretation in Kant: The Hermeneutical Import of the Critique of Judgment.* Chicago: University of Chicago Press.

7

A Cultural Critique of Cultural Relativism

By XIAORONG LI*

ABSTRACT. This chapter explores a certain line of critical analysis
according to which one can proceed to undermine the claim that
judgments approving freedom, and standards upholding human
rights, are culturally relativistic and cannot possibly have any universal
validity. This exploration begins with a scrutiny of common assumptions about the nature of culture itself. The author tries to demonstrate
that common misunderstandings of culture have provided ammunition to cultural relativists. Seeking clarity helps strengthen the philosophical objections to normative cultural relativism. The author refers
to such a line of analysis as the "cultural critique of cultural relativism."

I

Introduction

THE RECOGNITION THAT CULTURE has an ethical significance need not
undermine the plausibility of universal moral values and ethical
principles. The fact that cultures are different and particularistic does
not entail cultural relativism. To support these two propositions, I will
begin this chapter by discussing the controversies surrounding the
troubled relationship between culture, on the one hand, and the claim
to universal moral principles, on the other. More specifically, I will
examine those arguments that seek to undermine the philosophical
efforts to defend these universal principles. I shall argue that a careful

*Xiaorong Li is a research scholar at the Institute for Philosophy and Public Policy at
the University of Maryland, College Park. She has written articles on international
justice, the ethics of human rights, and democratization, and she is the author of the
new book *Ethics, Human Rights and Culture*, published by Palgrave Macmillan (2006).
American Journal of Economics and Sociology, Vol. 66, No. 1 (January, 2007).

scrutiny of common assumptions about culture helps to clarify certain misunderstandings that have provided ammunition to cultural relativists in the past, and it also helps to strengthen the philosophical objections to normative cultural relativism. In what follows, I shall refer to this line of analysis as the "cultural critique."

II

The Trouble with "Culture"

THE UNIVERSALISTIC PRINCIPLES of human rights prohibit, for instance, certain customary practices (e.g., honor killing or female circumcision). However, without being cultivated into a *cultural capital* in the form of particular customs or habits, such universal ethical norms as "equal respect for humanity" or "equal treatment of all as free and autonomous human beings" cannot be realistically implemented without the implementer using some highly coercive force that undermines the very norms that he or she seeks to implement. Also, the ideas upholding the human rights principles have evolved as integral parts of specific cultural traditions. These traditions, in turn, differ significantly from those traditions in which the above-mentioned customary practices (e.g., honor killings), as well as the ideas behind them, have evolved. Just as basic human rights principles protect freedom of expression and thought, they must also allow for cultural diversity and promote pluralism. Thus, the *culture factor* cannot be ignored or put on the back burner in any serious ethical thinking. Critical analysis of substantive ethical proposals benefits from a scrutiny of common assumptions about "culture," and it also benefits from an assessment of the extent to which culture is relevant to ethics.

"Culture" is generally spared the kind of careful scrutiny that such concepts as "personhood" or "human rights" are subjected to. Cultural relativists and universalists alike typically assume that "culture" is a self-evident or commonly agreed upon concept. "Culture," "tradition," or "community" are often used interchangeably as if they refer to the same thing. Moreover, an individual's understanding of these concepts informs, to a large extent, his or her substantive views about the relevant ethical topics under consideration. This normative ethical thinking, therefore, must begin with a rigorous analysis of how culture, tradition, and community are, or should be, understood. For example, it must begin by considering how, if at all, different cultures can commensurate or cohere with each other, or how their values and moral norms can be criticized and evaluated according to commonly held standards.

To avoid any lengthy digression into matters of definition, I shall argue below that what I term the *minimalist consensus* view about culture is the most promising alternative in clarifying these and other matters of normative importance. I understand "minimalist consensus" to be the view that most cultural anthropologists and sociologists seem to accept or could be reasonably expected to accept.[1] This is the view that *a culture is an inherited body of informal knowledge embodied in traditions, transmitted through social learning in a community, and incorporated in practices.*[2] This consensus view emerges from, but also transcends, the long disputes in the contentious fields of cultural theories and culture studies.

For some background on this issue, the main points of contention within these debates are worth mentioning briefly. At the risk of simplification, I shall describe the main disputes as being those among the *classic school* and the *contemporary school.* The classic school believes that culture is largely a bounded entity, homogeneous, holistic, and time-insensitive.[3] The contemporary school believes that culture is open and influenced from outside—its borders, if any, are porous and fluid; it changes over time; and it is internally heteroge neous. Suffice it to say that recent ethnographic work does not seem to favor the classic view.

The "minimalist consensus" view is attractive for my purpose here because it accommodates some incongruent insights of both the classic and contemporary schools. First, it gives "culture" a more definitive and concrete form as a body of informal knowledge, which the contemporary school does not. The contemporary view comes too close to simply dissolving culture altogether for comfort's sake. A borderless, changing, and internally divided body of knowledge would be too undefined and amorphous to be a "body" at all. Thus, unlike the classical view, the consensus view does not consider visions that are privately intuited or ideas solitarily contemplated as being genuinely "cultural." Moreover, it specifies culture as *historically* inherited over generations, rather than as newly minted. By contrast, the contemporary view would allow admission into "culture" by any knowledge that is untested by time and experiences. Third, the consensus view further narrows culture down to a body of knowledge that is incorporated into practices and turned into lived experiences, for example, by being embodied in customs, expressed in symbols, implemented in institutions, or codified in rules. It is not confined to those modes of transmission and circulation carried out by books or in classrooms. Fourth, people who are interconnected in a *collaborative* entity, such as a community, are the main actors who are both learning and practicing creatively the teaching, whereas authorities and elites are not the exclusive interpreters and authors of such instruction. The consensus view is thus more balanced and, as such, it can accommodate the contradictory social phenomenon that the term "culture" is intended to characterize.

Now, the consensus concept of culture, being minimalist, is also general in that it allows incongruent interpretations about what culture is, and permits one to characterize culture(s) in contradictory terms. This, however, may not necessarily argue against adopting the consensus concept. It may be that culture is characteristically incongruent or contradictory. For lack of a better phrase, I use "paradoxes of culture" to tease out the incongruence and contradictions. Three "paradoxes" are particularly relevant here. The first occurs when we see on the one hand that a culture can be unique to a community but on the other hand that it can also overlap and be compatible with other cultures. The second arises when we see that a culture can be uniform or have unity but that it can also have its own internal heterogeneity and permit individualization in the community. The final paradox comes into view when we see that a culture has its own roots, continuity, and conservation but that it also permits self-criticism by the members of the community, leading to (potential) transformations within it and to the formation of hybrid traditions with different origins or histories. These paradoxes have important implications for normative thinking about the compatibility of cross-cultural ethical norms and local cultural rules.

Consider the first paradox. It is common to cite cultural uniqueness as an obstacle to conceptualizing and validating cross-cultural moral principles. If moral universalists may be said to have a tendency to deny cultural uniqueness, cultural relativists tend to overemphasize it. Yet relativists are mistaken in insisting that uniqueness entails incommensurability. A body of knowledge can be unique if it has no exact copy elsewhere. Nevertheless, each overlapping body of knowledge can also be unique—each may have unique formations of mosaic and eclectic patterns in spite of having shared elements. Two overlapping eclectic patterns can be commensurable in spite of their uniqueness.

Consider the second paradox. Cultural uniformity is not necessarily present in a territorially finite community. Yet the sense of unity can surprisingly rise to the occasion. When the members of a community perceive an external discrimination made against them as a group, their sense of unity restores the community, leading them to embrace their common heritage for the purpose of solidarity. Cultural identity is historically fluid. One must balance unity with fluidity and internal diversity. Fluidity and diversity are constant and ubiquitous, while solidarity is occasional and contingent.[4] Intra-cultural diversity, despite unity, opens the possibility for intercultural communication and penetration, because internally divided groups can find common causes across boundaries.

The third paradox recognizes profound transformation as well as historical continuity. It does not assume that changes make culture into something ephemeral, having no durable reality and possessing only the fleeting moments of an illusion.

We must then fine-tune the consensus view with an important clause. *A culture is a body of informal knowledge that is historically inherited, transformed, embodied, and contested in traditions, incorporated and innovated in practices, and transmitted, altered through social learning, in a community of evolving and porous boundaries.*

This working concept helps clarify some of the confusions concerning what it means to speak of a cultural "tradition" or "community." It entails that a *cultural community* is a paradoxical social context—a socially organized population group with a shared identity, within which a body of informal knowledge is socially transmitted and contested. Being "paradoxical," this social context has identifiable yet contested and porous boundaries. It is unique yet commensurable with other social contexts. Its members have mixed feelings and clashing views about their inherited practices and rules. They relate to their heritage differently. Their heritage means different things and invokes different feelings in them. A cultural community differs from the simple notion of any given historical population; it also differs from an idealized, bounded, internally harmonious, and timeless group or society.

The working concept also entails that *cultural tradition* is the embodiment of paradoxical informal knowledge. The substance of a tradition consists in competing and clashing rules, customs, symbols, rituals, habits, and practices. This concept emphasizes renovation in spite of a people's inheritance of beliefs and the impact of their changing experiences. Philosophers tend to employ two notions of "tradition": one narrow and the other broad. The working concept favors the latter. The narrow view recognizes only intellectual or spiritual discourses, in which the educated elite deliberates and disputes the norms, rules, or standards. The broad view sees tradition as reflected knowledge, which has been reinterpreted, recreated, and enacted in the cultural practices of a community. On this broad view, tradition is not merely an intellectual discourse or its products but also contains practices and customary rules or ideas lived by people. Social learning, through which informal knowledge is transmitted and contested, involves more than understanding and reflection. It involves practicing acquired knowledge through experiences and internalizing it into habits, dispositions, and skills.

This scrutiny of "culture," I contend, helps elucidate its relevance or significance to ethics and, more specifically, it helps clarify some common presumptions about morality's relativity to culture.

III

The Ethical Significance of Culture

DOES CULTURE JUSTIFY or explain moral actions or judgments? If yes, how? If culture can explain or justify moral judgments or actions, I will consider culture *relevant* to, or *significant* for, morality or ethics.

The working concept of culture entails a twofold assessment of culture's presumed legitimating (normative) and explanatory (heuristic) significance. First, a paradoxical body of informal knowledge can potentially justify different positions concerning a moral problem because this body is internally conflicted and changes over time. Second, a paradoxical body of informal knowledge cannot provide a causal explanation of moral decisions made by those raised in or identified with it. This is because a member's moral views and motives are likely to have been developed under the influence of, or associated with, one of several contested visions within the culture or shared with those in other cultures. Factors other than cultural ones also play decisive roles. Hence, there exists no apparent causal chain whereby one can trace a person's moral decisions to his or her culture, either as a whole or alone. To spell out these implications of the working concept is to take an *analytic* approach to culture's ethical significance.

To proceed with this analytic approach, I will first consider two views of explanation: (1) explanation functions to identify a causal relationship between what explains and what is being explained; and (2) explanation functions to illuminate or confer intelligibility and coherence on what is being explained. I refer to (1) as a *strong* explanation and (2) as a *weak* one. If culture is able to perform function (1), it has a *strong heuristic significance* for ethics, and if it is able to perform (2), it has a *weak heuristic significance*. (I also assume, for later discussion, that if culture is able to *justify* moral views or actions, then it has a *normative significance* as well.)

First, I acknowledge culture's weak heuristic significance. As I see it, the acknowledgment of a weak heuristic significance agrees with the intuition that, to the extent that culture provides a source of informal moral knowledge, it shapes the judgments of moral agents, motivates them to act, and is therefore able to play a weak heuristic role in making sense of their actions or judgments. Next, I proceed to undermine culture's strong heuristic significance by *disaggregating culture* into some of its key components or entities, with which we tend to use "culture" interchangeably. Specifically, I examine "tradition" and "community." This exercise allows greater accuracy in identifying where and how culture might be ethically significant in the strong heuristic sense.

To what extent can we trace different judgments to their agents' distinctive cultural *traditions?* Tradition understood under the working concept of culture does not provide the *cause* of, or determine, the views (or judgments) of its practitioners. Individual members of the same tradition may have very different experiences, which can lead them to different moral judgments or motivations to act. As a result, even if the members of a community are raised in the same tradition—for example, their moral education is under Islamic law—this does not determine the same unanimity in their moral judgments, say, about the custom of amputating a thief's arm.[5]

An action may have multiple causes or diverse sources of impetus, including reasons or motives that do not spring directly or solely from a person's tradition. The man who saves a drowning child may have several possible motives. A person raised in the Inuit tradition may disagree with fellow members about the necessity for collective survival of leaving the elderly, who are too frail or sick to work, to die in the wilderness. Even if someone cites the Inuit tradition that allows this practice, that alone does not help determine the cause of this person's judgment about it. Likewise, an uncaring or greedy son's action in compliance with this custom may not be shaped or motivated by the tradition at all. Even when a group of people engages in a common action, they may do so for multiple, sometimes incongruent, motives and reasons.

Can one's "embeddedness" in a cultural community cause or determine one's moral judgment? The working concept of culture has implications for addressing this question, and hence it also has implications for assessing the communitarian contentions that communally "embedded" persons act or must act in accordance with the ends and commitments of their communities. Communitarians often criticize the liberal conception of the "self" for its unrealistic portrayal of persons. Some of them argue that liberalism is wrong to promote institutions or policies that shape "disembodied" individuals and allow autonomous choices.[6] In so arguing, they assume that "embeddedness" in community causally determines most people's ends and that their judgments or actions can always be traced back to their communal duties, loyalties, and purposes. In other words, people's judgments and actions can be explained with certainty in a causal nexus.

The working concept of culture entails that judgments and actions of communally "embodied" persons cannot always be exclusively traced to any shared norms in their own communities. Within any such community, there are likely to be diverse, conflicting, critically contested, and changing goals and commitments. Its members' reflections and debates about competing objectives are often influenced by ideas that have originated in other communities. The communitarian notion of the "self" as acting for some preset ends, which are adopted in the local community, is insensitive to the reality of diversity and to the activity of critical reflection and autonomous choice, as well as to the diverse interpenetrations of ideas across communities.

Is it plausible, then, to require that members must always judge or act according to communally adopted ends and commitments? But the members' judgments and actions cannot be meaningfully evaluated by norms found exclusively within their own community, in part because there is often a diversity of norms within any given community. Thus, the same judgment might be considered right according to some norms but wrong according to others. Because of this shared interpenetration among communities as well as the diversity within each one, the insistence that the members' moral decisions must always be determined by norms accepted within an agent's own community looks to be a false claim.

These considerations raise serious doubts about the strong heuristic, ethical significance attributed to any cultural community. So far, I have tried to raise some doubts about the strong heuristic claim in order to undermine its assumption about the members' *equal* "embeddedness" in a traditional community; in my view, cultural "embeddedness" is always "uneven." Members of the same community do not equally share traditional teachings, identify with authorities and fellow community members, make the same choices, or reflect in the same way on inherited customs. Membership in a community is no guarantee that all members acquire the same proficiency in learning the tradition. Moreover, the same enculturation is no guarantee of the same convictions or motives to act accordingly.

While it is perhaps true to say that no one is completely "disembodied," that is, not embedded in any cultural community, people nonetheless achieve different levels of enculturation. Their relationships with fellow members and authorities in their communities differ both in strength and durability. "Embedded" persons in a community are always capable of being *individualized in their "embeddedness."*

We may thus conclude that a person's judgments and decisions to act are not determined exclusively by his or her membership in a community. To confer on a community a weak heuristic significance to ethics, one must recognize and assess the unevenness of their "embeddedness" in the community. The unevenness in a community's embeddedness means that people are able to form autonomous judgments, which are not determined exclusively by their community's prescribed ends.

IV

A Cultural Critique of Cultural Relativism

To ADDRESS THE QUESTION as to whether or not culture has *normative* ethical significance, we must first revisit the issue of normative cultural relativism. What does the working concept of culture imply about the evaluation of cultural relativism? If "culture" were naturally relativistic, then any logical argument that seeks to refute cultural relativism would not be sound. Thus, cultural relativism may have a shelter in cultural studies. If this were the case, then philosophers would have to scrutinize the presumptions and empirical claims about "culture," and especially consider morality's presumed relativity due to culture.

Normative cultural relativism differs from descriptive cultural relativism.[7] This differentiation is sometimes blurred in the relevant discussions. *Descriptive cultural relativism* (DCR) describes a relativity of moral agents' judgments to their culture.[8] It describes the *differences* between cultures in their moral views and standards. By contrast, *normative cultural relativism* (NCR) requires that moral judgments and standards be considered valid or invalid only relative to an agent's own culture; in other words, his or her moral views or actions ought to be considered right if and only if they are judged so according to the cultural standards of the community. DCR alerts one to problems concerning the *feasibility* and effectiveness in implementing ethical principles. It challenges one to consider the question: Given the cultural differences in the world, how is it feasible to motivate compliance and implement ethical norms, such as human rights? In comparison, NCR poses a different set of questions: For example, since a judgment can only be valid or invalid according to standards in the culture in which it is found, should one assess the judgment by persons from other cultures by appealing to one's own cultural standards? Should one use only the local culture's standards?

I am primarily interested in developing a cultural critique of NCR.[9] NCR assumes that culture has normative ethical significance in providing moral justification. Without this assumption, the relativist would not be able to claim that the rightness of moral judgments and actions must be relative to the moral agents' own culture, and that culture must be the exclusive source of the standards for judging the rightness of its members' views and practices.

Philosophers tend to rely on the classical understanding of "culture."[10] They tend to refute normative relativism (NR) in its general form, rather than in its cultural variety form, NCR. Three influential arguments refuting NR can be strengthened to help refute NCR by considering critically the nature of culture.

Let us consider the first argument that NR commits the "naturalistic fallacy," in other words, the fallacy of arguing from "is" to "ought," or from observed states of affairs to normative principles or general laws. From observing how people behave, the relativists imply that people make moral judgments and use standards that they find in their own society, history, or culture, and that these standards are self-justifying. From these observations, NR makes the following normative proposition: One *should* judge people's moral beliefs based on their social norms, and it is wrong to use one's own social standards to judge others. According to this argument, for example, from the mere fact that some people value cultural diversity, we cannot infer that diversity must be valued and ought to be respected by all.[11]

In everyday life, however, we are more trusting of our observations than we are in the claims of the social sciences. Those who arrive at normative relativism from observations may argue that such a commonsensical trust is all that we have to go on in morality. Many people find nothing terribly wrong if somebody reasons in the following fashion: When it is repeatedly *observed* that "outsiders" criticize a local population on what they consider right and claim that it is wrong according to their own (outside) standards, the result has often been destructive. Based on this observation, then, the relativists claim that we *should* adopt a rule stating that we should always refrain from judging others according to our own standards. This sort of reasoning, even if strictly speaking it commits the naturalistic fallacy, is nonetheless appealing in everyday life and persuasive to many. Practically speaking, what this means is that to simply charge NR with the "naturalistic fallacy" is not as effective or persuasive as philosophers have commonly thought. In a cultural context, moral rules and principles are acquired from lived social experiences. We learn how to judge views and behaviors in different cultures through experiences that interact with them. If we are to specify any universal ethical rules that govern judgment making across cultures, we may have nothing more than such lived experiences as our guide. To abandon them would leave us impoverished when it comes to making our own ethical judgments and to setting our own norms.

Let us now consider the second argument, that NR is internally inconsistent. NR prescribes the following: (1) never judge someone else's views according to standards of one's own, or (2) judge others' views according to their own standards only. These two standards state prescriptions that the relativists use to judge other peoples' moral judgments universally; they are thus universal judgments.[12]

The relativist may try to respond, however, by revising (1) to the effect of (1*): Never judge others according to one's own standard, *except* when one's own standard is the one laid out here: (1); hence, one can judge others according to (1). Further, she can revise (2) to (2*): Judge others' views according to one's own standards, except when judging the behavior of making judgment about others, where the standard laid out here, in other words, (2), applies. Hence, according to (2*), one can use standards that are not the others' when judging these others' behavior of making judgment about other people. This revision has been suggested as a way to get out of the apparent self-contradiction. But it does not work. Neither (1*) nor (2*) alters the paradox of the relativist, who still has to use a universal standard or remain self-contradictory. Moreover, as some critics point out,[13] the relativist needs to give substantive arguments defending the provision of exception in (1*) and (2*) in order to avoid arbitrariness.

The relativist may try to avoid arbitrariness by restricting (1*) to (1**): Those in my own group (in which NR is accepted) should never judge morality in other groups (where NR is not accepted, including the universalists) according to our own standards as laid out here, that is, (1*). Now, (1**) may not appear to involve the troubling self-inconsistency, and it may not appear to make arbitrary exception. One price the relativist adopting (1**) is willing to pay, however, is a significant restriction on the scope of applicability of (1); for (1**) presumably no longer applies to anyone outside members of the group who are relativists. However, normative relativism still does not save itself from self-contradiction and arbitrariness. A relativist who adopts (1**) cannot say that her standard is true or her inferences from that standard are sound. If she makes any claim at all about her standard, then she is saying that the standard has truth-value. If there is truth-value to her standard, then that claim implies the opposing standard is false. She is still judging the universalists. In this case, the relativist remains caught in a self-contradiction. The only way out of the contradiction is to claim that "no claim I make is true," and then she is obviously caught in the liar's paradox![14]

Finally, let us now consider the third argument, that NR violates the generality requirement. According to this argument, ethical propositions are *by nature* general or universalistic.[15] Therefore, anyone who makes moral judgments is also making general claims applicable to anyone, anywhere, in similar moral situations. Accordingly, the relativist is mistaken about the nature of moral judgment making when she demands of us that we never make judgments across social and cultural boundaries. Some philosophers thus argue that relativists are unable to criticize past wrongs (e.g., slavery) and wrongs in other lands (e.g., fascism and neo-Nazism). This critique exposes the relativists' insincerity or hypocrisy. It has this effect, however, only if the relativists have claimed to be capable of criticizing such wrongs. The relativists may reply, with courage, that their point is precisely that no one is able to criticize "wrongs" in other societies or cultures, whether they are historical or are foreign "wrongs." To point out her inability to do so thus does not effectively reject her NR position—one also needs to go after the problem with the relativism's claim to its inability to make any judgment, which disqualifies relativism as a normative theory.

To enhance the effectiveness of the first argument above (the one involving the naturalistic fallacy), a "cultural" critique of cultural relativism questions the empirical claim that moral views and standards *are* "relative" to culture, namely, that they vary from culture to culture, that they are incommensurable, and that they are applicable only to the culture of their origin. The crucial premise for the inference made from the observations of cultural "relativity" to NCR will be seriously undermined if it is shown that such observations are defective and that they are contradicted by observations of commensurable judgments and standards that are found in different cultures. Even if the naturalistic fallacy does not suffice in persuading us to distrust observations in everyday moral judgment making and norm setting, the philosophers can still fault NCR's observation about morality's cultural relativity because their descriptions of moral decision making and behavior are inaccurate.

To enhance the second argument discussed above against relativists, the cultural critique advises us to reject (1**) by challenging its presumptions about the "cultural other." In particular, we can challenge its implicit assumptions about the clear-cut division between cultural groups—between a "relativists' culture" and a "nonrelativists' culture"—and the counterintuitiveness of this divide. By requiring members of the cultural relativist's own "cultural community" not to judge outsiders according to their own cultural standards, as discussed above, the relativist must assume that she is able to tell apart the members of her own culture from "outsiders." She must assume that there are clear borders between the "insiders" and "outsiders." She could therefore assume that a certain standard (i.e., NCR-1**) is uniquely applicable in her own "cultural community," and that all members in this one share this standard. These are implausible assumptions given the paradoxical nature of culture as discussed earlier in this essay.

To enhance the third objection against NCR, the cultural critique advises us also to challenge NCR's presumptions about "other cultures," as if cultures were impenetrable and incommensurable such that it would be impossible to apply any general standards to judging moral views and behaviors across their boundaries. For instance, one can pursue this line of critique by demonstrating that, due to the paradoxical nature of culture, Confucian moral views have found believers in dominantly Christian societies, that the Confucian morality has evolved, become internally divided, and been mixed with other schools of moral thought, such as Aristotelian virtue ethics, and that many in the once dominantly Confucian societies such as China, Japan, and other southeast Asian societies have accepted Christian or Islamic moral views.

In this manner, the *cultural critique* of NCR draws upon the working concept of "culture" to undermine the plausibility of morality's presumed cultural relativity. Its main insight is this: if there cannot always be any agreed upon moral standard inside a culture, and if nonlocals may share local standards, then one cannot plausibly prescribe NCR. Likewise, if the rightness of moral judgments cannot always be decided exclusively by standards found in a local culture, then it makes little sense to demand of people that they use local standards exclusively.

The cultural critique challenges NCR's key inference: since there cannot be any transcultural standards, then one should not accept any proposed transcultural standards. Moreover, since there can only be local cultural standards, then one ought to judge moral views or actions by standards in the moral agent's local culture. In so inferring, NCR assumes the impossibility of transcultural standards and incommensurability of standards found in different cultures. The validity of NCR is contingent on the validity of these assumptions. If these assumptions are invalid, that is, if there *can* be transcultural standards and if standards found in distinct cultures are commensurable, then NCR's foundation is weakened.[16] According to the cultural critique, the ambiguity of the cultural identities of moral agents and moral standards makes it difficult and sometimes impossible to apply NCR to judging the ways in which persons make moral judgments about others.

When a moral position, X, is judged both right and wrong according to opposing local standards in a culture Y, or if it is also judged right or wrong according to standards in other cultures, the rightness or wrongness of X, then, is not particularly relative to culture Y or to the other cultures. *To establish the relativity of moral judgments and standards to culture, one must establish a correspondence between variation in moral judgments/standards and variation in the cultures of their agents and, vice versa, one must establish that any such variations are so radical that the varying judgments and standards are incommensurable.*

Cultural relativity as such cannot be taken for granted. Given that a culture may contain conflicting judgments or standards, the variations among them do not correspond to one set variation from culture to culture. Given that two cultures may contain similar standards, their members may make similar judgments, and the variation from culture to culture does not correspond to any set variation in standards or judgments. This means that one cannot forecast or otherwise statistically infer how people will make their moral judgments and establish their moral standards; yet the variations continue to uphold general norms recognized and accepted by diverse societies.

The cultural critique effectively dissolves the presumed problem of morality's relativity to culture or the cultural relativity of morality. It demonstrates that, in moral judgment making and norm setting, there is no real problem of cultural relativity as such, though there can be problems with cultural misunderstanding, insensitivity, discrimination toward differences, and denial of inner-culture differences and similarities between cultures.

Is it possible to make concessions to the key points about the nature of culture while holding on to the thesis of cultural relativity? Let us suppose that the relativist admits intra-cultural diversity and intercultural connectedness, and that she tries to adjust NCR to the effect of NCR-1. NCR-1 states the following: *It is wrong to judge moral views or practices in a culture according to one's own standards and, accordingly, one should only apply standards in the cultures of those whom one judges, even if these cultures have internally divided moral views or externally shared views with other cultures.* NCR-1 departs from NCR because NCR-1 abandons the position that the *only* acceptable standard is *exclusively* found and uniformly shared in the moral agent's *own* culture. According to NCR-1, it is permissible to use standards that are disputed in the local culture or shared by some people in other cultures.

NCR-1 may be able to survive the cultural critique. But if one adopts NCR-1, which embraces this critique's basic insight about culture's internal heterogeneity and intercultural commensurability, then the relativist for all practical purposes leaves behind her insistence on morality's relativity to culture. Indeed, NCR-1 makes such important concessions that it no longer seems to qualify as a genuinely relativist position, for it no longer insists on a neat *correspondence* between variation in morality and variation in culture. Rather, NCR-1 states a position about the particularity of a local culture. It prescribes that the particular set of local standards should be considered, even though these are shared elsewhere and disputed locally.

Conceivably, the relativist may respond to the cultural critique by insisting that the relativity thesis can still apply to cultures that are bounded and homogenous, no matter how few there are, or how small they may be. For instance, the relativists may say, we can concede that in a local context there is agreement about the rightness of honor killing because those in agreement are all members of a bounded and homogenous culture. They can make this concession and still claim that such a "culture" may not be the same for all the tribes, villages, or communities where this practice is found, due to the internal disagreements about this practice in their social contexts. Accordingly, those who disapprove of this practice, whatever their social, religious, or national identities are, simply do not belong to such a "culture." The relativist may then claim that morality's relativity with respect to culture is salvaged in such cases since, wherever a moral disagreement occurs, a different "culture" or subculture would form among those who would agree.

This conceivable scenario allows for an exit, a kind of cultural secession, to those who do not accept the moral position of the fellow members in their group. The boundaries around the new group are supposedly unambiguous, and the makeup of the group is allegedly homogenous. This response by the relativist allows that a "culture" may consist in a very small group of like-minded individuals (or even one solitary individual) who agree about a single moral issue—a troubling ethical position, to say the least! It allows dividing any group into "cultures" along the lines of their disagreements or agreements over various moral issues.

If moral differences from culture to culture are understood, however, as belonging to groups of like-minded moral agents, this does not necessarily entail incommensurability among them. Moreover, it is not the case that cultures can be understood in such a schizophrenic portrayal of the social landscape in any real-world scenario. Cultural relativism, based on this portrayal of culture and its insistence on cultural incommensurability, collapses into its extreme form—individual relativism or solipsism: each person judges and acts "morally" only according to his or her own standards. Such an eventuality shows the impossibility of this view.

One may respond to this cultural critique by saying that it does not constitute a categorical rejection of NCR; rather, it merely demonstrates NCR's unrealistic or faulty presumptions about culture. One may try to show that it is possible to prescribe norms governing how we ought to judge others' moral views found in other people's "cultures"—even though "cultures" as such may not exist—just as it is possible to prescribe norms governing what we ought to do with regard to Meinong's hypothetical "golden mountain," for instance, by thinking of norms to either preserve or deplete it. One may make such a case, but my response is that norms governing behaviors toward nonexisting objects or in nonexisting contexts have little, if any, application in the real world. It is no trivial accomplishment if we can establish that NCR has little application in the real world, where cultures are internally divided and mutually commensurable and penetrable.

In our world of "creolized," hybrid, evolving, and internally clashing cultures, it is difficult, to say the least, to identify to which culture(s) exactly a moral agent's judgments or standards are relative. Along the lines of critical analysis pursued in this paper, we can proceed to undermine the claims that judgments approving human freedom and standards upholding human rights are culturally relativistic or cannot possibly have any universal validity.

Notes

1. This consensus has become the standard textbook concept today, that is, the view that "culture" is "distinctly human; transmitted through learning; traditions and customs that govern behavior and beliefs" (Kottak, C., *Anthropology: The Exploration of Human Diversity*, 5th ed. (New York: McGraw-Hill, 1991), 17); or as "the system of knowledge more or less shared by members of a society" (Keesing, R., *Cultural Anthropology: A Contemporary Perspective*, 2nd ed. (New York: Holt, Rinehart and Winston, 1981), 509).

2. One survey conducted half a century ago found over 150 diverse definitions of culture. Cf. Kroeber, A., and C. Kluckhohn, *Culture: A Critical Review of Concepts and Definitions* (New York: Random House, 1963), 357.

3. The classic views were popular among the postcolonial anthropologists like Franz Boas and his students Ruth Benedict, Melville Herskovits, and Margaret Mead. They were inspired by the 18th-century German intellectual Johann von Herder.

4. Jack Goody writes: "Actors generally define their culture in terms of the dominant political, linguistic, or religious units to which they owe affiliation, . . . presuming a bounded unity which is often problematic" ("Culture and Its Boundaries," in *Assessing Cultural Anthropology*, ed. Robert Borofsky, (New York: McGraw-Hill, 1994), 254).

5. For an argument for the compatibility of the judgment disapproving of this practice with fundamental beliefs in the Islamic tradition, see Abdullahi An-Na'im, *Human Rights in Cross-Cultural Perspectives*, (Philadelphia: University of Pennsylvania Press, 1992).

6. See, for instance, Michael Sandel, *Liberalism and the Limits of Justice* (Cambridge: Cambridge University Press, 1982), 15–23.

7. See Richard Brandt, "Ethical Relativism," in *The Encyclopedia of Philosophy*, ed. Paul Edwards (New York: MacMillan and Free Press, 1967) for a three-way distinction: descriptive, normative, and meta-ethical.

8. For a sympathetic view of descriptive cultural relativism, see An-Na'im, "Toward a Cross-Cultural Approach to Defining International Standards of Human Rights," in An-Na'im (ibid.).

9. A "cultural critique" of DCR would question its empirical foundation. Cultural anthropologists have yet to conduct any survey of all cultures in the world to warrant the claims that morality differs from culture to culture and that morality is relative to culture. See Michele Moody-Adams, *Fieldwork in Familiar Places* (Cambridge: Harvard University Press, 1997).

10. Bernard Williams, for instance, uses "culture" to refer to comprehensive "forms of life"; hence any two cultures are "incommensurable" in that they have different concepts, references, and notions of what counts as evidence and in that one could not "combine accepting" both or "work within both of them." He goes on to say that the incommensurability of cultures, however, should not leave room for cultural relativism. This is because when two incommensurable cultures exclude each other, those in one culture can still "reject" ideas in the other. Cf. Williams, *Ethics and the Limits of Philosophy* (Cambridge: Harvard University Press, 1985), 157–158.

11. As Elvin Hatch points out, "[t]he fact of moral diversity no more compels our approval of other ways of life than the existence of cancer compels us to value ill-health" (Elvin Hatch, *Culture and Morality: The Relativity of Values in Anthropology* (New York: Columbia University Press, 1983), 68).

12. For this refutation, see Bernard Williams, *Morality: An Introduction to Ethics* (New York: Harper and Row, 1972) and (1985, ch. 9); and David Lyons, "Ethical Relativism and the Problem of Incoherence," *Ethics* 86 (1975–1976):107 and 109. Also, see Carlos Nino's critiques of moral relativism in Nino, *The Ethics of Human Rights* (Oxford: Clarendon Press, 1991).

13. For example, see Teson, F., "International Human Rights and Cultural Relativism," *Virginia Journal of International Law* 25(4) (1985): 869–898.

14. Daniel Shannon commented on this point, which helped me in presenting my thoughts more clearly.

15. Bernard Williams writes: "The fact that people can and must react when they are confronted with another culture, and do so by applying their existing notions—also by reflecting on them—seems to show that the ethical thought of a given culture can always stretch beyond its boundaries. . . . Each outlook may still be making claims it intends to apply to the whole world, not just to that part of it which is its 'own' world" (1985: 159). Also, as Marcus George Singer put it, "the generalization principle is involved in or presupposed by every genuine moral judgment, for it is an essential part of . . . [any] distinctively moral terms" (*Generalization in Ethics: An Essay in the Logic of Ethics* (New York: Knopf, 1961), 34).

16. Meanwhile, the validity of NCR does not depend on the (empirical) validity of DCR. Even if DCR is unconfirmed on empirical grounds, NCR can still be plausible. If gold mountains have not been confirmed to exist, one can still make normative propositions prescribing what one ought to do or not do with regard to gold mountains.

References

An-Na'im, A. (1992). "Toward a Cross-Cultural Approach to Defining International Standards of Human Rights." In *Human Rights in Cross-Cultural Perspectives*. Philadelphia: University of Pennsylvania Press.

Brandt, R. (1967). "Ethical Relativism." In *Encyclopedia of Philosopohy*, ed. Paul Edwards. New York: Macmillian Press.

Goody, J. (1994). "Culture and Its Boundaries." In *Assessing Cutural Anthropology*, ed. Robert Borofsky. New York: McGraw-Hill.

Hatch, E. (1983). *Culture and Morality: The Relativity of Values in Anthropology*. New York: Columbia University Press.

Kessing, R. (1981). *Cultural Anthropology: A Contemporary Perspective*. New York: Holt, Rinehart and Winston.

Kottak, C. (1991). *Anthropology: The Exploration of Human Diversity*. New York: McGraw-Hill.

Kroeber, A., and C. Kluckhohn. (1963). *Culture: A Critical Review of Concepts and Definitions*. New York: Random House.

Moody-Adams, M. (1997). *Fieldwork in Familiar Places*. Cambridge: Harvard University Press.

Nino, C. (1991). *The Ethics of Human Rights.* Oxford: Clarendon Press.

Sandel, M. (1982). *Liberalism and the Limits of Justice.* Cambridge: Cambridge University Press.

Singer, M. (1961). *Generalization in Ethics: An Essay in the Logic of Ethics.* New York: Knopf.

Teson, F. (1985). "International Human Rights and Cultural Relativism." *Virginia Journal of International Law* 25(4): 869–898.

Williams, B. (1972). *Morality: An Introduction to Ethics.* New York: Harper and Row.

——. (1985). *Ethics and the Limits of Philosophy.* Cambridge: Harvard University Press.

8
Culture, Evil, and Horror

By PAUL SANTILLI*

ABSTRACT. This chapter develops a concept of aesthetic and existential horror and suggests its importance for understanding modern and
postmodern culture. It makes three distinct claims. First, the experience of horror signifies a breakdown in the symbolic categories and
valuations of a culture. Second, this experience has ontological significance because in horror the human is exposed to the naked fact of
being. This latter point is derived from Heidegger's comments on
anxiety and Emmanuel Levinas's notion of the "*il y a*" or "there is." A
third claim follows from these two, namely, that horror is distinct from
evil. Evil is defined within a cultural matrix; horror is the undefined
other of a culture. Evil represents the negation of being; horror shows
the sickening presence of being as being. The essay concludes with a
reflection on the possibility of a postmodern ethics that takes responsibility for the "horrors of being" generated by globalization.

I

Introduction

A CULTURE IS A WAY in which human beings represent their lives to
themselves through language and other symbolic systems.[1] With
culture, the human separates from the animal and enters an order of
discriminations by which the beautiful is distinguished from the ugly,
the noble from the shameful, and the pure from the defiled. Inherent
in the establishment of cultural coordinates is a logic that excludes
those elements of reality that have no defined location according to
these coordinates. Since a culture gets its bearings by names for

*Paul Santilli is Professor of Philosophy at Siena College, where he specializes in
ethics and cinema studies. His recent publications include a book chapter in *Philosophy,
Genocide, and Human Rights*, edited by John Roth (Palgrave Macmillan, 2005), as well
as articles in *Film and Philosophy* and the *Journal of Aesthetics and Art Criticism* on the
films of the Polish director Krzysztof Kieślowski.

American Journal of Economics and Sociology, Vol. 66, No. 1 (January, 2007).
© 2007 American Journal of Economics and Sociology, Inc.

things, then we could say that what is outside the culture has no name as well. This is not to say, however, that the non-acculturated remainders of the symbolizing process cannot be represented or experienced in any way. It is the purpose of this essay to show that the experience of horror evokes elements of *the real* that have not been assimilated into a culture (and so into "normal" *reality*). We shall try to understand the philosophical significance of horror for modern and postmodern culture by situating it in three contexts—the aesthetic, the existential-ontological, and the ethical—and by drawing a contrast between horror and evil. Modern culture has tended to identify as evil the horror of what is unassimilated to universal norms and rational principles. The question posed at the end of this essay is whether a better philosophical understanding of horror in the context of a late-modern global economy and culture may point the way to an ethics that accepts, loves, and takes responsibility for the monstrous (but not evil) Other.

II

Culture and Horror

THE COUNTERPART OF CULTURE, I would like to suggest, is not nature but horror. The natural usually has a well-defined place in a culture. Defined, and domesticated by a system of signifiers, nature is given a *name* as something original, wild, spontaneous, restorative, dangerous, and so forth. There is nothing so cultivated, for example, as the nature of romantic poets. Of course, culture itself has several meanings. When culture is used to refer to that which is refined and educated, *Kultur* and *Bildung*, then the raw, primitive drives of nature can be seen as polar opposites to culture. But this demarcation is itself a cultural act of language and symbolization. Strictly speaking, I would say that the antithesis of culture is not nature but the *unnatural*—that is, the *monstrosity* that does not fit into any categories or names. As Andrew Gibson has noted, "monstrosity transgresses the metaphysics underlying symbolic boundaries, the boundaries that determine all those categories and classifications that separate kinds of being off from one another."[2] This is echoed by Richard Kearney, who says that monsters "ghost the margins of what can be legitimately thought and said. . . . By definition unrecogniz-able, they defy our accredited norms of identification."[3] Another way of making this point is to think of culture in terms of binary oppo-sitions holding, for example, between the living and the dead, the raw and the cooked, male and female, the human and the nonhu-man, and so on, but also between culture and nature. In that case, then, what is truly "outside" culture would not simply be a member of yet another binary pair, but a sort of "third" indeterminate being or event, in some way present *to* but not re/presented *within* any cultural scheme.

A culture's ontological and axiological categories, defining the real and the good, are also opposed to alternative cultural formulations of the real and the good. In that sense, every coherent human culture is alien to every other culture. But there is a kind of absolute alienage as well that does not consist simply of rival symbolic representations of being, but of being that cannot be represented. This would be monstrous horror, outside the margins, ab-normal, and a leftover from the cultural order of entities and values. Some contemporary thinkers, following the lead of Julia Kristeva and her concept of the "abject," have thought of this monstrous horror as something like the *chora*, which Plato identifies in the *Timaeus* as the "mother and receptacle of all visible and sensible things" (*Timaeus* 49–51).[4] Kearney suggests that c*hora* is a "pre-verbal semiotic space, [a] placeless place before language, law, or cognition proper."[5] This origin, which is strictly speaking preontological and preaxiological since it precedes and is excluded from the *logos* by which beings are named and values are set out, is "what is on the border, what does not respect borders . . . what threatens identity; it is neither good nor evil, subject nor object . . . but something that threatens these very distinctions," according to Kelly Oliver.[6] This is what I regard as the monstrous, unnatural real lingering on the other side of any cultural matrix. By its very act of defining reality and instituting meanings, a culture must seal itself off from what it cannot acknowledge as real or meaningful, and that we shall call the realm of horror.[7]

Nevertheless, the horror with no name, which a culture bars from entering its symbolic domain, is not entirely absent. It literally haunts the edges of the culture, as an indeterminate menace and potential violation of the established norms. In his interesting reflections on Franz Kafka, Mish'Alani observes the following:

> Every collective human order, insofar as it comprises an understanding of itself, is also haunted by figures and shapes with which it tries to identify its Other. It suffers from the phantasms of what lies outside its comprehension, alien figures, obscure, dangerous, or contemptible denizens of those amorphous regions defined only by its own primal silences, exclusions, and rejections.[8]

The cultural imagination strives to represent what is in principle impossible for a culture to represent to itself, preontological and precategorical domains of existence that are separated off as soon as any cultural formation is instituted. One way modern culture does this is through art, especially through a particular genre of art-horror consisting of literary fiction and films.[9] Art-horror is a cultural product through which the culture imagines the other that menaces its central norms and categories. Although art-horror, unlike tragedy, traditionally has received little attention from philosophers, it is worth looking at in order to learn how our culture envisions its rejected or abjected other.

III

Art-Horror and Evil

ART-HORROR IS A TERM coined by the aesthetician Noël Carroll, who offers a three-part definition. First, art-horror provokes, or ought to provoke, a particular emotional state, that of horror. This emotional state is an "abnormal, physically felt agitation (shuddering, tingling, screaming, etc.)."[10] Second, the emotion of horror is generated by beliefs, thoughts, or judgments about a particular kind of object. Carroll is a cognitivist and holds that an emotion is not simply a physical reaction to environmental stimuli but a physical state brought by a cognitive evaluation. So, although the emotion of horror is indeed visceral, its presence in a person is contingent upon that person's having the requisite sorts of judgments about objective states of affairs. Third, the object that arouses horror is judged to be so because it is both dangerously threatening and impure.[11] This object or being Carroll calls a "horror monster," whose monstrosity is characterized not only by its fearsome nature but also by the fact that it is in some way unclean and disgusting. Monsters, says Carroll, borrowing from Mary Douglas's analyses in *Purity and Danger*, are "categorically intersti- tial." That is to say, they are beings who have no place in a culture's schematic maps and are loathsome for that very reason: "For they are beings or creatures that specialize in formlessness, incompleteness, categorical interstitiality, and categorical contradictoriness."[12]

Following Carroll, then, what is important for an understanding of horror is to recognize that the monster's violence not only endangers but also *confuses* the very schemes we ordinarily use to judge vio- lence. The emotion of horror is distinguished from that of fear or dread by additional elements of repugnance or visceral disgust at a figure that does not fit our standard pictures of the madman, murderer, or devil. To take an iconic emblem of horror in 20th-century imagina- tion, Dracula or the Vampire, we note that its monstrosity is mani- fested in ways that mix up our deepest cultural assumptions. In F. W. Murnau's 1922 moving picture *Nosferatu: A Symphony of Horror*, the vampire is portrayed as an awful blend of the living and the dead, male and female, man and animal, nourishment and blood, sexuality and death. Wherever this creature materializes, there are filthy rats, pestilence, and plagues. A culture has no site for such a being, and the shudder one experiences in its presence is not simply the dread of a killer but of revulsion toward something unclean or polluted, belong- ing neither to nature nor to human society. As Carroll puts it, "[mon- sters] are un-natural relative to a culture's conceptual scheme of nature. They do not fit the scheme; they violate it. Thus, monsters are not only physically threatening; they are cognitively threatening. . . . For such monsters are in a certain sense challenges to the foun- dations of a culture's way of thinking."[13]

With this definition, Carroll has made a valuable contribution not only to the aesthetics of art-horror, but also to an understanding of the relation horror bears to cultural norms in general. It allows us to distinguish *nonhorrific* violations of cultural values, which the culture itself can name and define, from those that are *horror inducing*. Not every violation of a cultural norm is monstrous. Steven Smith has stated in an essay on "Rational Horror" that "[t]he repugnance of horror is its protesting recoil from a violation."[14] This designation, however, obscures the difference between emotional responses to cultural violations that are specifically immoral or criminal and responses that are more properly called ones of "horror." A culture can classify many transgressions of its norms using the resources of its symbolic system—its criminal codes or religious commandments, for example. Adultery or theft, even when committed by very wicked persons, need not be strictly speaking described as monstrous or horrifying because such an act can be mapped out and understood within the cultural milieu. Although we do in ordinary language refer to particularly gruesome crimes or evils of great magnitude as "monstrous" and may describe ourselves as "horrified" by them, it is still the case that while they transgress moral norms, they do not fall outside normal linguistic procedures for assessing such transgressions. We may be shocked and morally sickened by a serial child killer, but we know exactly what this killer is and where he belongs within our society's value structure.

The link I am now tentatively drawing between horror as an aesthetic concept and the relevance of horror for moral judgments, and to which I shall return, can also be looked at in another way. Artistic representations of murder, rape, war, or genocide, as awful as these things are, would not ordinarily be thought to belong to the specialized genre of horror literature or cinema. The reason for this, I think, is that evil is defined within the coordinates of a symbolic system the way crimes are defined by laws. Evil itself is not anticultural, but is located within the normative parameters organized by the community. Child murder and incest, for example, have a place within the cultural framework precisely as abominations. They are the exceptions that help the normal system function; they *are* exceptions and evil only in relation to systematic forms of legitimacy. We should not confuse, however, this sort of negativity with the monster who has no operational standing within the system. The genre of art-horror as described by Carroll envisions an infestation of cultural forms by disgustingly unclean and dangerous beings for which there are no standard means of judgment or response. The monstrous other of culture does not so much violate specific ideals within the system— the positive value of life, marriage, religious ritual, and so forth—but the whole system itself. Horror is not merely the shock of radical evil or suffering, as William Earle has maintained.[15] Rather it is the shock of that which cannot even be defined or located in a spectrum of values, which includes at its borders even deeds of extreme evil.

For Carroll, therefore, horror is what Heideggerians would call an *ontic* threat, deriving from some particular entity that falls through the cracks, as it were, of standard epistemological and ontological categories. Horror, in Carroll's theory, also designates a specific emotion aroused by the fictionalized possibility of such a threat's existence. But these *aesthetic* encounters with horror, I believe, are rooted in a more fundamental *ontological* (or perhaps preontological) experience of horror, which is neglected in Carroll's work. Horror is not only a peculiar emotion arising from time to time in response to a possible monstrosity, but it is an enduring feature of our being in the world. It is a basic mood and orientation, or *Stimmung*, with respect to existence. When Marlow echoes the famous last words of Kurtz in the *Heart of Darkness*—"The horror! The horror!"—Conrad's narration makes clear that the horror lies not in Kurtz's own heart, but in the very depths of reality itself. Indeed, the distinction between a subjective feeling and objective monstrosity collapses in those words: "The dusk," writes Conrad, "was repeating them in a persistent whisper all around us, in a whisper that seemed to swell menacingly like the first whisper of a rising wind. 'The horror! The horror!' "[16] It is not as though Conrad is referring to a something, a particular item in the world that horrifies; rather, it is being itself that is the horror.

To develop this idea of horror as a *phenomenon of being*, in distinction to its incarnation in a monstrous object or its status as an emotional state responding to this object, we shall draw on Levinas's idea of the "*Il y a*," or "there is," as he presents it in some early writings before *Totality and Infinity*, and provide, by way of context, a brief look at Heidegger's account of anxiety and the uncanny in *Being and Time*.

IV

Ontological Horror

ALTHOUGH HEIDEGGER HIMSELF does not employ the terms "monstrous" or "horror," his phenomenological ontology allows us to broaden and deepen Carroll's account of art-horror. The horror story or horror film, in its efforts to imagine the unthinkable "other" of a culture, does not always depict a monster as such. What art-horror often shows us is that it is being in the world itself in any or all of its manifestations that has become uncanny and monstrous. In what way can our being in the world be regarded with horror?

According to Heidegger's analysis in *Being and Time*, anxiety is a basic mode of our being in the world, our *Dasein*, characterized as a disturbance before an indefinite and unnamed presence.[17] It is not a particular thing or event *in* the world that one fears in *Angst*, not an ontic object like a criminal, a disease, or an accident. Rather, in anxiety one is unsettled before the world itself, before the very fact of the world's being there at all: "the world as world is disclosed first and foremost by anxiety, as a mode or state-of-mind."[18] This anxiety discloses the world as something open and possible for which the human being (*Dasein*) has to take responsibility. Heidegger interprets anxiety as a kind of uncanniness, or the *unheimlich*. For Heidegger, the uncanny nature of anxiety discloses the disturbing absence of permanence, solidity, and naturalness in our everyday existence: "Everyday familiarity collapses."[19] The uncanny before which one feels anxiety is not any specific kind of entity and therefore is often referred to by Heidegger as a nothing, *ein Nicht*. The occasion of the uncanny need not be due to the appearance of a cultural oddity, even one that is gruesome or terrifying. The normal objects of the world are enough; any "thing" or "no-thing" can provoke an awareness of the contingency and alien nature of existence. An ordinary kitchen or hallway, the most banal item in one's living room, can take on the presence of the uncanny, a phenomenon that Alfred Hitchcock exploited so well in his films.

Emmanuel Levinas takes another but related approach to the phenomenological ontology of horror. Levinas identifies our being in the world with the experience of the *il y a* or the "there is." In *Time and the Other*, Levinas describes the *il y a* as that which remains after we "imagine all things, beings and persons, returning to nothingness." What remains is not a void, but a kind of sheer presence, an "atmospheric density," a plenitude, "or the murmur of silence."[20] Obviously, the *il y a* can only be evoked or intimated, since it stands for what is left over from the direct perception or vocalization of an intentional consciousness. It underlies and is behind every item in existence because, for Levinas, it is nothing but the bare, anonymous, and impersonal fact of existing. What characterizes the *il y a* above all is—*horror.* "The rustling of the there is . . . is horror."[21] What does Levinas mean by this?

Alluding to the Latin root of horror, *horrēre* or "bristling," Levinas indicates that it is not we who "rustle" but Being. Horror is not an emotion a human being feels in the face of something terrifying, impure, or dreadful; it is a rather a phenomenon of Being itself (or "Existing," as Levinas sometimes prefers), in its anonymous, impersonal, and utterly indifferent presence. In the encounter with the *il y a*, conceptual distinctions like subject and object break down, so that horror belongs neither to an affective state of conscious selves nor to objective things, but to an "existence without existents" in which neither we nor things matter very much. Levinas speaks of this encounter as an "insomnia" in the "night"—"the darkness of the night which is neither an object nor the quality of an object. . . . There is no longer *this* or *that*; there is not 'something.' " The "I" of the subject is "submerged by the night, invaded, depersonalized, stifled by it."[22] "Night" is employed by Levinas metaphorically to capture the thick and stifling weight of being that shows up when we suspend our active participation in the world and simply sit and watch, without sleep, without the passing of time, and with horror, the dissipation of meaning and value. Here, he echoes Heidegger, who says: "In the dark there is emphatically 'nothing' to see, though the very world itself is *still* there and 'there' *more obtrusively.*"[23] Not only do the standard symbolic forms by which we orient ourselves in the world melt down, but our very consciousness of being a distinct self collapses. In this existential experience we feel the presence of pure being without the safety net of cultural constructs to sort out objects and subjects. Horror happens when nothing has an identity or a name except the pure nondifferentiated identity of Being.

Levinas himself thought that the encounter with the *il y a* was not quite the same as Heidegger's uncanny anxiety in the face of the being of the world:

> The pure nothingness revealed by anxiety in Heidegger's analysis does not constitute the there is. There is horror of being and not anxiety over nothingness, fear of being and not fear for being; there is being prey to, delivered over to something that is not a "something".[24]

For Heidegger, the contingency and uncanniness of the ordinary world are revealed or intimated in anxiety. Nothing need be as it is; anything could break apart at any moment. Through anxiety I become aware that I bear the responsible burden of sustaining my life projects until death. As Jacques Rolland has noted, the nothingness exposed in anxiety is a negation of the solidity and certainty of the world and the opening of pure indefinite possibilities for existing.[25] For Levinas, however, the basic experience of horror stems not from anxiety but from *nausea*. In an essay from 1935, *De L'evasion* [*On Escape*], Levinas describes nausea as follows:

> In nausea—which amounts to an impossibility of being what one is—we are at the same time riveted to ourselves, enclosed in a tight circle that smothers. We are there, and there is nothing more to be done . . . *this is the very experience of pure being.* . . . As such, nausea discovers only the nakedness of being in its plenitude and in its utterly binding presence.[26]

As Rolland has pointed out, the term *nausea* in its root meaning refers to seasickness (*le mal de mer*). In nausea we are disoriented as though we were at sea, deprived of our habitual landmarks, the frames and parameters by which we dwell in and make sense of the world: "Nausea must therefore be understood as the feeling of our being when at sea, such that in the loss of earth's shores and the disappearance of the vessel, the sea itself draws back as sea, and we remain alone, floating in the pure element."[27] Although Levinas thought it important to distinguish his reflections from those of Jean-Paul Sartre, there is little doubt that he is getting at the same experience described by Sartre in his novel *Nausea*, published in 1938. For example, Sartre writes about the main character Roquentin's nauseous experience of Being in terms that evoke Levinas's own description of the *il y a*: "This veneer had melted, leaving soft monstrous masses, all in disorder— naked, in a frightful obscene nakedness."[28]

Levinas also takes a different position than Heidegger on the relation of horror to death. For Heidegger, an authentic recognition of the unsurpassable possibility of one's own annihilation in death is crucial for *Dasein's* disclosure of being as being. In contrast, making one of his most intriguing observations about horror, Levinas states: "Horror is nowise an anxiety about death."[29] Horror is rather "the impossibility of death." For Levinas, the encounter with being as *il y a* does not arouse in us an authentic, anxious awareness of the burden of freedom and subjectivity unto death. Death, even violent, murderous death, is not what horrifies, popular opinion and Hollywood movies to the contrary. In fact, death actually offers the human being hope of an escape from Being's imposing, oppressive presence and its horrifying shudder. By a suicidal gesture or an actual killing, the subject may intend to escape the anonymity and anomie of existence by reasserting, through a negation, his or her own individual freedom. But in the very act of death-dealing there is a leftover and, as it were, a negation of the negation: "Horror is the event of being which returns in the heart of this negation." What remains after death is the corpse itself, an ineluctable remainder of the act, representing the triumph of being over the subject's free negation. Says Levinas: "A corpse is horrible; it already bears in itself its own phantom, it presages its return. The haunting spectre, the phantom, constitute the very elements of horror."[30]

The key to understanding this approach to ontological horror is to see it as the *death of death*. Levinas says that "horror carries out the condemnation to perpetual reality, to existence with 'no exits.' "[31] The mass murders of the Holocaust or genocides in Rwanda and Sudan, for example, fill us with a moral revulsion that sometimes is described as horror because such acts exceed all that we understand to be "normal" crimes. But, in truth, such unimaginable deaths, even in their excess, still have a place within standard ontological and axiological horizons. Because we have, thanks to our culture, a kind of existential foothold, normative stance, and security, we can be moral witnesses to our time's atrocities. We can "know" death, its time, its place, and its meaning. We can condemn and punish the evildoers, mourn and remember their victims with all the resources of our cultural and religious traditions, however inadequate they may be. Levinasian horror, in contrast, lies elsewhere, in the crumbling of all our resources for managing death and in the brute confrontation with the meaningless glut of being. If there can be genuine horror in the spectacle of genocide, then it would lie not in the twisted use of human freedom to commit such evils, but rather in the persistent remainders of the acts, those unintegrated remnants of the slain corpses, the bones and skulls, for example, at the Tuol Sleng museum in Cambodia or in the church of Nyarubuye in Rwanda.[32] The *horror*, in contrast to the *evil*, of genocide lies not in the crime and the deaths per se, but in the crimes against crime and in the death of deaths. In crime and death the dignity, pride, and freedom of the human subject may still manifest themselves, however perversely. The horror of the carcass is something else, that before which we are nauseated and filled with revulsion. The horror of the 20th century's undead rises up from the twisted anonymity of beings that have not been allowed to die (really) or to be at rest and that, instead of passing into the past, persist in sickening us with their irremissible presence.

V

Modern and Postmodern Horror—The Ethical Challenge

To RECAPITULATE: we have observed, first of all, that horror refers to an experience of those aspects of the real that are not yet slotted into any particular cultural schema. That experience is like fear, but it is not the kind of fear one feels before a specific danger. Rather, it is an anxiety about the instability and contingency of the world itself. Jerome Miller writes: "[I]t is precisely this world, whose solidity I never question, that momentarily shudders when horror awakens in me."[33] Although it is common to regard horror as an emotion among many other emotions that come and go, like fear, terror, or dread, I have drawn on Heidegger's analysis of uncanny anxiety and Levinas's philosophy of the *il y a*, insomnia, and nausea to suggest that there is a primary horror in the human being's way of being in the world that is never entirely exorcised by acculturation and that is never quite absent in our daily existence. Part of the appeal, I think, of art-horror is that it taps into this existential ground and exhibits it in a recognizably chilling story or scary movie. I have also argued that while evil often does have elements of horror and horror, in turn, elements of evil, it is neither necessary nor sufficient for horror to be joined with evil. Indeed, if evil in its classic Augustinian version refers to the annihilation of being or death in its broadest possible construal, then horror may be regarded as the obverse of evil. For it is the *presence* of the real as that indefinite, murky leftover of cultural integration and rational syntheses that arouses horror, not the *absence* of being. Whereas we experience evil in what has been taken away from us and destroyed, we encounter horror as that which *refuses* to pass away, haunting existence as literally the *refuse* of what has been destroyed.

With this understanding of the ontological nature of horror and its difference from evil, we could deepen Noël Carroll's aesthetic analyses of art-horror to consider other features of the genre than that of a culturally anomalous monster. Many horror films, such as Alfred Hitchcock's *Psycho* (1960), Jonathan Demme's *Silence of the Lambs* (1991), or Roman Polanski's *Repulsion* (1965), do not feature unnatural monsters like the vampire. What makes them horrifying and, in part, what also makes vampire movies so horrific, is that they show us, to the point of revulsion, not only a killing but the *remains* of the killing. In the famous shower scene of *Psycho*, for example, the shock of the stabbing of Marion Crane (Janet Leigh) by Norman Bates (Anthony Perkins) mutates into the horror of the lingering, almost caressing shot of the victim's body and her open eye on the tiled floor, as the blood swirls down the drain. What is monstrous about art-horror from this perspective is not simply the *evil* of violent murders, which we find aplenty in gangster films and westerns, but the fact that that the dead do not quite pass away, continuing to exist in a grotesque and perverse way as an unburied corpse, a undead zombie, or a cannibalized body. And this death of death applies as well to the death of the killer-monster. Even when it is finally "killed off" by the end of the film, the horror genre usually teases us with the possibility that it may come back, that such beings can never really be extinguished. The dead do not stay dead.

I would like to conclude these reflections, however, by taking both Carroll's and Levinas's accounts of horror in another direction than that of aesthetics by asking whether the recognition of horror assists us in any way in coming to terms with modernity, and especially with recent cultural crises provoked in large measure by the globalization of market capitalism, as analyzed especially by the sociologist Zygmunt Bauman. Some cultures include the monstrous within their borders and so, paradoxically, are less susceptible to horror than others. Premodern and non-Western societies embrace within their symbolic imaginaries, often as part of their religion, fantastic figures, hybrids of humans and animals, demons, and other unnatural or supernatural creatures. Such beings are not strictly speaking what I would call horror entities. The reason for this is that the mythologies and imaginative terrains of these cultures have named such beings and have located them within the symbolic system. If the borders are open to a liberal exchange between the living and the dead, gods and mortals, or beast and men, then what may look to us like monstrous manifestations are not, in fact, truly monstrous or horrific because they are constituted within a particular cultural matrix itself, being named and understood as such. A good example of this is the marble faun described by Nathaniel Hawthorne. Praxiteles's sculpture of a faun, says Hawthorne, was "neither man nor animal and yet no monster, but a being in whom both races meet on friendly ground."[34] Here the hybrid is itself a cultural entity, not a categorical interstitiality, in Carroll's sense. It would be so even if it were less gentle and more violent than a faun.

In contrast, modern scientific culture has had few such regions in its categorical schemes for the acknowledgment of that which cannot fit into those schemes. In fact, modern culture, from its onset in the 17th century, has aspired to enmesh without remainder all of being within its conceptual nets. The Cartesian ideal of total knowledge and total control, as expressed in the sixth part of the *Discourse on Method*, lives on in 21st-century science, technology, and global markets. Modern culture as such has no place in its coding apparatus for hybrids, mixtures, and other loose entities that extend the horizons of the real beyond the reach of rationality or utility. Its margins are not soft but hard. If a faun were suddenly to appear in a modern corporate office, it would be, indeed, a thing of horror, for there would be literally no *accounting* for it. Modernity wants a place for everything and everything in its place; it dislikes fuzzy borders or the thought that being could be somehow inaccessible.

This totalizing dream of modernity is, of course, bound to fail. The universal language of mathematics, the controls of technology, and the globalization of markets always leave a residue that will not be absorbed by the culture. It is that residue that continues to inspire the genre of art-horror, whose initial appearance during the late 1700s in the form of gothic novels and then, a century later, in the first horror movies, has shadowed not only the growth of science, technology, and industrial capitalism but also the rise of modernist high culture's novels, poetry, drama, and paintings. As Nick Capasso says: "Monsters also appeared as the obverse of the now common coin of Reason."[35] The recognition of the fact that modernity has not captured and controlled everything in its disciplinary structures is one of the distinguishing features of *postmodern culture*, which does not so much supersede as creep along the edges of modernity. Not only does postmodern culture recognize the fact of being's nonassimilation to reason's rules and to the social order's symbolic maps, it often *celebrates* this fact in philosophy and art. The postmodern is strangely attracted to the hybrids, monsters, ambiguous species, open borders, and mixtures that flourished in premodern societies. As Zygmunt Bauman has insightfully observed, postmodernity is "*modernity without illusions.*" He writes: "The illusions, in question, boil down to a belief that the 'messiness' of the human world is but a temporary and repairable state, sooner or later to be replaced by the orderly and systematic rule of reason."[36] The postmodern intellectual, by contrast, believes that "messiness" goes all the way down. Symbolic systems and rational norms are but temporary ways of holding the chaos at bay.

Could the postmodern acknowledgment of the ineluctable monstrousness of being offer us an ethics more suited to what Bauman has called the emerging *"liquid," global phase of late modernity* than the classical enlightenment ethics of rational subjects attuned to universal, rational principles?[37] For example, in a Kantian or neo-Kantian morality, the monstrous exception to the order of reason or rational discourse cannot be truly human, and when it manifests itself in the human it becomes identified with a kind of radical evil. But what if we regarded the inhuman itself as an element of the human, as the drive or desire that eludes civilizing and symbolizing categories, or as the body that refuses to transform itself into spirit and remains, like the bodies in Todd Browning's film *Freaks* (1939), grotesque, unruly, and horrible in the eyes of the established order? If we reject modernity's efforts to cleanse the world of ambiguous and ambivalent beings for the sake of science and efficiency, we may be open to acknowledging the humanity of the deformed body, of the "refuse" of wars, genocides, and merciless economies, and of the unnerving outsiders who haunt the borders of our civilized neighborhoods. This acknowledgment cannot dispense with horror, pretending that the mutilated body or the cadaver is something other than a monster, but it can be an opening to an ethics of love and responsibility for the other.

As Zygmunt Bauman has argued in a number of recent books, the current global economy has generated a new form of waste, a multitude of human beings who are made superfluous by the relentless movement of late modern capitalism and who are unable to fit into the demands of an extraordinarily fluid consumer society.[38] In the liquid era of digital information, telecommunication, and deregulated markets, there are no fixed territories for manufacture and distribution and no permanent set of rules or norms to limit the harsher effects of capitalism. The global economy and the weakening of the welfare state bring a multitude of material benefits that stimulate and gratify (temporarily) the desires of consumers, who are (momentarily) succeeding in the new order. But its unregulated freedoms also bring new forms of insecurity, misery, and violence, as evidenced by the millions of unemployed, abandoned in the rush to "downsize" and "outsource," and the millions of refugees, asylum seekers, and so-called illegal economic migrants who are left homeless in city streets, in camps, in holding cells, and prisons as the financial, managerial, and intellectual elite whiz around the globe in constant motion. Globalization, says Bauman, creates excess human beings who do not fit into basic categories by which the elite define their own humanity.[39] They are new kinds of monstrosities, ambiguous, "interstitial" creatures, new embodiments of the fundamental ontological insecurity that afflicts all humans. As such, they are also convenient targets and scapegoats, beings regarded with revulsion, suspicion, and bewilderment as parasites or potential terrorists.

But they are also the "real" that intrudes upon the consumerist fantasyland that so many of us in the "Westernized" parts of the planet have come to identify with happiness. As I have argued in this essay, the "real" that does not fit into any scheme of culture is a monstrous horror. The human byproducts of modernity's globalization, industrial catastrophes, and ethnic cleansings tend to be stripped of their social identity and placed, like the inmates at Guantanamo Bay, outside the scope of any nation's system of rights and laws; and so they are the "monsters" for our time. But they are not the embodiments of evil or simply nonhuman. They are, in the deepest and oldest sense, our "neighbors," and they could be any one of us at any time given the uncertainties and unpredictabilities of the risk society.[40] While there is, of course, still a great need for modern institutions of international law, human rights, and basic justice to resist the evils done to persons displaced by globalization—and the evil that they themselves can do—I believe there is also a need for a postmodern ethic of personal responsibility and love for that which horrifies, disgusts, and eludes our understanding. Such an ethics has not yet been written, although core ideas can be found in the best of postmodern thinkers like Levinas, Bauman, Slavoj Žižek, Julia Kristeva, Jacques Derrida, and Niels Lógstrup. It was, and still is, the illusion of modernity to think that rational science, efficient economics, and smart political programs could in time overcome and eliminate the horror of the human condition. What, in fact, modernity has often done is simply add to the horror of being, leaving us with the debris of its history. How to love, take responsibility for, and in some way redeem that debris is the urgent challenge still facing a postmodern ethics.

Notes

1. Here I am assuming without elaboration the perspective on culture developed by Ernst Cassirer in the *Philosophy of Symbolic Forms*. "Cassirer has held to a singular sense of culture, with multiple basic or 'symbolic forms' that underlie the diversity of culture." Donald Verene, "Foreword" in Ernst Cassirer, *The Logic of the Cultural Sciences* (New Haven: Yale University Press, 2000), vii. A version of this paper was read at the Sixth World Congress of the International Society for Universal Dialogue (ISUD) in Helsinki, July 2005. I want to thank members of the ISUD for their encouraging and helpful comments on this essay.

2. Andrew Gibson, *Towards A Postmodern Theory of Narrative* (Edinburgh: Edinburgh University Press, 1996), 237.

3. Richard Kearney, *Strangers, Gods, and Monsters* (London and New York: Routledge, 2003), 4.

4. See, especially, Julia Kristeva, *Powers of Horror: An Essay on Abjection*, trans. Leon S. Roudiez (New York: Columbia University Press, 1982), 1–15.

5. Kearney, 196.

6. Kelly Oliver, *Subjectivity Without Subjects: From Abject Fathers to Desiring Mothers* (Lanham, MD: Rowan and Littlefield, 1999), 60. Cited by Kearney, 195.

7. As Jerome Miller notes: "There is no impregnable structure of meaning because every structure, in order to function as such, must create that very distinction between inside and outside which makes a rupture of itself by the outside possible. In short, there is no way to foreclose the possibility of horror." "Horror and the Deconstruction of the Self," *Philosophy Today* (Winter 1988): 289.

8. J. K. Mish'Alani, "Being and Infestation," *Graduate Faculty Philosophy Journal* XVI(1) (1993): 235.

9. I owe the term "art-horror" to Noël Carroll, *The Philosophy of Horror or Paradoxes of the Heart* (London and New York: Routledge, 1990). Carroll is one of a growing number of philosophers who are starting to develop an aesthetics of so-called popular culture, recognizing that well-made horror films, for example, may have something significant to tell us about human beings' experiences of self and the world.

10. Ibid., 27.

11. Ibid., 27.

12. Ibid., 32.

13. Ibid., 34.

14. Steven J. Smith, "Rational Horror," *Philosophy Today* (Winter 1983): 310.

15. In William Earle, *The Autobiographical Consciousness* (Chicago: Quadrangle Books, 1972). "[H]orror, we shall say, is a shocked fascination with some disastrous choice of possibility of suffering that appears to us as radically evil" (205).

16. Joseph Conrad, *Heart of Darkness and the Secret Sharer* (New York: New American Library, 1910), 142.

17. Martin Heidegger, *Being and Time*, trans. John Macquarrie and Edward Robinson (New York: Harper & Row, 1962), 231.

18. Ibid., 233.

19. Ibid., Although the term *unheimlich* had been used eight years before by Freud in "On the Uncanny" (1919), Heidegger in *Being and Time* does not make any connection to or acknowledge the Freudian sense of the term.

20. Emmanuel Levinas, *Time and the Other*, trans. Richard A. Cohen (Pittsburgh: Duquesne University Press, 1987), 46.

21. "Le frôlement de l'*il y a*, c'est l'horreur." Emmanuel Levinas, "There is: Existence Without Existents," in *The Levinas Reader*, ed. Sean Hand (Oxford: Blackwell, 1989), 32.

22. Ibid., 30–31.
23. Heidegger, 234.
24. Levinas, 1989, 34.
25. Jacques Rolland, "Getting Out of Being by a New Path," in Emmanuel Levinas, *On Escape*, trans. Bettina Bergo (Stanford: Stanford University Press, 2003), 20.
26. Levinas, *On Escape*, 66–67 (emphasis in original).
27. Rolland, 19.
28. Jean Paul Sartre, *Nausea*, trans. Lloyd Alexander (New York: New Direction, 1964), 171–172. As an illustration of this experience of the *il y a*, consider Roman Polanski's film *Repulsion* (1965). The film is about a woman, Carol LeDoux (Catherine Deneuve), who lives with her sister in a London flat. The film at the outset reveals Carol to be a disturbed, withdrawn personality, childishly dependent on her sister and phobic about the world, especially male sexuality. Essentially, the film tries to convey the way Carol experiences her being in the world as one of horror, nausea, and disgust, as she descends into madness. She appears to see grotesque cracks opening up in the walls and ceiling of her apartment. Her rooms lose their solidity, bulging and contorting in menacing ways. A corridor becomes a nightmarish zone of rubbery hands groping her body. The kitchen becomes disgusting with remnants of meals and a slowly rotting rabbit carcass. The audience experiences horror not because of a worry that a specific thing that might harm her, but because of an unsettling glimpse into the alien thingness of things themselves.
29. Levinas, 1989, 33.
30. Ibid., 33. Here again Sartre's character, Roquentin, sheds light on Levinasian horror: "But even my death would have been *In the way. In the way*, my corpse, my blood on these stones, between these plants, at the back of this smiling garden . . . *In the way.* I was *In the way* for eternity." Sartre, 173 (emphasis in original).
31. Ibid., 34.
32. For details about the Tuol Sleng museum, see Judy Ledgerwood, "The Cambodian Tuol Sleng Museum of Genocidal Crimes: National Narrative," in *Genocide, Collective Violence, and Popular Memory: The Politics of Remembrance in the Twentieth Century*, eds. David E. Lovey and William H. Beezley (Wilmington, DE: Scholarly Resources, 2002), 103–122. On Nyarubuye, see Philip Gourevitch, "Among the Dead" in *Disturbing Remains: Memory, History, and Crisis in the Twentieth Century*, eds. Michael S. Roth and Charles G. Salas (Los Angeles: Getty Research Institute, 2001).
33. Miller, 288. Levinas says of the encounter with the *il y a*: "things and beings strike us as though they no longer composed a world, and were swimming in the chaos of their existence" (Levinas, 1989, 31).
34. Nathaniel Hawthorne, *The Marble Faun* (Mineola, NY: Dover Publications, 2004), 4.

35. Cited by Kearney, 118.

36. Zygmunt Bauman, *Postmodern Ethics* (Oxford: Blackwell, 1993), 32.

37. See Zygmunt Bauman's *Liquid Life* (Cambridge: Polity Press, 2005). According to Bauman, unlike the period of "solid" modernity, late "liquid" modernity no longer confines economic and social powers to any locale, but allows them to roam with incredibly rapid mobility all over the globe. A national corporation bound to a specific state is becoming an anachronism. In the liquid world what are valued are flux and change, not lasting identity or definition: "The sole purpose of being on the move is to remain on the move" (*Liquid Life*, 133).

38. See, for example, Z. Bauman's *Globalization: The Human Consequences* (New York: Columbia University Press, 1998) and *Wasted Lives: Modernity and its Outcasts* (Cambridge: Polity Press, 2004).

39. See *Wasted Lives*, 38–41. " 'Surplus population' is one more variety of human waste . . . the superfluous are not just an alien body but a cancerous growth gnawing at the healthy tissues of society . . ."

40. Interestingly, Slavoj Žižek has titled a recent essay "Neighbors and Other Monsters: A Plea for Ethical Violence," in *The Neighbor: Three Inquiries in Political Theology*, with Eric Santer and Kenneth Reinhard (Chicago: University of Chicago Press, 2005). Žižek writes that the face of the neighbor should be encountered as a monstrous thing and not a "gentrified" spirit (162–163).

References

Bauman, Z. (1993). *Postmodern Ethics*. Oxford: Blackwell Publishers.

———. (1998). *Globalization: The Human Consequences*. New York: Columbia University Press.

———. (2004). *Wasted Lives: Modernity and its Outcasts*. Cambridge: Polity Press.

———. (2005). *Liquid Life*. Cambridge: Polity Press.

Carroll, N. (1990). *The Philosophy of Horror or Paradoxes of the Heart*. London and New York: Routledge.

Conrad, J. (1910). *Heart of Darkness and the Secret Sharer*. New York: New American Library.

Earle, W. (1972). *The Autobiographical Consciousness*. Chicago, IL: Quadrangle Books.

Gibson, A. (1996). *Towards A Postmodern Theory of Narrative*. Edinburgh: Edinburgh University Press.

Gourevitch, P. (2001). "Among the Dead." In *Disturbing Remains: Memory, History, and Crisis in the Twentieth Century*, eds. Michael S. Roth and Charles G. Salas, pp. 63–73. Los Angeles: Getty Research Institute.

Hawthorne, N. (2004). *The Marble Faun*. Mineola, NY: Dover Publications.

Heidegger, M. (1962). *Being and Time*, trans. John Macquarrie and Edward Robinson. New York: Harper & Row.

Kearney, R. (2003). *Strangers, Gods, and Monsters*. London and New York: Routledge.

Kristeva, J. (1982). *Powers of Horror: An Essay on Abjection*, trans. Leon S. Roudiez. New York: Columbia University Press.

Ledgerwood, J. (2002). "The Cambodian Tuol Sleng Museum of Genocidal Crimes: National Narrative." In *Genocide, Collective Violence, and Popular Memory: The Politics of Remembrance in the Twentieth Century*, eds., David E. Lovey and William H. Beezley, pp. 103–122. Wilmington, DE: Scholarly Resources.

Levinas, E. (1987). *Time and the Other*, trans. Richard A. Cohen. Pittsburgh, PA: Duquesne University Press.

——. (1989). "There is: Existence Without Existents." In *The Levinas Reader*, ed., Sean Hand, pp. 29–36. Oxford: Blackwell.

Miller, J. (1988). "Horror and the Deconstruction of the Self." *Philosophy Today* no. 32 (Winter): 286–298.

Mish'Alani, J. K. (1993). "Being and Infestation." *Graduate Faculty Philosophy Journal* 16(1): 227–243.

Oliver, K. (1999). *Subjectivity Without Subjects: From Abject Fathers to Desiring Mothers*. Lanham, MD: Rowan and Littlefield.

Rolland, J. (2003). "Getting Out of Being by a New Path." Introduction to Emmanuel Levinas, *On Escape*, trans. Bettina Bergo, pp. 3–48. Stanford: Stanford University Press.

Sartre, J. P. (1964). *Nausea*, trans. Lloyd Alexander. New York: New Directions.

Smith, S. J. (1983). "Rational Horror." *Philosophy Today* no. 27: 307–316.

Verene, D. (2000). "Foreword" to Ernst Cassirer, *The Logic of the Cultural Sciences*. New Haven: Yale University Press.

Žižek, S. (2005). *The Neighbor: Three Inquiries in Political Theology*, with Eric Santer and Kenneth Reinhard. Chicago: University of Chicago Press.

9
Persons

Natural, Functional, or Ethical Kind?

By JOHN P. LIZZA*

ABSTRACT. In this paper, I examine alternative views of personhood
and how they affect our understanding of life and death. Building on
David Wiggins's insight that our concept of person tries to hold in a
single focus our nature as a biological being, a subject of consciousness, and a locus of moral values, I argue against views that try to
reduce persons to one of these aspects at the expense of the others.
Thought experiments that have been prominent in the literature on
personal identity are criticized on grounds that they sunder persons
from the moral and cultural context in which they appear and ignore
an essential relational aspect of persons. I argue for a substantive view
of persons that understands persons as "constituted by" but not
identical to human organisms, and that treats persons as having
essential relational properties. Persons are thus beings whose nature is
not determined entirely by their biology or psychology but is, in part,
a matter of individual, moral, and cultural construction. I argue that
such a view provides the best theoretical grounding to answer the
more practical, bioethical questions concerning the beginning and end
of life.

*John Lizza is Professor and Chair of Philosophy at Kutztown University of Pennsyl-
vania. His main philosophical interests are in metaphysics, philosophy of mind,
and bioethics. He is the author of *Persons, Humanity, and the Definition of Death*
(Baltimore: Johns Hopkins University Press, 2006).
American Journal of Economics and Sociology, Vol. 66, No. 1 (January, 2007).

I

Introduction

ADVANCES IN medical technology have posed significant challenges to how we fix the boundaries of the beginning and end of life. When does a person begin and cease to exist? Are embryos, artificially sustained whole-brain-dead bodies, individuals in permanent vegetative state (PermVS)[1], and anencephalics[2] living persons? In short, who should be counted among the living "we"?

Alternative positions on these issues have been assumed or implied by different views of the nature of persons. This has been evident in the debate over the definition of death and criteria for its determination. Simplifying the account somewhat, three alternative views of the person have been prominent in this discussion: (1) a "species" or natural kind concept that identifies the person with the human organism;[3] (2) a "qualitative" or "functionalist" view that identifies the person with certain abilities and qualities of awareness;[4] and (3) a "substantive" view that treats the person not as some qualitative or functional specification of some more basic kind of thing, such as a human organism, but as a primitive substance that has psychological and corporeal characteristics.[5]

Since the identification of the person with the biological organism leads to defining the beginning and end of life in strictly biological terms, this view has led some bioethicists to reject "brain death" as death.[6] Pointing to cases of postmortem pregnancy[7] and the extraordinary case of a whole-brain-dead body sustained for over 13 years,[8] these theorists argue that the human organism may continue to exist even if it has lost all brain functions. Persons may retain their organic integration, albeit through artificial life support, and thus continue to exist despite the loss of all brain functions. Accordingly, these theorists reject the whole-brain neurological criterion for determining death and accept only the traditional criterion of irreversible cessation of respiration and circulation. For example, Shewmon states, "as long as the human body is alive (from the biological perspective of somatic integrative unity) then the person is alive."[9]

Other bioethicists who identify the person with the human organism, however, accept "brain death" as death. For example, Alexander

Capron writes that "the accepted criterion for being a person . . . [is] live birth of the product of human conception."[10] In Capron's view, when we artificially sustain whole-brain-dead pregnant women, we are sustaining collections of human organs rather than the person, in other words, the human organism as a whole. If all brain functions are lost, including the integrative functions of the brainstem, then the person has died. Death is defined as the irreversible loss of organic integration. Capron and others hold that individuals in PermVS and anencephalics are living persons. Death has not occurred because these individuals retain brainstem functions and thus the human organism, that is, the person, has not lost its organic integration.

In contrast to those who accept a "species" concept of person, bioethicists who identify the person with a set of psychological functions define a person's life and death in terms of the beginning, continuation, and cessation of certain psychological functions. Thus, Green and Wikler (1980) argue in favor of a consciousness-related or "higher-brain" formulation of death that would consider individuals who have lost all brain function, as well as individuals in PermVS, as dead. Since individuals in PermVS are no longer psychologically continuous with their former selves, those former selves have ceased to exist, that is, they have died.

It is worth noting that some prominent critics of this higher-brain formulation of death, such as James Bernat, Charles Culver, and Bernard Gert, accept the functionalist or qualitative view of the person that Green and Wikler invoke, but reject the implication that individuals who have irreversibly lost consciousness and every other mental function have "died." Bernat, Culver, and Gert (1981) distinguish the person from the human organism and hold that individuals in PermVS are not persons. However, they object to characterizing individuals in PermVS as "dead" on grounds that this would be an incorrect use of the term "dead." They define "death" as "the permanent cessation of functioning of the organism as a whole" and claim that "death" is a strictly biological concept, applicable to human organisms but not to persons. Thus, they criticize the consciousness-related, neurological formulation of death as involving a metaphorical use of "death," "applying it to an organism which has ceased to be a person but has not died."[11] In their view, "death" cannot be applied literally to persons because death is a biological concept appropriate to biological organisms, not to roles, functions, abilities, or qualities of awareness. Just as a human organism may cease to be a banker or basketball player without dying, Bernat, Culver, and Gert hold that a human organism can cease to be a person without dying.

The third view, the "substantive" concept of person, treats the person neither as some qualitative or functional specification of some more basic kind of thing, such as a human organism, nor as identical to a human organism. Instead, in this view, a person is a primitive substance that necessarily has psychological and corporeal characteristics. P. F. Strawson's definition of a person as an individual to which we can apply both predicates that ascribe psychological characteristics (P-predicates) and predicates that ascribe corporeal characteristics (M-predicates) is an example of the use of "person" in this substantive sense.[12] In Strawson's view, it is neither a category mistake nor a metaphor to predicate death to persons. This view of the person is reflected in common expressions such as "people die every day," and differs from the "species meaning" in that it entails that the person must have the capacity or realistic potential for psychological functions. This cannot be said about a corpse or about some living members of the biological species *Homo sapiens*, such as anencephalics and individuals in PermVS.

In the context of the debate over the definition of death, Tristam Engelhardt (1975), Karen Gervais (1986), and I (1999, 2004) have invoked this substantive view of the person and have distinguished the death of the person from that of the human organism. In this view, since persons must have the capacity or realistic potential for consciousness and other mental functions, the irreversible loss of that capacity or potential would mean the ceasing to exist or death of the person. Persons whose brains have been destroyed to the point where they have lost the potential for consciousness and every other mental function are therefore dead. Technology may sustain human or humanoid bodies that have irreversibly lost the potential for consciousness, but this should not obscure the reality that the person, understood as a substantive being, has died.

Because the concept of person is pivotal in this discussion, an assessment of which concept of person makes the most sense is unavoidable. Failure to address the issue would leave us with parties in the debate over the definition of death essentially talking past each other by proposing definitions of death for different kinds of things. A similar challenge appears in the debate over abortion. Disagreement on the issue of whether a human embryo or fetus is a person may lead to irreconcilable disagreement over the morality of abortion. Indeed, when the discussion of personhood in the debate over abortion was perhaps at its height, Ruth Macklin (1983) concluded that we had reached an impasse on differences over the concept of personhood and that continued focus on personhood would be of little help in making progress or reaching any kind of consensus on abortion. Although Macklin provides a perceptive account of certain aspects of the disagreement over concepts of personhood and the role that the concept has played in bioethics, I think that her conclusions were premature.

While I agree with Macklin that there will probably always be disagreement over the concept of person, I am generally skeptical about calling disagreement at any point "fundamental" or incapable of making progress toward consensus.[13] Further analysis often reveals how our beliefs are tied to other beliefs, and critical reflection on those other beliefs may lead to revision in the beliefs that we thought were different in a "fundamental" or foundational sense. We sometimes find that what we initially consider to be a "fundamental disagreement" turns out to be a not-so-fundamental disagreement or not even a disagreement after all. Indeed, because the concept of personhood is so central to our moral, metaphysical, and cultural systems of thought, it has a depth to it that we have only begun to explore. If our concept of personhood is tied to other descriptive and prescriptive beliefs, we need to examine exactly what those beliefs are and whether they are consistent with how we wish to use the term "person."

Daniel Callahan (1988) has pointed out that persons cannot be understood or defined by a single character or essential nature. Callahan[14] cites Ernest Becker, who observes: "In the human sciences man must be seen at all times in the total social-cultural-historical context, precisely because it is this that forms his 'self' or nature." This social-cultural-historical depth to the concept of person has been insufficiently explored, especially in the context of advances in life-sustaining technology that affect our understanding of when a person dies. Instead of uncritically accepting what James Bernat (2002) has called the "biological paradigm of death," we need to explore our social-cultural-historical traditions and see how "brain death" fits with those traditions.

In addition, instead of examining how the social-cultural-historical context informs our notions of persons and personal identity, contemporary philosophers addressing issues of personhood, personal identity, and abortion have spent much more time considering conceptual puzzles about personal identity that ignore the social-cultural-historical context in which persons appear. While some theorists, such as G. H. Mead (1925, 1934), Jean-Paul Sartre (1942, 1945, 1946), Ludwig Wittgenstein (1953), Clifford Geertz (1964, 1965, 1966), Rom Harré (1984, 1989), and Ken Gergen (1991a, 1991b), have emphasized the relational and cultural nature of persons, most contemporary debate over criteria for personhood and personal identity in the philosophical literature has assumed that the criteria must be something internal to the person, for example, internally related psychological or bodily states. Much less attention has been paid to how external factors, such as cultural factors or an individual's relation to others, may determine the nature and identity of persons. Examination of such factors may lead to a greater consensus or an acceptance of pluralism concerning the nature of persons and what it means for them to die. In fact, one of the main reasons for accepting a particular version of the substantive view of persons, that is, that persons are "constituted by" human organisms, is that it allows external factors to play an essential role in the identity and individuation of persons.

Moreover, personhood is a dynamic concept that is subject to change in light of new knowledge and possibilities. If our nature is not fixed and we can create, at least in part, who we are, personhood and personal identity should be approached more as open-ended projects, rather than as realities that are determined by factors independent of the choices that we make. Thus, although examining our tradition is important for evaluating the new phenomena created by advances in medical technology, especially when it poses challenges to our basic concepts of life, death, and who we are, it is insufficient. We need to also ask what it is that we want to become.

As Christopher Gill (1990: 156) and David Wiggins (1987) have suggested, our theory of personhood tries to hold together in a single focus three aspects of persons:

(1) an object of biological, anatomical, and neurophysiological inquiry;
(2) a subject of consciousness; and
(3) a locus of all sorts of moral attributes and the source or conceptual origin of all value.

Wiggins's approach is helpful because it suggests that when faced with problematic cases that challenge the range of our concept of person, such as the whole-brain dead body, individuals in PermVS, or human embryos, we need to examine to what extent these beings are like ourselves in the three senses that inform our concept of person. We also need to examine how these three features are interconnected. Too often, theorists will focus on one of these aspects and ignore the others. This is particularly evident in the philosophical discussion about personal identity over the last 50 years. As noted above, the thought experiments that challenge our concept of persons and personal identity and that have dominated contemporary philosophical discussion of personal identity tend to sunder persons from the cultural and moral context in which they appear. If Wiggins is right, we should not expect to have a purely metaphysical or value-free account of the nature of a person.

In the remainder of this chapter, I will provide a sketch of my argument that the species and qualitative views of personhood are mistaken because they fail to do justice to one or more of these dimensions of persons. Accordingly, the support that some have thought these views provided for accepting their position on the definition and criteria for death is undermined. I shall argue in favor of the substantive view of personhood that understands persons as constituted by, but not identical to, human organisms. I believe that this substantive view provides the best theoretical framework for bringing together an understanding of ourselves as biological, conscious, and moral beings. It also supports a more pluralistic approach to the definition and criteria for death.

II

Persons as Identical to Human Organisms

THE MAIN DIFFICULTY for the species view of persons is that it entails beliefs that most of us reject. For example, in F. Feldman's version, all members of the species *Homo sapiens*, regardless of whether they are alive or not, are persons. However, as David Wiggins has pointed out, this view seems to commit us to counting "among present persons Jeremy Bentham, and even the Pharaohs, presumably more competently preserved."[15]

Indeed, little thought seems to have been given to the moral implications of identifying ourselves with human organisms, dead or alive. For example, David Mackie (1999) observes that the formulation of animalism that identifies the person with the human organism in Feldman's "dead or alive" sense invites the question, "Who are 'we'?" Mackie then states: "To this question, the answer must be that 'we' means you, me, and those persons who are of the same substantial kind as us."[16] Since Mackie and Feldman identify persons with members of the biological kind *Homo sapiens*, and since they believe that human corpses are still members of that biological kind, they count human corpses among the "we." One wonders what company Feldman and Mackie keep! They appear not to have the "discomfort" that Wiggins says most of us feel about any straightforward identification of ourselves with our bodies. They also ignore the relevance of subjectivity and reciprocity that Wiggins, Gill, Harré, and others identify as central to personhood.

This resistance to identifying ourselves with our bodies can be extended to other cases. For example, although many believe that we accept the loss of all brain functions as death because it entails the irreversible loss of organic integration, this is mistaken. Likewise, cases of postmortem pregnancy and the extraordinary case of a whole-brain-dead body sustained for over 13 years challenge the idea that brain function is necessary for organic integration. Instead, the real reason we accept the loss of all brain functions as death is that it entails the irreversible loss of consciousness and every other mental function. Most of us would not identify ourselves with our whole-brain-dead bodies even though those bodies may be artificially sustained because those bodies lack the potential for any mental functions. The same could be said about many people's intuitions about anencephalics and individuals in PermVS, although I suspect that there may be more uncertainty about these cases. However, this uncertainty may have to do mostly with an uncertainty about whether individuals in PermVS or anencephalics have any potential for consciousness.

When we come to human organisms who have the potential for consciousness and other mental functions or who demonstrate minimal awareness and sentience, I think there is much greater disagreement about whether to include them among the "we." Consideration of the moral significance of sentience and potentiality complicates matters. While few moral theories accord any moral standing to beings that utterly lack the potential for consciousness, awareness, and sentience (Warren 2000), some moral theories, such as utilitarianism, assign moral value to beings with consciousness and sentience. Whether such value is sufficient for the high moral standing that is usually accorded to persons, however, is an open question.

Thus, the initial intuitions that we have about whether we should count individuals in PermVS and the artificially sustained whole-brain dead as among the "we" may receive support from more reflective moral considerations. While Feldman is right that consideration of the biological structure of dead specimens of the human species, that is, dead persons, may lead us to consider them to be human beings or persons (compare butterflies carefully preserved and mounted), biological structure is only one aspect of human beings and persons. Unless we think that our ontology is completely independent of having a perspective on the world, values, and interests, there is no reason why these biological aspects should take precedence over the psychological and moral aspects of persons.

III

Persons as Qualities of Human Organisms

THERE ARE FOUR main difficulties with the qualitative or functionalist view of person. First, as I have pointed out elsewhere,[17] it conflicts with what many ordinary people, as well as philosophers, have always said about persons and death. Whereas Bernat, Culver, and Gert claim that we commit a category mistake by predicating death literally to persons, most of us normally think of persons as the kind of thing that can literally die. We also think of them as the kind of thing that can literally live, eat, sleep, jump, breathe, and so on. However, according to Bernat, Culver, and Gert, these predicates apply literally to human organisms and only metaphorically to persons. To say that these common expressions are metaphorical departs from ordinary usage and the standard understanding of the terms.

Second, the functionalist concept of person fails to do justice to the moral dimension of persons. Locke's proposal to treat the person as a mode or set of psychological qualities of a substance was challenged by Molyneux ([1693] 1794: 329) and Reid (1785), precisely on such grounds. For example, Molyneux pointed out that Locke's memory criterion of personal identity entailed the unacceptable implication that there would be no reason to hold someone responsible for an immoral act that he or she committed while drunk, if the person had no memory of having done the act. Locke, himself, believed that the concept of person was a "forensic" term and ultimately recognized the force of Molyneux's criticism (Allison 1966). Christine Korsgaard (1989) has similarly challenged Parfit's qualitative view of the person on grounds that it fails to adequately account for moral responsibility.

Third, proponents of the functionalist view, such as Locke ([1694] 1975) and Parfit (1986), have relied heavily on intuitions about certain thought experiments that they claim show that "what matters" to us about personal identity is psychological continuity. However, critics, such as Lockwood (1985), Wiggins (1980), Unger (1990), and McMahan (2002), have challenged these intuitions and argued that bodily or brain continuity is a significant part of what matters to us about our identity. The upshot of these criticisms is that only a view that treats the person as a substantive entity, not as a mode or quality of some substantive entity, can provide adequate grounding for the moral dimension of persons.

Finally, the functionalist view relies on a notion of "qualitative similarity" that makes the substantive matter underlying the psychological states irrelevant to personal identity or survival. Locke's view is a precursor to the contemporary functionalist theory of the mind that rejects the idea that the mind is a substantive entity, whether material or immaterial. Instead, the mind is conceived as a function that can be described abstractly by a machine table of inputs, internal states, and outputs. While the function needs to be embodied in some medium, such as the neurophysiological processes of the brain, the function can be described independently of whatever underlies or instantiates it.[18]

In his thought experiments involving replication and "teletransportation," Parfit (1986) assumes that teletransportation would preserve the qualitative similarity of one's psychological properties. Just as a photocopy machine may make many qualitatively identical copies of a document, the teletransporter may make qualitatively identical copies of a person's psychological states. He then claims that such qualitative similarity would be "all that matters to us" about our identity. This assumes, however, that there are no essential, relational properties of persons that might not be preserved by replication. For if persons have essential relational properties, then even though an original and replica may be qualitatively similar in many internal or nonrelational respects, they may not be qualitatively similar in their relational respects. For example, a forged $20 bill may be qualitatively similar in many respects to a real $20 bill, but all that matters to us about the real $20 bill would not be preserved by replicating it. Persons, like $20 bills, have essential relational properties insofar as they are essentially social and cultural beings. Moreover, the instantiation of these properties depends on conventions, moral and legal theory, and other aspects of culture.[19] In other words, persons and their identity are in part defined by the moral and cultural context in which they appear. The conclusions that Parfit draws from the thought experiments are faulty because they sunder persons from their social and cultural context and ignore their relational dimension.

IV

Persons as Substances

SINCE THE SUBSTANTIVE VIEW maintains that a person is neither identical to a human organism nor simply a functional or qualitative specification of a human organism, the relation between the person and the human organism must be understood in terms of something other than identity or as a relation between a substance and a quality. In an earlier work (Lizza 1991), I argued that the relation between the person and human organism should be understood as one of constitution.[20] More recently, Lynne Rudder Baker (2000) has developed much more fully the view that persons are constituted by human beings.[21] She, too, treats subjectivity as essential to persons and has shown how relational factors play a role in their constitution. In particular, persons cannot exist independently of their having and being related to beings with propositional attitudes. While not all constituted things have intentional properties—for example, genes are constituted by DNA molecules but existed before there were propositional attitudes—other constituted objects, such as persons and works of art, are dependent on their relation to beings with intentionality.[22] This last factor provides the conceptual space to do justice to the role that social and cultural factors play in fixing the boundaries of our concept of person, factors that theorists such as G. H. Mead, Sartre, Geertz, and Harré have emphasized in their work.

In the constitutive view, persons are biological beings, and our understanding of their biology should inform our understanding of their nature. It would thus be a mistake to treat persons as simple artifacts whose nature is a matter of mere stipulation. Not anything can be a person. Indeed, as with all natural kinds, the lawlike regularities associated with the concept *human being* place restrictions on the possible development of members within its extension. These same restrictions apply to persons insofar as they are constituted by a natural kind. For example, if our neurophysiology tells us that a certain amount of brain matter is required for consciousness, then, assuming that such potential is necessary for something to be a person, human organisms without the requisite neurophysiological structures would be ruled out of the class of persons.

However, persons are not identical to human organisms, and the concept *person* is not a natural kind concept. Because of their essential psychological, moral, and cultural nature, persons are not reducible to their biological being. Our understanding of them is informed not only by biological theory, but by psychological, moral, sociological, and cultural theories as well.

Since psychological, moral, and cultural considerations take us beyond biology, the nature of persons is *in part* a matter of interpretation within those theories. Persons are not beings whose nature we can discover in the same way that we can discover that water is H_2O. Nor are persons simply artificial, functional constructions such that the matter constituting them is irrelevant to their individuation and identification. Instead, following David Wiggins, the concept of person is a "hybrid concept." By this, I mean that the concept *person* is partly determined by the biology of the natural kind that constitutes a person and partly by psychological, moral, and cultural considerations. In this interpretation, the fundamental substantial kind under which we are individuated and identified would be neither person *simpliciter*, nor human organism. Rather it would be the hybrid concept *human-person*. Moreover, such a view would make the identity and individuation a matter of arbitrary stipulation only if one thought that one's psychological, moral, and cultural theories were arbitrary. If these theories can have rational support (and I believe that they can), then they can provide rational support for our judgments about persons and personal identity.

Developing Strawson's insight on how our sense of personal identity is tied to bodily considerations and our recognition (or interpretation) of other persons, Rom Harré suggests that our social being is reflected in our system of personal pronouns and how we come to use them. He writes:

> The indexicality of "I" depends, it might be argued, upon the grasp of the simple referential function of "you." Since "myself" is not a thing I could discover, it seems I cannot first experience myself and then attach the personal pronoun "I" to that experience. I must be learning the pronoun system as a whole through the ways in which and the means by which I am being treated as a person by others. So that, by being treated as "you," or as a member of "we," I am now in a position to add "I" to my vocabulary, to show where, in the array of persons, speaking, thinking, feeling, promising and so on, is happening. In order to be addressed as "you," I must be being perceived as a definite embodied person, that is, as a distinct human but material individual by others. This unity of the pronoun system might be one of the things that is meant by the social construction of the self. But it depends upon the recognizable bodily identity that I have even as an infant. I have identified these as the indexical uses of "I."[23]

Harré further observes that we are treated by other people as having a distinct point of view and as being a locus of agency. The very conditions of bodily identity that are necessary conditions for having the idea of ourselves as persons are, he states, "embedded in all kind of social practices . . . in such practices as moral praise and blame."[24] He concludes:

> So the acquisition of the idea of a personal identity for oneself, through which one develops a sense of identity, is at least in part a consequence of social practices which derive from the fact of identity as it is conceived in a culture. Our first preliminary conclusion, then, must be that a human being learns that he or she is a person from others and in discovering a sphere of action the source of which is treated by others as the very person they identify as having spatiotemporal identity. Thus, a human being does not learn that he or she is a person by the empirical disclosure of an experiential fact. Personal identity is symbolic of social practices not of empirical experiences. It has the status of a theory.[25]

Harré's point that personal identity, at least in part, is a matter of social and cultural interpretation and practice and is not purely an empirical fact to be discovered is significant to the problem of defining the beginning and end of life. If social and cultural factors inform our sense of personal identity, then those same factors are relevant when we are confronted with cases that challenge whether some individual should be counted among the living "we." Thus, an individual who is minimally conscious would not necessarily be ruled out of the class of persons, since others may sympathize with the individual and extend compassion and recognition. However, the situation is much different when we consider an individual in PermVS or one who has lost all brain function. *Assuming* that these individuals have lost their ability to experience the world, they have lost their subjectivity, and hence fall outside the boundaries of persons. They are mere material beings. Sympathy, compassion, and social recognition are no longer appropriate responses. This, of course, does not mean that these individuals should not be treated with some respect. However, the respect accorded to these individuals should be more in line with the respect that we accord corpses. Sympathy and compassion are inappropriate moral responses to corpses. Since corpses lack feeling and interests, there is nothing to sympathize with. The same can be said about our relation to individuals in PermVS and those who have lost all brain function.

It is important to note that the inappropriateness of sympathy, compassion, and other moral emotions in these cases is predicated on the belief that these human organisms have lost their potential and capacity for subjectivity. This belief, of course, is based on an assumption that subjectivity in human organisms is dependent on certain brain functions and that those functions are irreversibly destroyed in cases of PermVS and whole-brain-dead human organisms. If one were to reject these assumptions, then the responses of sympathy and compassion toward these individuals and other moral beliefs about them might be appropriate. For example, D. Alan Shewmon (1997) rejects the assumption that the potential for consciousness and other mental functions resides in the brain. According to Shewmon, individuals who have lost all brain function still retain the potential for intellect and will and therefore have not died. Shewmon's view is based on a specific understanding of potentiality—one that I believe we have good reason to reject but that Shewmon believes is supported by the Catholic philosophical and theological tradition.[26]

Other examples of how different metaphysical beliefs embedded in cultural practices may affect whether an individual gets treated as a living person are reflected in why some Japanese, Jews, and Native Americans reject whole-brain death as death. Some members of these groups believe that the spirit has not left the body as long as respiration is present, regardless of whether respiration is maintained by natural or artificial means. Since they understand death as the separation of the spirit from the body, death has not occurred until respiration has ceased. In the case of the Japanese, the traditional concept of *kokoro* as an "inner" stable self or core of the person may play a role in why some Japanese reject brain death as death. Lock[27] explains that *kokoro* is thought to lie in the depths of the body, but it is not an anatomical organ. It is neither identified with the brain, nor is it associated exclusively with the mind. Yet it is regarded as the source of the stable "inner" self or person. Since *kokoro* may be thought to remain even in a body that has lost all brain function, some Japanese do not accept brain death as death. Finally, Vera Kalitzkus (2004) points out that within Hinduism, *atman* or the soul is not released from the body until the main mourner, usually the eldest son, smashes the skull of the person who has undergone cremation. Kalitzkus states: "With the postponement of the final point of death to the smashing of the skull, death falls under the control of the social: it is transferred from the realm of the natural to that of the cultural."[28]

The point of these examples is to show how different metaphysical beliefs are embedded in different cultural practices and how those practices affect whether and when a person is treated as dead. We should expect that people will continue to differ on whether certain individuals should be considered dead because they will continue to differ on their view of the nature of persons. However, I am not suggesting that we should accept a naïve relativism about persons or that cultural practice cannot be changed. The new cases dished up by advances in medical technology should force us to reflect on our beliefs and practices and, in some cases, to revise them. Thus, upon reflection, some practices may be determined to be inconsistent with other things we believe about persons and how they should be treated. The practices may also be based on mistaken beliefs about other matters. Indeed, I have tried to show how a view that treats persons as constituted by material beings (in our case, human organisms) and as essentially having a subjective, moral, and social nature is inconsistent with treating human organisms that have irreversibly lost the capacity for subjectivity as living persons.

In conclusion, whether anencephalics, individuals in PermVS, the artificially sustained whole-brain dead, and embryos are persons may not be readily answered by some discovery about the nature of persons. Because "person" is not a univocal term and there is no universally agreed upon theory about the nature of persons, it may only be possible to criticize alternative views about persons by showing how those views conflict with the rules of usage of the terms within a given theory of personhood or how they conflict with other accepted ethical or metaphysical beliefs. In other words, the question may be answered by how consistent our application of the term is with other things that we want to say about persons. In this view, it is a mistake to treat persons as exclusively a natural, functional, or ethical kind. This exclusivity generates inconsistencies among the beliefs that we have about persons and what we wish to say about the borderline cases. Instead, the adequacy of any concept of person depends on how successfully it manages to hold in a "single focus" our nature as biological, psychological, and moral beings.

Notes

1. I use the term "permanent vegetative state (PermVS)" to refer to extreme cases of persistent vegetative state (PVS) in which the diagnosis of the irreversible loss of consciousness and other cognitive functions can be determined with a high degree of clinical certainty (Multi-Society Task Force on PVS 1994: 1501). Guérit (1994, 1995, 2004) identifies such cases pathophysiologically by their absence of all primary components of cortical-evoked potentials. However, there is some debate over whether we can know that individuals in PVS lack consciousness, temporarily or irreversibly. See, for example, Howsepian (1994, 1996), Borthwick (1996), Shewmon (2004b), and Laureys et al. (2004).

2. Anencephaly is defined as "a severe and uniformly fatal abnormality resulting in the congenital absence of skull, scalp, and forebrain. Although some telencephalic tissue may be present, by the time of birth, there is no functional cortex but only a hemorrhagic mass of neurons and glia" (Shinnar and Arras 1989: 730). Guérit (2004: 19–20) expresses the widely accepted view in neurology that anencephaly constitutes a "pathophysiological process known to be incompatible with consciousness, irrespective of whether the brain stem is functioning or not." There is, however, some debate over whether the plasticity of the brain may enable some infants lacking cortical structures to have experiences that would normally be mediated by them in adults (Shewmon 1988, 1992, 2004b). Indeed, D. Alan Shewmon (2004b) reports three remarkable cases in which children without cortical structures exhibited conscious behavior.

3. Olson (1997); Feldman (1992); Snowdon (1990).

4. Locke ([1694] 1975); Hume ([1739] 1978); Parfit (1986).

5. Strawson (1959); Wiggins (1980).

6. Jonas (1974); Becker (1975); Shewmon (1997, 1998b, 2004a); Taylor (1997).

7. Field et al. (1988); Anstötz (1993).

8. Shewmon (1998a).

9. Shewmon (1997: 74).

10. Capron (1987: 8).

11. Bernat, Culver, and Gert (1981: 182–183).

12. Strawson (1959: 87–16); Strawson (1958).

13. Macklin does not explicitly say that the disagreement over personhood is "fundamental." However, her conclusion that no further progress can be

made through further investigation of the alternative concepts of personhood appears to imply as much.

14. Callahan (1988: 47).

15. Wiggins (1980: 162).

16. Mackie (1999: 230).

17. Lizza (1999).

18. As K. T. Maslin (2001: 275) points out, "the Lockean/Parfit proposal is analogous to treating you as a function or program run on the hardware of the brain, the material embodiment being strictly irrelevant to your identity and survival. You could go from body and brain to body and brain, just as information on a floppy disc can be transferred intact to another disc if the original becomes damaged."

19. See Lizza (1991); Harré (1984); and Baker (2000).

20. As far as I am aware, the first person to propose that persons may be constituted by but not identical to bodies was Sidney Shoemaker (Shoemaker and Swinburne 1984: 113–114).

21. One of the most significant aspects of Baker's theory is her treatment of constitution as a "unity relation,"that is, when *x* constitutes *y* there are not two things that happen to spatiotemporally coincide, but a single thing, *y* as constituted by *x* (Baker 2002: 46 ff.). This leads to a distinction between how things can have properties derivatively and nonderivatively (cf. Persson 1999), a distinction that enables her (2002: 191–212) to fend off some of the more forceful objections leveled from the animalist camp by Olson (1997) and Snowdon (1990). For Baker's further defense of the constitutive view, see Baker (1999, 2002).

22. Baker (2000: ch. 2).

23. Harré (1984: 211).

24. Ibid., 211.

25. Ibid., 212.

26. I critique Shewmon's view of potentiality in Lizza (2005).

27. Lock (2002: 227–228).

28. Kalitzkus (2004: 144).

References

Allison, H. (1966). "Locke's Theory of Personal Identity: A Re-Examination." *Journal of the History of Ideas* 27: 41–58.

Anstötz, A. (1993). "Should a Brain-Dead Pregnant Woman Carry Her Child to Full Term? The Case of the 'Erlanger Baby'." *Bioethics* 7(4): 340–350.

Baker, L. R. (1999). "What Am I?" *Philosophy and Phenomenological Research* 59: 151–159.

———. (2000). *Persons and Bodies.* Cambridge: Cambridge University Press.

——. (2002). "The Ontological Status of Persons." *Philosophy and Phenomenological Research* 65(2): 370–388.

Becker, L. (1975). "Human Being: The Boundaries of the Concept." *Philosophy and Public Affairs* 4(4): 335–359.

Bernat, J. (2002). "The Biophilosophical Basis of Whole-Brain Death." *Social Philosophy and Policy* 19(2): 324–342.

Bernat, J. L., C. Culver, and B. Gert. (1981). "On the Definition and Criterion of Death." *Annals of Internal Medicine* 94: 389–394.

Borthwick, C. (1996). "The Permanent Vegetative State: Ethical Crux, Medical Fiction?" *Issues in Law and Medicine* 12(2): 167–185.

Callahan, D. (1988). "The 'Beginning' of Human Life." In *What is a Person?* ed. Michael F. Goodman, pp. 29–55. Clifton, NJ: Humana Press.

Capron, A. M. (1987). "Anencephalic Donors: Separate the Dead from the Dying." *Hastings Center Report* 17(1): 5–9.

Engelhardt, H. T., Jr. (1975). "Defining Death: A Philosophical Problem for Medicine and Law." *American Review of Respiratory Diseases* 112: 587–590.

Feldman, F. (1992). *Confrontations with the Reaper.* New York: Oxford University Press.

Field, D. R., E. A. Gates, R. K. Creasy, K. R. Jonsen, and R. K. Laros. (1988). "Maternal Brain Death During Pregnancy." *Journal of the American Medical Association* 260(6): 816–822.

Geertz, C. (1964). "The Transition to Humanity." In *Horizons of Anthropology,* ed. S. Tax. Chicago: Aldine.

——. (1965). "The Impact of Culture on the Concept of Man." In *New Views on the Nature of Man,* ed. J. Platt. Chicago: University of Chicago Press.

——. (1966). "Religion as a Cultural System." In *Anthropological Approaches to the Study of Religion,* ed. M. Banton. New York: Frederick A. Praeger.

Gergen, K. J. (1991a). "The Social Construction of Self-Knowledge." In *Self and Identity,* ed. D. Kolak and R. Martin. New York: Macmillan.

——. (1991b). *The Saturated Self: Dilemmas of Identity in Contemporary Life.* New York: Basic Books.

Gervais, K. (1986). *Redefining Death.* New Haven, CT: Yale University Press.

Gill, C. (1990). "The Human Being as an Ethical Norm." In *The Person and the Human Mind,* eds. C. Gill. Oxford: Oxford University Press.

Green, M., and D. Wikler. (1980). "Brain Death and Personal Identity." *Philosophy and Public Affairs* 9: 105–133.

Guérit, J.-M. (1994). "The Interest of Multimodality Evoked Potentials in the Evaluation of Chronic Coma." *Acta Neurol Belg* 94: 174–182.

——. (1995). "Multimodality Evoked Potentials in the Permanent Vegetative State." In *Brain Death,* ed. C. Machado. Amsterdam: Elsevier.

——. (2004). "The Concept of Brain Death." In *Brain Death and Disorders of Consciousness,* eds. C. Machado and D. A. Shewmon. New York: Kluwer.

Harré, R. (1984). *Personal Being: A Theory for Individual Psychology.* Cambridge: Harvard University Press.

——. (1989). "The 'Self' as a Theoretical Concept." In *Relativism: Interpretation and Confrontation,* ed. M. Krausz. Notre Dame, IN: University of Notre Dame Press.

Howsepian, A. A. (1994). "Philosophical Reflections on Coma." *Review of Metaphysics* 47(4): 735–755.

——. (1996). "The 1994 Multi-Society Task Force Consensus Statement on the Persistent Vegetative State: A Critical Analysis." *Issues in Law and Medicine* 12(1): 3–29.

Hume, D. ([1739] 1978). *A Treatise of Human Nature,* ed. L. A. Selby-Bigge, 2nd rev. ed. Oxford: Clarendon Press.

Jonas, H. (1974). "Against the Stream: Comments on the Definition and Redefinition of Death." In *Philosophical Essays: From Ancient Creed to Technological Man.* Englewood Cliffs, NJ: Prentice Hall.

Kalitzkus, V. (2004). "Neither Dead-nor-Alive: Organ Donation and the Paradox of 'Living Corpses.' " In *Making Sense of Death and Dying,* ed. A. Fagan. Amsterdam: Rodopi.

Korsgaard, C. M. (1989). "Personal Identity and the Unity of Agency." *Philosophy and Public Affairs* 18(2): 101–132.

Laureys, S., M.-E. Faymonville, X. De Tiège, P. Peigneux, J. Berré, G. Moonen, S. Goldman, and P. Maquet. (2004). "Brain Function in the Vegetative State." In *Brain Death and Disorders of Consciousness,* eds. C. Machado and D. A. Shewmon. New York: Kluwer.

Lizza, J. P. (1991). "Metaphysical and Cultural Aspects of Persons." Ph.D. diss. Ann Arbor, MI: University Microfilms.

——. (1999). "Defining Death for Persons and Human Organisms." *Theoretical Medicine and Bioethics* 20: 439–453.

——. (2005). "Potentiality, Irreversibility, and Death." *Journal of Medicine and Philosophy* 30: 45–64.

Lock, M. (2002). *Twice Dead.* Berkeley: University of California Press.

Locke, J. ([1694] 1975). *An Essay Concerning Human Understanding,* 2nd ed. Oxford: Clarendon Press.

Lockwood, M. (1985). "When Does a Life Begin?" In *Moral Dilemmas in Modern Medicine,* ed. M. Lockwood. Oxford: Oxford University Press.

Mackie, D. (1999). "Personal Identity and Dead People." *Philosophical Studies* 95: 219–242.

Macklin, R. (1983). "Personhood in the Bioethics Literature." *Milbank Memorial Fund Quarterly/Health and Society* 6(1): 35–57.

Maslin, K. T. (2001). *An Introduction to the Philosophy of Mind.* Cambridge, UK: Polity Press.

McMahan, J. (2002). *The Ethics of Killing: Problems at the Margins of Life.* Oxford: Oxford University Press.

Mead, G. H. (1925). "The Genesis of Self and Social Control." *International Journal of Ethics* 35: 251–273.

———. (1934). *Mind, Self and Society from the Standpoint of a Social Behaviorist.* Chicago: University of Chicago Press.

Molyneux, W. (1794). "Letter of Molyneux to Locke," 23 Dec. 1693. In *The Works of John Locke VIII.* London: n.p.

Multi-Society Task Force on PVS. (1994). "Medical Aspects of the Persistent Vegetative State Parts 1 and 2." *New England Journal of Medicine* 330: 1499–1508, 1572–1579.

Olson, E. T. (1997). *The Human Animal.* Oxford: Oxford University Press.

Parfit, D. (1986). *Reasons and Persons.* Oxford: Oxford University Press.

Persson, I. (1999). "Our Identity and the Separability of Persons and Organisms." *Dialogue* 38: 519–533.

Reid, T. ([1785] 1969). *Essays on the Intellectual Powers of Man.* Cambridge: MIT Press.

Sartre, J.-P. ([1942] 1994). *L'Être et le néant: essai d'ontologie phénoménologique [Being and Nothingness]*, trans. H. E. Barnes. New York: Gramercy Books.

———. ([1945] 1955). *Huis clos [No Exit]*, trans. S. Gilbert. New York: Vintage Books.

———. ([1946] 1970). *L'existentialisme est un humanisme.* Paris: Les Editions Nagel.

Shewmon, D. A. (1988). "Anencephaly: Selected Medical Aspects." *Hastings Center Report* 18: 11–18.

———. (1992). "Brain Death: A Valid Theme with Invalid Variations, Blurred by Semantic Ambiguity ." In *Working Group on the Determination of Brain Death and its Relationship to Human Death*, eds. H. Angstwurm and I. Carrasco de Paula. Vatican City: Pontificia Academia Scientiarum.

———. (1997). "Recovery from 'Brain Death': A Neurologist's Apologia." *Linacre Quarterly* 64(1): 31–96.

———. (1998a). "Chronic 'Brain Death': Meta-Analysis and Conceptual Consequences." *Neurology* 51(6): 1538–1545.

———. (1998b). " 'Brainstem Death,' 'Brain Death,' and Death: A Critical Reevaluation of the Purported Evidence." *Issues in Law and Medicine* 14(2): 125–146.

———. (2004a). "The 'Critical Organ' for the 'Organism as a Whole': Lessons from the Lowly Spinal Cord." In *Brain Death and Disorders of Consciousness*, eds. C. Machado and D. A. Shewmon. New York: Kluwer.

———. (2004b). "The ABC of PVS." In *Brain Death and Disorders of Consciousness*, eds. C. Machado and D. A. Shewmon. New York: Kluwer.

Shinnar, S., and J. Arras. (1989). "Ethical Issues in the Use of Anencephalic Infants as Organ Donors." *Neurologic Clinics* 7(4): 729–743.

Shoemaker, S., and R. Swinburne. (1984). *Personal Identity.* Oxford: Basil Blackwell.

Snowdon, P. F. (1990). "Person, Animals and Ourselves." In *The Person and the Human Mind: Issues in Ancient and Modern Philosophy*, ed. C. Gill. Oxford: Clarendon Press.

Strawson, P. F. ([1958] 1991). "Persons." In *Minnesota Studies in the Philosophy of Science*, vol. 2, eds. H. Feigl, M. Scriven, and G. Maxwell, pp. 330–353. Minneapolis: University of Minnesota Press. Reprinted in D. M. Rosenthal, ed., *The Nature of Mind*. New York: Oxford University Press, 1991.

———. (1959). *Individuals*. London: Methuen.

Taylor, R. M. (1997). "Re-Examining the Definition and Criteria of Death." *Seminars in Neurology* 17: 265–270.

Unger, P. (1990). *Identity, Consciousness and Value*. New York: Oxford University Press.

Warren, M. (2000). *Moral Status: Obligations to Persons and Other Living Things*. Oxford: Oxford University Press.

Wiggins, D. (1980). *Sameness and Substance*. Cambridge: Harvard University Press.

———. (1987). "The Person as Object of Science, as Subject of Experience, and as the Locus of Value." In *Persons and Personality: A Contemporary Inquiry*, eds. A. Peacocke and G. Gillet. Oxford: Oxford University Press.

Wittgenstein, L. (1953). *Philosophical Investigations*, trans. G. E. M. Anscombe. Oxford: Blackwell.

10

The Subject of Freedom at the End of History

Socialism Beyond Humanism

By John Sanbonmatsu*

ABSTRACT. The postmodernist turn in theory left the status of *humanism* in some doubt. This chapter argues that a recuperation of a specifically socialist humanism is both possible and desirable, but only by overcoming the anthropocentrism of radical humanism. Renaissance and Enlightenment conceptions of the subject were rooted in an untenable dichotomy between the human and the animal, in ways that vitiated the idea and ideal of universal freedom. By conflating subjectivity as such with *human* subjectivity, humanism created a diremption in the world that placed the knower (human consciousness) on one side, and the merely known (objectified Nature) on the other. Marxism and socialist humanism reproduced this error in ways that have undermined the socialist vision of universal emancipation, misconstrued the nature of the subject, and overlooked the significance of human domination of other animals. The author advocates a new approach, what he calls *metahumanism*, to affirm a "two-sided" freedom in which the liberation of other animals from human oppression, and the emancipation of ourselves *as animals*—that is, the restoration of the sensual dimension of existence, free sexual expression, and valorization of the labor and love of the body—would become central features of a new movement for civil and cultural reform.

*John Sanbonmatsu is Assistant Professor of Philosophy at Worcester Polytechnic Institute in Massachusetts. He is the author of *The Postmodern Prince: Critical Theory, Left Strategy, and the Making of a New Political Subject* (2004) and co-editor with Renzo Llorente of *Animal Liberation and Human Freedom* (forthcoming).

American Journal of Economics and Sociology, Vol. 66, No. 1 (January, 2007).

I

Introduction

MY OBJECTIVE IN THIS SHORT ESSAY is to clarify the nature of the subject and its relationship to historical possibilities of freedom. My purpose in doing so is to help prepare the ground for a comprehensive new theory and practice of liberatory politics, what I have elsewhere called *metahumanism.*[1] Metahumanism is my term both for an emergent social movement—the world historical movement to establish a new form of civilization based on social equality, justice, and reconciliation with nature—and for the *theory* that seeks to ground that movement. In essence, metahumanism is simply the ethical ontology, and political practice, of *universal freedom.*

My project, in a sense, takes up where humanist critical theory left off 40 years ago, when Anchor Books published *Socialist Humanism: An International Symposium* (1965). Conceived and edited by Erich Fromm, the symposium included essays from practically every significant critical or socialist theorist in Europe and the United States, including Raya Dunayevskya, Herbert Marcuse, Lucien Goldmann, Bertrand Russell, Ernst Bloch, Galvano della Volpe, Bronislaw Baczko, Norman Thomas, and Mathilde Niel, among others. What bound this otherwise diverse set of contributors together was consensus on a single point: that socialism entailed humanism, and that humanism entailed socialism. The tenor of the collection was optimistic and forward-looking. As Fromm wrote in the book's introduction, the symposium was intended to demonstrate "that socialist Humanism is no longer the concern of a few dispersed intellectuals, but a movement to be found throughout the world, developing independently in different countries."[2]

As it turned out, however, the socialist humanist movement was already at its apogee, and it swiftly declined in the years that followed. The explosive growth of the New Left movement in the late 1960s, with its sudden spontaneous energy and critique of alienation, both concretized socialist humanist ideals and at the same time privileged practice over theory in a way that tended to militate against the kind of grand theoretical synthesis Fromm and others had hoped for.[3] With the collapse of the New Left in the 1970s, and the further weakening of working-class movements throughout the world over the next two decades, the Left as such went into retreat and socialism all but disappeared from political discourse. The Marxist theory of revolution was seen to be a dead letter issue, and Marx's conception of the historical subject was criticized for leaving out, among others, women, people of color, and gays and lesbians. By the 1980s, many critical philosophers had also turned against the very idea of humanism and "the human." Structuralist and poststructuralist theories decentered the subject and in effect reduced it to the status of a thing. With Enlightenment exposed as a destructive myth and Reason shown to be little more than an idealist conceit disguising the will-to-power of a particular historical subject (the white European man), postmodernists held that we were now free to embrace the more liberatory discourse of "difference." The dis-integration of the unitary subject, on this view, yields a multitude of political and aesthetic possibilities, an infinite play of identity *as* multiplicity.[4] Anti-humanist poststructuralism is still seen by many to be an improvement over totalizing conceptions of the subject in classical Marxism, as well as a tonic to the liberal myth of a self-identical subject immune to historical contingency and power.

The main trouble with the postmodernist rejection of the subject in theory, however, is that it has fatefully coincided with the obliteration of the individual human and nonhuman subject in social or historical *fact*. That subject is faced today with annihilation from two sides. On one side lies the threat of outright biological extinction from any combination of ecological catastrophe, natural or human-produced plague, or nuclear war. On the other lies alienation, the destruction of autonomous thought and culture, and the reduction of life-world to the commodity. Renunciation of the subject in theory, while originally intended as a radical gesture, is in the present context thus all but indistinguishable from celebration of reification. As the systemic ecological and social contradictions of capitalism as a world system intensify, undermining every basis for future ecological survival, democracy, the comity of nations, and, in a word, the possibility of human happiness and nonhuman well-being, the objective need for an alternative form of human civilization becomes ever more *existentially* urgent. Without proper philosophical ground beneath its feet, however, any attempt by critical praxis to transform the world is likely to be doomed to strategic incoherence and a lack of fundamental clarity on the ethical dimensions of its own practice. Hence the urgent need, not for further celebration of fragmentation and chaos (which is largely what passes for "critical" theory today) but, on the contrary, for a robust conception of the subject and a general phenomenology of its freedom.

Traditional humanism is based on two ideas: that humankind strives toward unity with itself, and that we human beings alone are endowed with ontological freedom, hence with the potential to perfect ourselves.[5] As a comprehensive theory of the subject, in contrast, *meta*humanism (as the neologism implies) represents the sublation of traditional humanism: it is the movement simultaneously to *negate* the anthropocentric subject of traditional humanism and to *recuperate* the subject *qua* subject as an object of *human* consciousness and practice. Such a sublation is necessary because humanism is at once the inescapable horizon of our thought and the ultimate source of our alienation from ourselves and from other animals. Metahumanism also represents the sublation of *socialist* humanism. Fromm and other Western Marxists saw socialist humanism as the general movement to realize the unity of humankind (in a classless society) and to perfect society by negating or overcoming that which negates free human labor or creative activity (capitalism). On the one hand, metahumanism, *as* a socialism, concurs with socialist humanism that freedom cannot be meaningful without the "discovery" and realization of *what we already are, but also what we must become,* namely, a "species being" capable of seizing our own destiny and creating a just and harmonious order in which the antagonisms that prevail under conditions of universal alienation—for example, between self and society, and culture and nature—are overcome. At the same time, however, metahumanism modifies the earlier socialist humanist project in two ways. First, metahumanism rejects the conceit that humankind is identical to itself, an expressive unity that works *upon* nature to achieve self-recognition. Second, and relatedly, metahumanism rejects the notion that human self-realization is freedom *as such,* that is, a *universal* freedom. In particular, metahumanism affirms the fundamental evolutionary continuity between human and nonhuman animal life and consciousness, and hence

rejects a conception of unity, and self-perfection, that would deny our ontological connection to animal others. Only in this manner, I argue, can socialist humanism lose its "one-sided" nature to become the struggle against *unfreedom* in all its manifestations.

II

Humanism and Hatred of the Animal Other

WITH THE NOTABLE EXCEPTION of Max Horkheimer (who alone among Frankfurt School critics openly supported animal welfare movements), socialist humanists in the the 20th century based their theory of liberation on a conception of freedom that purged the world of all *nonhuman* subjectivity. The contributors to Fromm's 1965 *Symposium* were in agreement on this point. Mihailo Markovic, for example, argued that "humanist *ontology* is a philosophical theory of the objects of the *human* world, whose boundaries are constituted by all kinds of human activity, including sense-perception, the construction of theories, . . . etc., as well as the physical operations of the human body."[6] Another critic similarly described alienated human consciousness as "animal vegetation," a surreal but characteristic ontological conflation of being-in-the-world (sentience) with plant matter. Fromm himself wrote: "Man can find unity by trying to regress to the animal stage, [only] by doing away with *what is specifically human (reason and love)*."[7] This latter view, of animal nature or being-in-the-world as "regression"—indeed as the *negation* of what it means to be human— was symptomatic of a fundamental error that has compromised the entire humanist conception from the very beginning.

In the 1486 *Oratio de hominis dignitate* (*Oration on the Dignity of Man*), Pico della Mirandola affirmed the essential unity of humankind and the possibility of achieving moral perfection through reason, chiefly by portraying the human being as *the* protean subject, a nothingness whose divinity derived from his ability to be his own creator—" 'the molder and maker of thyself,' " as God says, admiring His handiwork.[8] A "chameleon," Man "fashions, fabricates, transforms himself into the shape of all flesh, into the character of every creature."[9] In Pico's conception, "man," though ostensibly the mediate being, the being "at the midpoint of the world," nonetheless possesses a rational essence that places him in infinitely greater proximity to the divine, to God, than to the animal. "[L]et us compete with the angels for dignity and glory," he wrote. "When we have willed it, we shall not be at all below them."[10] In Pico's synthesis, God's universe itself is portrayed as nothing more than the backdrop of "man himself," or rather of his own miraculous unfolding and self-making (a view that would later find new expression in Hegel's *Geist*). The wonder of human self-realization *is* the glory of God.

In suggesting that "the knowledge of all nature" is within reach of consciousness, and that the entire natural universe is merely the storybook of a grand human *Bildungsroman*, Pico prepared the way for the experimentalism of Francis Bacon and for the idealist metaphysics of Descartes, both of which proved ruinous for the ecology of the West (not to mention for the social status of women in early modern Europe).[11] In point of fact, Pico's ontology, like all other forms of humanism, rested on unfreedom—the violent appropriation of nature and the domination of other animals. In this regard, while Renaissance humanism represented in many ways a real advance for human freedom over the stultifying categories of medieval theology and feudalism—and thus prepared the way for an even greater advance in individual European freedom via the Reformation—nonetheless, vis-à-vis our relation to the nonhuman world, the anthropocentrism of the Renaissance also represented a step *backward* from the medieval Aristotelian and Catholic view of Nature as God's creation. While Aristotle's naturalism in *De Anima* had rested on a hierarchy of souls, it had also emphasized the continuity and mutual resonances between different kinds of ensouled beings. By contrast, the return to Neoplatonism signaled by Pico and Marsilio Ficino reduced being to an onto-theological hierarchy, with reason or mind placed *in opposition* to sensuous existence.

It is worth taking a moment to trace the path by which this conception later insinuated itself into modern philosophical and social theory. The Renaissance ideal of humankind as a "self-determining" creature whose freedom lay ontologically in its capacity for quasi-divine reason (the transcendent being of Greek myth and Christian metaphysics) achieved its apotheosis with the Enlightenment. The *philosophes* extended the humanist idea in two new ways. First, as

Bronislaw Baczko reminds us, humankind was now seen "to treat the entire world as an object that can be changed." Second, "the efficacy of human endeavors" was seen to be "guaranteed by nature itself and by the fact that man belongs to and is part of the world of nature."[12] In his reaction against the positivist and naturalist strains of this latter conception, Kant posited reason as an autonomous metaphysical force, hence as the sole ground of freedom and *value*. What is key for our purposes here is that Kant accepted Pico's view of an ontological hierarchy of beings in which all "earthly things" were to be placed at an infinite remove from the transcendental realm of thought. The "rational being," Kant wrote, "must regard himself qua intelligence (and hence not from the side of his lower powers) as belonging not to the world of sense but to the world of understanding [*Verstand*]."[13]

Hegel later sought to dissolve both Kantian and Cartesian dualism between subject and object by affirming a higher synthesis in which the dialectical movement of mind (*Geist*) reconciled the metaphysical and social antinomies of reality. Like Kant, however, Hegel too reduced the meaning and becoming of nature (Substance) to the movement of *human* consciousness (*as* divine Spirit, or God); or as he put it, world and " 'its relations and determinations are the work of . . . man's self-development.' "[14] Significantly, Hegel explicitly tied the progress of human freedom and reason to the development of "superior" forms of civilization that negated the animal as such. He thus reserved his greatest condemnation for premodern forms of religious culture that combined "the harshest bondage in the fetters of superstition" with "man's degraded subservience to animals." As Hegel wrote: "The Egyptians and the Hindus, for instance, revere animals as beings higher than themselves."[15]

In fact, not merely Hegel but the Western tradition as a whole came to see the expression of "reverence" for animals as crypto-hatred for human life and for God Himself—in short, as a form of *nihilism*. (This view is defended to this day by neohumanists like Luc Ferry.[16]) So thoroughgoing and universal is contempt for "the animal"—and Derrida rightly suggested that this formulation is already a mystification,[17] since there is not simply "us" and "them," but "us" amidst myriad other beings-in-the-world, each unique—that one could argue that *contempt* as such constitutes the epistemological ground or *episteme* not merely for humanist thought but indeed for modern humanity's every existential and existentiell modality. As Wilhelm Reich observed in his study of the mass psychology of fascism, having "developed the peculiar idea that he was not an animal," man took "great pains to disassociate himself from the vicious animal and to prove that he 'is better' by pointing to his culture and his civilization, which distinguish him from the animal." This fundamental outlook, Reich suggests, lies at the heart of the repressive functions of society itself:

> Man's entire attitude, his "theories of value," moral philosophies . . . all bear witness to the fact that he does not want to be reminded that he is fundamentally an animal, that he has incomparably more in common with "the animal" than he has with that which he thinks and dreams himself to be. . . . His viciousness, his inability to live peacefully with his own kind, his wars, bear witness to the fact that man is distinguished from the other animals only by a boundless sadism and the mechanical trinity of an authoritarian view of life, mechanistic science, and the machine. If one looks back over long stretches of the results of human civilization, one finds that man's claims are not only false, but are peculiarly contrived to make him forget that he is an animal.[18]

The contrivances to make us "forget" that we are animals are many; in a sense they constitute the totality of the modern built and representational human world.

What I have been arguing is that humanism from the start was based on a conception of freedom defined as *the negation of nonhuman subjectivity.* By conflating subjectivity *as such* with *human* subjectivity, humanism created a diremption in the world that placed the knower (human consciousness) on one side, and the merely known (objective Nature—in Cartesianism, the *res extensa*) on the other. There were two main consequences. The first was to reify a colossal species solipsism that effectively subsumed all Being, and all *beings,* to the godlike human ego. The second was to construct social and political thought on the basis of a profound misapprehension of our *own* nature and its possibilities. Both problems, the reduction of nature and other animals to thinglike status, and the reduction of human being itself to an abstraction—mind—can be traced back, in various forms, to Greek metaphysics. Marcuse rightly observed that the Greek view of Logos "as the essence of being," both in Platonic

thought and Aristotelian logic, made reason "antagonistic to those faculties and attitudes which are receptive rather than productive, which tend toward gratification rather than transcendence."[19] The "subjugation" of Eros or sensuous life became "a constitutive element of human reason, which is thus in its very function repressive."[20] Continual repression of desire and feeling "culminates in the conquest of external nature, which must be perpetually attacked, curbed, exploited in order to yield to human needs."[21] The struggle between reason and emotion and appetitive desire in this way came to constitute the core antagonism in Western culture. Mastery of self and other, especially the Other of Nature, becomes the *leitmotif* of civilization.

Colonialism and genocide, among the true innovations of modernity, can only be understood in the context of this dialectic of repression. To take a familiar literary example, the pathos of Kurtz's imperative to "exterminate all the brutes" at the end of Conrad's *Heart of Darkness* emerges not from the brutality of the gesture but from the comic grandiosity of Kurtz's bad faith. Unable to reckon with the dark, "bestial" side of his own nature—to tame it—Kurtz seeks to cover over his own crimes with renewed genocidal fury. A thoroughly bad conscience can only be corrected through the Absolute: only in extermination of "the beasts" can the killer be cured of the moral corruption within. The "animal" within, in other words, is projected onto the animal *without*, onto the "Other" whose very existence is a reminder of the hatred and ugliness of the exterminating subject himself. And this dialectic, of repression and extermination, which conditions *human* social relations, that is, relations between and among human beings, also undergirds the political economy of meat production and the overall domination of animals, the unending "cycle" (in Carol Adams's words) "of objectification, fragmentation, and consumption."[22] What is at issue is not "animal rights" per se—an abstract, sterile term that barely hints at the extent and scale of our civilizational pathology—but the need for a comprehensive critique of an entire modality of existence rooted in unceasing exploitation, systematic brutalization, and, ultimately, the logic of mass killing and extermination. Simply, no doctrine of "universal" liberation that ignores the plight of the thousands of millions of beings enslaved and slaughtered by human beings can avoid collapsing in moral and political self-contradiction.

III

Escaping the *Nous*: Freedom Unbound

LET US NOW RETURN to the problem of socialism and the question of the subject today. Notwithstanding his avowed interest in a praxis that would "humanize" nature, Marx, too, based his dialectic of history (if unconsciously) on Pico's onto-theological hierarchy. Marx affirmed the view that freedom is nothing other than " 'the development of human power, which is *its own end*,' " a view he took virtually intact from Feuerbach.[23] Achieving our "species being"—that is, our capacity for self-transcendence—would hence mean negating and transcending our "crude" animal senses. As Ted Benton suggests, however, Marx's humanism was in essence a form of *speciesism*.[24] This anthropocentric conception of the ontology of freedom has remained the basis of socialist thought ever since. Yet as long as freedom, both as ideal (concept) and as practice, continues to be constituted in humanist socialist thought on the basis of *unfreedom* and *domination*—control of nature, and natural others, through instrumental reason—critical thought will leave the central mechanism of repression untouched.[25] The problem with traditional socialist humanism was never, *pace* postmodernism, that it was too universalist—that it was based, in short, on a totalizing meta-narrative of freedom grounded in a single universal subject—but rather that its ontology of freedom was too *limited* and *one-sided*. We will therefore need to complicate our notion of what freedom is if we are to provide socialism with a more reliable basis for a transformative ethics and radical democratic vision.

Here, ironically, Marxism can learn something useful about the relationship between freedom and ontology from Plato. Among the central themes of *The Republic* is the notion that the subjugation of Eros is the precondition for justice and the good life. According to Plato, the realm of ideas, the realm of *nous* and hence of the divine, exists in stark opposition to the "merely" sensual, visible realm (the "odious ooze," as Socrates terms it, of sense perception—i.e., the knowledge obtained through our animal body). One of the

consequences of Socrates' argument is that perfect freedom is *unnatural*, hence anathema to the truly just order, both within the soul and without (i.e., in society). Thus, in a pure democracy or state of absolute freedom, Socrates warns in Book VII, not only would slaves treat their masters as equals and women ask to be treated as the equals to men, but even the animals would clamor for equality. "Unless you've seen it," he says, "you'd never believe the freedom that even animals subject to man enjoy in a democracy. Dogs behave like the proverbial masters—why, the very horses and mules stalk about in stately freedom and shoulder aside anyone who doesn't step out of their way, and everything else is equally bristling with freedom." To which Glaucon replies, with a shudder, "You're telling me my own nightmare."[26] Unbounded, Plato implies, freedom threatens the existing social order and the state because it challenges natural ontological hierarchies of male vs. female, mind vs. body, human vs. animal. Or to put it another way, freedom is dangerous because it points to an *indifference to ontological boundaries*.

While Socrates makes the case of animals the basis for his *reductio ad absurdum* against democracy, we might take the opposite tack—to defend a conception of freedom that is truly universal rather than one-sided, that is, which construes *defense of the freedom of the subject* in the broadest possible terms. As we have seen, Fromm asserted that only human beings are capable of reason and of love. In reality, however, many other animals have minds, and experience and share love, a fact known for centuries to many ordinary people, if only now being "demonstrated" to the satisfaction of Western science through elaborate empirical experiments in cognitive ethology.[27] It is therefore unsatisfactory to continue to define universal freedom in the traditional way, viz. (a) as *human* freedom alone and (b) as the negation of the nonhuman or "animal" as such. Mikhail Bakunin noted that "[e]very living being strives for prosperity and freedom, and in order to hate an oppressor, it is not necessary to be a man, it is enough to be an animal."[28] Freedom and hatred of oppression are identical to one another, and just as animals can be, and are, *oppressed* by human beings, the subject of freedom need not be a member of *homo sapiens*. The significance of this insight could not be more profound, coming at a time of widening ecological destruction, mass species extinction, and the mass killing of literally billions of our fellow animal beings in slaughterhouses no less brutal and unconscionable than the concentration camps of Eastern Europe a few generations ago.[29] True or universal freedom would indeed be indifferent to species boundaries.

What distinguishes animals (including us) from plants is that for the former, becoming what we "are" is always already subjective and intentional (in Husserl's sense), not simply objective (in the sense of realization of a biology, an evolutionary impetus, etc.—in crude, positivistic terms, programmed "behavior" or "genetic information").[30] That is, for every being that takes the world as an object of its own consciousness and experiential embodiment, the content of freedom is always individual, the content not of an abstraction ("species") but of a particular *suffering* being. No two animals are like, each is individual, each is thrown back on itself to make sense of the world, each is therefore *a subject.* Self-consciousness and logos are attributes of a particular *kind* of subjectivity; however, they are not subjectivity *as such*, just as my pleasure of sitting in the sun or making love is no less *essential* to my identity and subjectivity, and no less a source of value and meaning, than my ability to perform calculus or analyze Kant. (What makes us *distinct* does not necessarily give us our *essence.*)

Our first interpolation of the humanist conception of freedom, therefore, must be to affirm the intuitive, primordial understanding of freedom as *freedom from* oppression. We are perhaps accustomed, since Hegel, to see so-called negative liberty as an inferior kind of freedom, on the grounds that its quality seems to be based in the realm of *necessity*, which would seem to make it indifferent to or even opposed to what we conceive to be our *ontological* freedom, that is, autonomous reason and free will. However, it is only because thought has devalued the realm of necessity and embodiment, or sensuous life, that freedom *from* has come to be so devalued. In fact, not only is freedom *from* not in contradiction to essence, it is often the sine qua non for what we call positive freedom, freedom *to*, which is nothing other than the free creative fulfillment of our natural capacities— including, in the case of homo sapiens, to exist as a *becoming*, as political, social beings burdened with the responsibility of self-making as a species being. We can and must go further, to note that freedom from oppression is essentially a "positive" conception, insofar as it implies a robust sense of well-being of the organism, and even of *happiness*. On closer examination, in fact, it becomes clear that freedom to and freedom from are two moments or sides of the same fundamental identity, the same phenomenon, which is the drive of all living things to be what they "are," that is, to unfold their inherent possibilities. Freedom and its natural cognate *justice* meet here, in *eudaimonia*, and not just for members of homo sapiens.[31]

Second, we must acknowledge that universal or metahumanist freedom, as liberation of the subject *qua* subject, is ontologically two-sided. First, freedom logically and substantively entails liberation of other animals from human oppression. If socialism truly represents the negation of the negation—that is, the overcoming of unfreedom— then a properly *meta*humanist ethics and practice entails negating our destruction of all other beings on earth. Second, freedom entails liberation of ourselves *as* animals: in other words, restoration of the sensual dimension of existence, free sexual expression, valorization of the labor of the body, overcoming of "animal" (physical and mental) suffering, and so forth. Restoration of subjectivity to nature is thus also the restoration of *subjectivity* to ourselves. In particular, reclaiming our sensuous nature would allow us to recover those affective ("feminine") capacities within ourselves that have been systematically denigrated by the patriarchal, onto theological assumptions deep in the marrow of our thought: empathy, compassion, simple being-with-others (what Nietzsche contemptuously dismissed as "herd instinct").

This double movement of freedom brings us to the threshold of new self-understanding, a new *Bildung* in which we recognize ourselves, our "humanity"—our own fragility and mortality as individuals—in the bodies and minds of animal others. Self-recognition in this manner becomes mediated *through* the animal other. We are they, and they are us. Yet what we do to them, they do not therefore do to us (to paraphrase Hegel).[32] That is, our recognition of animal others is not yet *self*-recognition because our relation with our other remains one of mastery or domination. Each new ecological emergency, however (the avian flu epidemic comes to mind), forces us to see our distorted selves—our agency and activity—reflected back to us in the suffering of animal others at *our* hands. Confronted with the devastation our own hubris has wrought, we are thus thrown back into and onto ourselves, but now in a way that takes us out of our radical species solipsism. As we become aware of our participation in extermination, we enter a new liminal ethical space in which the distinction between ourselves and our "other" can be confronted and, through construction of a new modus vivendi, dissolved.

It is only in coming *outside* ourselves, through care for others, that we develop an ethical self. As Norman Geras points out, interest alone, "whether class or some other type of interest"—and here we must add *species* interest—cannot substitute for an ethical framework. "On its own, self-interest, even if this is the interest of a group, offers an improbable route towards a state of things in which sympathetic care and support for others will have come to occupy a much more prominent place." For this reason, "[a]n ethic of mutual concern and care has to inform any worthwhile politics of justice, or equality, or socialism, as much as the politics and economics of a different kind of society would be needed to underpin and envelop the widespread practice of that ethic."[33] As a comprehensive form of political praxis, therefore, metahumanism is to be conceived not as the immanent expression of "interests" but as the general project of freedom of self *and other*. Radical politics might in this way find its proper ethical ground—by expanding the subject of liberation from the working class, and even from human beings as such, to encompass *all suffering beings*. In this manner, socialism casts off its claim to being a "science" and assumes its rightful but heretofore unappreciated place as a major world religion, or rather a *meta*-religion, in the sense of a movement for moral and spiritual, not merely social, redemption. Once we conceive the struggle for freedom not merely as the realization of an abstract capability or essence, but as a struggle that emerges out of *caring* about the suffering of embodied beings, human and nonhuman alike,[34] we at once introduce a crucial, missing ethical dimension into praxis and affirm the need for the reenchantment of the world, which is a form of spiritualism.

Marcuse, who as we have seen sought to recuperate the suppressed sensual, hence "animal" dimension of our existence, hinted at the possibility of just such a new way of living with ourselves and others in the natural world in *Eros and Civilization*. Drawing on the myths of Orpheus and Narcissus, he gestured toward a future civilizational mode in which the false antinomies of head and heart, nature and culture, human and animal might at last be overcome. In resisting the technologization of the world, the impulse to dominate and kill the other (Thanatos), humanity might come to resemble Orpheus, singing the world to life. "In being spoken to, loved, and cared for, flowers and springs and animals appear as what they are—beautiful, not only for those who address and regard them, but for themselves, 'objectively.' "[35] Marcuse's ecstatic vision of nature sung back to life—reenchanted—is suggestive of a metahumanist conception of freedom. True overcoming of nihilism would entail not the negation or denial of the animal, but the reverse: a reconceptualization of ourselves as subjects for whom subjectivity is always-already *inter*subjectivity, *mitsein*, being-with other beings-in-the-world.[36] The old humanist ideal of realization of expressive unity would thus take on new meaning, as unity *with other subjects in nature*, rather than (as in the Romantic as well as contemporary deep ecology approaches) unity with "nature" in the abstract, as Concept. In contradistinction, however, to Marcuse's socialist humanism, "singing" nature to life also implies "listening" to the nonhuman other as well: attending to the suffering of the nonhuman other, whether that other is a whale trapped in a harbor, a spider monkey dying of thirst in the rain forest because of global warming, or a mouse being administered electric shocks by a scientist in a laboratory.

Historical humanism remains true in that we are always-already engaged in a project of self-overcoming, including overcoming our own capability to overcome (our will-to-domination). Ours is still the project of human praxis, human collective consciousness, and human existential choice—in short, the project of *history*. At the same time, we must take care not to read other animal beings *out of* temporality or history. Animal others have constituted our history from the beginning, in the sense that we have built our civilization on their backs, our flesh out of their flesh, and our identity and imagined "dignity" on the basis of what we think they are not. They have been, in short, our negation—the other against which we have rebelled. Today, however, as we come face to face with the real possibility of the end of history, we must confront the fact that humanism itself has not been innocent of the making of our disaster. For in negating our other we have negated the earth, and life, itself. If we are to find a way beyond our global crisis, then, we will have to preserve *and* overcome "the human." Only in this way might we begin to formulate a consistent and universally valid conception of the subject and its freedom, hence to find a way to achieve that so-called dignity we imagine to be our unique birthright, and that continues to elude us.

Notes

1. John Sanbonmatsu, *The Postmodern Prince: Critical Theory, Left Strategy, and the Making of a New Political Subject* (New York: Monthly Review, 2004). See especially 203–223.

2. Erich Fromm, ed., *Socialist Humanism: An International Symposium* (New York: Doubleday, 1965), x.

3. Nigel Young, *An Infantile Disorder? The Crisis and Decline of the New Left* (London: Routledge and Kegan Paul, 1977).

4. E.g., James M. Glass, *Shattered Selves: Multiple Personality in a Postmodern World* (Ithaca, NY: Cornell University Press, 1993).

5. Fromm, vii.

6. Mihailo Markovic, "Humanism and Dialectic," in Fromm, 84.

7. Erich Fromm, "The Application of Humanist Psychoanalysis to Marx's Theory," in Fromm, 243.

8. Ibid., 5.

9. Pico Della Mirandola, *On the Dignity of Man*, trans. Charles Glenn Miller (Indianapolis, IN: Bobbs-Merill, 1940; reprinted 1965), 5, 6.

10. Ibid., 7.

11. Carolyn Merchant, *The Death of Nature: Women, Ecology, and Scientific Development* (Indianapolis, IN: New York: Harper and Row, 1980).

12. Baczko, in Fromm, 184.

13. Immanuel Kant, *Grounding for the Metaphysics of Morals*, 3rd ed., trans. James W. Ellington (Hackett Publishing, 1993), 53.

14. G. W. F. Hegel, quoted in Herbert Marcuse, *Reason and Revolution* (Boston: Beacon Press, 1960), 39.

15. G. W. F. Hegel, *Philosophy of Right*, trans. T. M. Knox (London: Oxford, 1967), 165.

16. Luc Ferry, *The New Ecological Order*, trans. Carol Volk (Chicago: University of Chicago, 1995).

17. Jacques Derrida, "The Animal That Therefore I Am," in *Animal Philosophy: Ethics and Identity*, ed. P. Atterton and M. Calarco (London: Continuum, 2004).

18. Wilhelm Reich, *The Mass Psychology of Fascism*, trans. Vincent R. Carfagno (New York: Noonday Press, 1970), 334–335.

19. Herbert Marcuse, *Eros and Civilization: A Philosophical Inquiry into Freud* (New York: Vintage Books, 1955), 111.

20. Ibid., 110.

21. Ibid.

22. Carol Adams, *The Sexual Politics of Meat* (New York: Continnuum, 1990), 47.

23. Quoted by Dunayevskaya in Fromm, 78.

24. Ted Benton, "Humanism = Speciesism: Marx on Humans and Animals," *Radical Philosophy*, 50(1988): 4–18.

25. Isaac D. Balbus, *Marxism and Domination* (Princeton, NJ: Princeton University Press, 1982), 11–60. See also Theodor Adorno and Max Horkheimer, *Dialectic of Enlightenment*, trans. John Cumming (New York: Continuum, 1976).

26. Plato, *Republic*, Book VIII, trans. Raymond Larson (Arlington Heights, IL: Harlan Davidson, 1979), 221 (563c–d).

27. See, for example, Lesley Rogers, *Minds of Their Own: Thinking and Awareness in Animals* (Boulder, CO: Westview, 1998).

28. Mikhail Bakunin, *The Political Philosophy of Bakunin*, ed. G. P. Maximoff (New York: Free Press, 1953).

29. Charles Patterson, *Eternal Treblinka: Our Treatment of Animals and the Holocaust* (New York: Lantern Books, 2002).

30. Maurice Merleau-Ponty, *The Structure of Behavior* (Boston: Beacon Press, 1967).

31. For a capabilities approach to an interspecies conception of justice, see Martha B. Nussbaum, "Beyond 'Compassion and Humanity': Justice for Nonhuman Animals," in *Animal Rights: Current Debates and New Directions*, eds. Cass Sunstein and Martha Nussbaum (Oxford: Oxford University Press, 2004), 299–320.

32. G. W. F. Hegel, *Phenomenology of Spirit*, trans. A. V. Miller (Oxford: Oxford University Press, 1977), §191, 116.

33. Norman Geras, *The Contract of Mutual Indifference: Political Philosophy After the Holocaust* (London: Verso, 1998), 76–77.

34. On a trans-species care ethic, which I am implicitly invoking here, see Josephine Donovan, "Attention to Suffering: Sympathy as a Basis for Ethical Treatment of Animals," in *Beyond Animal Rights*, eds. Josephine Donovan and Carl Adams (New York: Continuum, 2000), 147–169.

35. Marcuse, *Eros and Civilization*, 166.

36. Peter Steeves, *Animal Others: On Ethics, Ontology, and Animal Life* (Albany, NY: SUNY Press, 1999). See also Charles S. Brown and Ted Toadvine, *Eco-Phenomenology: Back to the Earth Itself* (Albany, NY: SUNY Press, 2003).

References

Adams, C. (1990). *The Sexual Politics of Meat.* New York: Continuum.

Adorno, T., and M. Horkheimer. (1976). *Dialectic of Enlightenment,* trans. J. Cumming. New York: Continuum.

Bakunin, M. (1953). *The Political Philosophy of Bakunin,* ed. G. P. Maximoff. New York: Free Press.

Balbus, I. D. (1982). *Marxism and Domination.* Princeton: Princeton University Press.

Benton, T. (1988). "Humanism = Speciesism: Marx on Humans and Animals." *Radical Philosophy* 50: 4–18.

Brown, C. S., and T. Toadvine, eds. (2003). *Eco-Phenomenology: Back to the Earth Itself.* Albany, NY: SUNY Press.

Derrida, J. (2004). "The Animal That Therefore I Am." In *Animal Philosophy: Ethics and Identity,* eds. P. Atterton and M. Calarco, pp. 111–128. London: Continuum.

Donovan, J. (2000). "Attention to Suffering: Sympathy as a Basis for Ethical Treatment of Animals." In *Beyond Animal Rights,* eds. J. Donovan and C. Adams, pp. 147–169. New York: Continuum.

Ferry, L. (1995). *The New Ecological Order,* trans. C. Volk. Chicago: University of Chicago Press.

Fromm, E., ed. (1965). *Socialist Humanism: An International Symposium.* New York: Doubleday.

Geras, N. (1998). *The Contract of Mutual Indifference: Political Philosophy After the Holocaust.* London: Verso.

Glass, J. M. (1993). *Shattered Selves: Multiple Personality in a Postmodern World.* Ithaca, NY: Cornell University Press.

Hegel, G. W. F. (1967). *Philosophy of Right,* trans. T. M. Knox. London: Oxford University Press.

——. (1977). *Phenomenology of Spirit,* trans. A. V. Miller. London: Oxford University Press.

Kant, I. (1993). *Grounding for the Metaphysics of Morals,* 3rd ed., trans. J. W. Ellington. Indianapolis, IN: Hackett Publishing.

Marcuse, H. (1960). *Reason and Revolution.* Boston: Beacon Press.

——. (1966). *Eros and Civilization.* Boston: Beacon Press.

Merchant, C. (1980). *The Death of Nature: Women, Ecology, and Scientific Development.* New York: Harper and Row.

Merleau-Ponty, M. (1967). *The Structure of Behavior.* Boston: Beacon Press.

Nussbaum, M. B. (2004). "Beyond 'Compassion and Humanity': Justice for Nonhuman Animals." In *Animal Rights: Current Debates and New Directions,* eds. C. Sunstein and M. B. Nussbaum, pp. 299–320. London: Oxford University Press.

Patterson, C. (2002). *Eternal Treblinka: Our Treatment of Animals and the Holocaust.* New York: Lantern Books.

Pico della Mirandola, G. (1940). *On the Dignity of Man*, trans. C. G. Miller. Indianapolis, IN: Bobbs-Merrill.

Plato. (1979). *Republic*, trans. R. Larson. Arlington Heights, IL: Harlan Davidson.

Reich, W. (1970). *The Mass Psychology of Fascism*, trans. V. R. Carfagno. New York: Noonday Press.

Rogers, L. (1998). *Minds of Their Own: Thinking and Awareness in Animals.* Boulder, CO: Westview.

Sanbonmatsu, J. (2004). *The Postmodern Prince: Critical Theory, Left Strategy, and the Making of a New Political Subject.* New York: Monthly Review Press.

Steeves, P. (1999). *Animal Others: On Ethics, Ontology, and Animal Life.* Albany, NY: SUNY Press.

Young, N. (1977). *An Infantile Disorder? The Crisis and Decline of the New Left.* London: Routledge and Kegan Paul.

PART V: CONCLUSION: THE CHALLENGES OF
GLOBALIZATION—A NON-WESTERN PERSPECTIVE

11

A Rediscovery of
Heaven-and-Human Oneness

By KEPING WANG*

ABSTRACT. The history of Chinese intellectual thought shows a constant and continuous probing into the chiasmatic encounters between *tian* (heaven or nature) and *ren* (humankind). This is conducive, in turn, to a core conception of *tian ren heyi* (heaven-and-human oneness) that largely embodies the general *ethos* or *Geist* of Chinese philosophy. Owing to its functional indication and dynamic character, the polysemy of the conception is apt to be extended along with the passage of time and according to the current situation or sociocultural context. At the present day, there is a tendency to rediscover the relevance of "heaven-and-human oneness" by reading new and even modern messages into the old conception. This has become an open-ended activity, inviting and involving a second reflection, transcultural exposition, and even creative transformation due to its hidden universality for the common good. This chapter attempts to look into the essential bearings of this "heaven-and-human oneness" concept employed as a *Dao* (*Tao* or Way) to deal with the interaction between nature and humanity. It also explores the complex history of the concept, with a particular reference to Li Zehou's recent reinterpretation as well as my own personal understanding. Some

*Keping Wang (1955–, Ph.D.) is a university professor (Beijing International Studies University), research fellow (Chinese Academy of Social Sciences), and visiting fellow (St. Anne's College, University of Oxford). His academic interests include aesthetics and comparative philosophy. His main publications are: *Plato's Poetics in* The Republic (2005); *Chinese Philosophy on Life* (2005); *Towards a Transcultural Aesthetics* (2002); *Essays on Sino-Occidental Aesthetic Cultures* (2000); *The Classic of the Dao: A New Investigation* (1998); and *Sightseeing as an Aesthetic Activity* (1992).

American Journal of Economics and Sociology, Vol. 66, No. 1 (January, 2007).

contemporary pragmatic implications of the concept are also examined with particular reference to eco-environmental concerns.

> Man is fallen; nature is erect, and serves as a differential thermometer, detecting the presence or absence of the divine sentiment in man.
>
> —Ralph Waldo Emerson

I

Introduction

IT IS CHIEFLY DUE to issues of eco-environmental degradation that people today tend to be more concerned with the interaction between nature and humankind. However, if one examines the history of Chinese intellectual thought, one finds a constant probing into the chiasmatic encounters between *tian* (heaven or nature), on the one hand, and *ren* (humankind) on the other. These encounters, in turn, are conducive to the development of a core conception of *tian ren heyi* (heaven-and-human oneness), which arguably forms the general *ethos* of Chinese philosophy. Even in present-day China, there is a tendency to try to rediscover the relevance of "heaven-and-human oneness" by reading new and updated messages into the old conception, thus reflecting on its hidden universality for the common good. In what follows, I will attempt to examine the essential bearings and relevance of this core concept of "heaven-and-human oneness" by tracing out its historical development while, at the same time, making frequent references to updated reinterpretations. The whole argument is intended to cover three main subtopics: the threefold significance of the concept, the two-dimensional orientation, and a pragmatic alternative.

II

The Threefold Significance

CHINESE CULTURE ORIGINATED from a nomadic tradition followed by a more settled agricultural counterpart. This being the case, *tian* (heaven) was first worshipped because it was seen to be both a dominant force and a dependent means for food production and human survival. According to the ancient view, *tian* (heaven) is above, and *di* (earth) is below, and together they make up the universe or nature as a whole in which all things or beings are begotten and conserved. This tri-part interaction has been the focus of consideration in Chinese thought from ancient times to the present. Confucianism, for instance, is preoccupied with "*san cai*" (three basic substances) that involve *tian* (heaven), *di* (earth), and *ren* (humankind); and Daoism is concerned with "*si da*" (four great parts) that comprise *tian, di, ren,* and *Dao (Tao).* It is owing to the Shaman or magic heritage that *tian* is regarded as an embodiment of a divine mandate and thus conceptualized as the Lord of Heaven. Yet, the Lord of Heaven stays and communicates with humans, things, tribes, or societies through magic force; it is neither beyond the empirical domain nor personified into a transcendental power like the Christian God. This is why *tian* as Heaven and *ren* as human interact with each other so closely that the conception of the oneness between the two came into shape in the pre-Qin period. Generally speaking, the conception itself can be dated back to Mencius (c. 372–289 BCE) and Chuang-tzu (c. 369–286 BCE), further developed by Dong Zhongshu (179–104 BCE), and metaphysically moralized by Neo-Confucianism in the Song Dynasty, especially from the 11th to 13th centuries CE. Over the passage of time, the idea of *tian* extended into a cluster of concepts such as *tiandi* (heaven and earth), *tianming* (the mandate of Heaven), *tianyi* (the will of Heaven), *tiandao* (the way of Heaven), and *xianxia* (the land under heaven), among many others. Three of them, I think, are especially important and relevant to the general eco-environmental concerns of humanity today. They are *tiandi* as nature, *xiandao* as the Heavenly Way, and *tianxia* as the land under sky or the world; together, they form the threefold significance in the Chinese notion of *tianren heyi*, or "heaven-and-human oneness."

A. Tiandi *and Its Naturalistic Aspects*

The literal translation of *tiandi* is heaven and earth that make up the universe or nature as a whole. The term is frequently used in many Chinese classics, and it is almost always set in a context where nature and humankind are interrelated.

In *A Taoist Classic of Chuang-tzu* (*Zhuang zi*), for instance, we read the following: "Heaven and Earth and I came into existence together, and the myriad things with me are one."[1] In addition, "Heaven and Earth have great beauty but remain in silence. . . . The myriad things have perfect principles but say nothing of them. The sage is a person who is in pursuit of the great beauty and the perfect principles."[2] Heaven and earth (*tiandi*) are viewed as the producer of the myriad things (*wanwu*). The myriad things take shelter in heaven and earth. They all gather together to form up the entirety of nature that is then synthesized with humankind into oneness. By such oneness, Chuang-tzu tries to equalize all things and justify his principle of making no distinction. He believes that the cosmic order or harmony is to be attained in no other way than this. In many cases, he advises those who attempt to pursue the Dao of absolute freedom and independent personality to follow the course of nature. This is not simply because nature operates characteristically in spontaneity or naturalness (*zi ran er ran*), but because nature also has great beauty and virtuous silence. Under such circumstances, nature is not only the place to live and act, but also an object for aesthetic appreciation. Accordingly, the sage as the idealized personality in Daoism is not merely the follower of natural law, but the discoverer of natural beauty as well. For example, in *The Happy Excursion* and other works, Chuang-tzu gives much credit to the aesthetic value of natural beauty owing to its nourishment of spiritual freedom. He readily bestows the natural with a joyous charm, whereas he rejects the artificial (e.g., the bull tamed by man for plowing) as being an evil distortion. All of this leads to his philosophy of aesthetic naturalism.

When it comes to Dong Zhongshu's *Rich Dews in Spring and Autumn* (*Chunqiu fanlu*), the natural beauty is said to embody the harmony of heaven and earth, and anyone who has a peaceful mind and right conduct is able to nourish his body by means of this beauty.[3] In a rather affectionate tone, Dong assumes that nature is the "grandfather of man," creating man *qua* man as it bears the virtue of "human-heartedness" (*ren*).[4] It follows that nature and man share a strong resemblance. For example, nature has the sun and the moon, man has the left and right eye; nature has four seasons, and man has four limbs; nature has four kinds of emotional power such as joy revealed in spring, happiness in summer, anger in autumn, sorrow in winter, and so does man. Nature and man are therefore one in a classificatory sense. Accordingly, a harmonious order comes into being when man identifies himself with nature. By contrast, a terrible disorder arises when man separates himself from nature.[5] Of course, to the modern way of thinking, the above comparison is ostensibly far-fetched and logically ridiculous, but it aims to remind humankind of their dependent position and inborn connection with nature. The emphasis on the strong resemblance between nature and man is not meaningless, since it encourages man to attend to nature as much as he attends to himself. This is hopefully conducive to an emotional caring for nature. Historically, Dong is the first to coin this concept of "heaven-and-human oneness." He acknowledges natural beauty underscored by the principle of proper harmony. But he also finds such beauty beneficial in a number of ways; for example, it is not simply aesthetically satisfying but also physically rewarding and morally generating. In other words, it satisfies aesthetic needs, nurtures the body, and facilitates the becoming of man as man via its rich resources and varied functions. However, Dong's preoccupation represents a mystical naturalism of sorts: his approach to the "oneness" is essentially based on the school of Yin and Yang; his personification of heaven exemplifies a kind of mystification instead of divination; and his contemplation of natural beauty reveals some mystical rapture.

Mencius is one of the early Chinese thinkers who promote the notion of heaven-and-human oneness. He views the notion mainly from a Confucian point of view, and he therefore seeks to maintain a balance by exposing the reciprocal interaction between the two sides. From a cognitive perspective, however, Mencius claims that the "One who has exhausted *xin* as his mental constitution knows *xing* as his own nature. Knowing his own nature, he knows *tian* as Heaven. To preserve his mental constitution, and nourish his own nature, is the way to serve Heaven."[6] This shows how humanity and heaven interact with each other. On the human side, it requires a sense of mission and more initiative, not only to develop one's cognitive power and cultivate one's character but also to do one's utmost for heaven. In this context, heaven (*tian*) implies abstractly an inborn destiny (*tianming*), and substantially the myriad things (*wanwu*). What is meant by "to serve

Heaven" is related to fulfilling the inborn destiny and looking after the myriad things. From a more pragmatic viewpoint, Mencius proposes the ideal of "loving people and treasuring things" (*ren min er ai wu*).[7] "Loving people" (*ren min*) is the result of extending affection from one's parents to others in general. "Treasuring things" (*ai wu*) signifies the caretaking of all beings according to the law of reciprocity. For instance, "if the farming seasons be not interfered with, the grain will be more than can be eaten. If close nets are not allowed to enter the pools and ponds, the fishes and turtles will be more than can be consumed. If the axes and bills enter the hills and forests only at the proper time, the wood and timber would be more than can be used."[8] Consequently, things are protected and multiplied at the same time, and people, in turn, are enabled to enjoy sufficient means for a good life. Otherwise, there would be a detrimental outcome of abusing natural resources and depriving nature of its generative capacity, which is sometimes metaphorically depicted, in Chinese literature, in terms of a greed-ridden farmer killing the hen for her eggs.

For all of the three thinkers discussed above, nature is perceived to be good and beautiful a priori. But whereas Chuang-tsu's preoccupation is with aesthetic naturalism, and Dong Zhongshu's concern is with mystical naturalism, Mencius seems to favor a pragmatic naturalism. Simply put, aesthetic naturalism tends to exaggerate the perfect beauty of nature while ignoring the active role of humankind; mystical naturalism tends to reinforce the heaven-and-human resemblance in order to project human affection into nature; and pragmatic naturalism tends to stress the mutual independence and reciprocal interaction between nature and humankind in order to secure a balanced development for the sake of human existence as its ultimate *telos*.

In China during the 1990s, there was a revival of interest in the rationale of heaven-and-human oneness. This occurred against the background of increased eco-environmental pressures in China and the world over. Some thinkers reexamined the rationale in order to build up a greater awareness of the problematic relations between human and nature. They regarded nature as an organic whole of the cosmic scheme, and proposed a new operation of heaven-and-human oneness for eco-environmental protection in terms of "sustainable development." According to this way of thinking, the organic whole ought to be taken care of because no part of it is a separate island, and everyone is accountable for its protection. Moreover, the general objective of sustainable development was not seen as merely economy based, but morality based as well, because it was also intended for the welfare of later generations.

B. Tiandao *and Its Moralistic Expectations*

THE CHINESE CONCEPTION of *tiandao* means "the Heavenly Way" concretized through its counterpart of *rendao* as "the Human Way." The former poses a higher frame of reference for the latter as it is directed toward moral development. Historically, this idea can be traced back to *The Book of Changes* (*I Ching*) in the following statement:

> The great man is someone whose virtue is constant with Heaven and Earth, his brightness with the sun and the moon, his orderly procedure with the four seasons. . . . When he precedes Heaven, Heaven will not act in opposition to him; and when he follows Heaven, he obeys the timing of its motion.[9]

What is emphasized in this passage appears to be the interactive oneness between heaven and humankind. In reality, however, the key message is hidden in human virtue and consistency with heaven and earth. As one can see in the commentary to the first two hexagrams of *qian* (symbol of heaven) and *kun* (symbol of earth), human virtue is expected to assimilate the counterpart of both heaven and earth. For "the action of Heaven is strong and dynamic. In the same manner, the noble man never ceases to strengthen himself."[10] Moreover, "the disposition of Earth bears sustaining power. The noble man, in accordance with this, supports all beings with his generous virtue."[11] Here, it can be observed that the dynamic action of heaven is demonstrated through the ceaseless cycle of the four seasons, and the sustaining power of earth through the carrying capacity of mountains, waters, and all other beings. Such activities suggest *tiandi zhide* as respective virtues of both heaven and earth. These virtues then come together to form *tiandi zhidao* as the "Way of Heaven and Earth," which is shortened into *tiandao* as the "Heavenly Way." The noble man as an idealized personality becomes what he is by learning from the Heavenly Way. He strives to develop himself persistently like heaven; and, like earth, he tries to achieve the generous virtue to help all other beings grow properly. Such deeds help to establish *rendao* as the Human Way for moral accomplishment.

This line of thought has been extended throughout the Chinese history of ideas. Mencius, for instance, pushes it further as a moral requirement for character training.[12] In his mind, the Human Way is embodied in what the noble man does, and the Heavenly Way is represented by heaven and earth. When the former reaches the corresponding level of the latter, the heaven-and-human oneness is accomplished and so is the idealized personality of the noble man. A similar idea is also found in *The Doctrine of the Mean* (*Zhong yong*). Herein the noble man is assumed to be a person with the most complete sincerity. When he gives full development to his own nature, he can also help others do the same. And when he helps others give full development to their nature, he can also help give full development to all other beings. In doing so, he can be said to assist the transforming and nourishing powers of heaven and earth.[13] This process demonstrates a hypothesized sequence about how the Human Way mingles with the Heavenly Way. It commences with the virtue of sincerity, capable of transforming oneself and others for the better; and then it goes through a number of stages by applying altruism to other beings and things. Finally, it arrives at the highest possible state of forming a union, of sorts, among the three components including heaven, earth, and humankind. Once again, this points to the core conception of "heaven-and-human oneness" as well as a sense of mission on the part of man as man.

Confucianism pays more attention to the reciprocal interaction between the Heavenly Way and the Human Way. This has been the case both in the past and at present. Among the Neo-Confucianists in the Song Dynasty was a general agreement on cancelling out the distinction between the Heavenly Way and the Human Way. That is to say, they tended to identify the former with the latter and ascertain the oneness between the two. For example, Zhang Zai (1020–1077 CE) argues that the Heavenly Way and the Human Way seem to be different in size, but remain the same in essence because it is genuinely human to be able to know and experience heaven.[14] Cheng Yi (1033–1107 CE) goes even further to define the relationship in concise terms: The Way (*dao*) is freed from any distinction between heaven and human. Yet, it is called the Heavenly Way when it is with heaven, the Earthly Way when it is with earth, and the Human Way when it is with human. The Way is one only. It is shared by heaven, earth and humankind together.[15]

In recent decades, modern Confucianists have attempted to revive the pathway of Neo-Confucianism for the sake of moral reconstruction. Mou Zongsan (1909–1995), for example, made tremendous endeavors to reinterpret the moral expectation of heaven-and-human oneness. He places much emphasis on integrating the virtue of heaven with its human counterpart. To his way of thinking, the individual life ought to be completely in reconciliation with the cosmic life. He thus affirms that the attainment of this reconciliation leads to the accomplishment not merely of moral being but also of inward sageliness. In order to fulfill this *telos*, one must follow the Heavenly Way and model one's own nature upon it. But how is that possible? Mou's illustration gives rise to a circle of development. The circle consists of four components. At the bottom of the circle is the becoming of individual life filled with possibilities. High above is the working of the Heavenly Way that is both religiously "transcendent" (*chaoyue*) and morally "immanent" (*neizai*). On the right-hand side stands the process of moral praxis relating to the virtues of human-heartedness (*ren*) and truth (*dao*). On the left-hand side stands the mandate of heaven in constant movement. It is thought that the process of moral praxis and the movement of the mandate make possible the transformational interaction between the individual life and the Heavenly Way. On this occasion, the individual life will rise up to combine itself with the Heavenly Way as a result of the praxis of the virtues of human-heartedness and truth. Meanwhile, the Heavenly Way has turned itself into a "metaphysical reality" (*xingershang de shiti*), and penetrated into human nature, thus breaking the estrangement and causing the reconciliation between the individual life and the Heavenly Way.[16] In plain language, the individual life of humankind below will ascend upward to meet the Heavenly Way through moral praxis, whereas the Heavenly Way will descend downward to meet the individual life of humankind through constant movement. Jointly, they will create the reconciliation or "heaven-and-human oneness" in which the Heavenly

Way is transformed into a "metaphysical reality" and the individual life into a moral being or "real self." The key to this idealized outcome lies in the sincere and persistent practice of such virtues as human-heartedness and truth. Otherwise, the above-mentioned reconciliation is not possible at all.

In the final analysis, Confucianists of whatever type use such terms as the Heavenly Way (*tiandao*) and the Human Way (*rendao*) in discourse. But very often they identify them with one another by illustrating the Heavenly Way in light of the Human Way for moral purposes. This line of thought is derived from a learning strategy recommended by Confucius, which starts from what is down below and gets through to what is up above.[17] By "what is down below" is meant human affairs or social commitment, and by "what is up above" is meant such virtues as human-heartedness and righteousness (*ren yi*). As learning is both a cognitive and a practical process, it begins with knowing human affairs and social deeds, but its perceptiveness must rise higher to facilitate the attainment and praxis of the afore-mentioned virtues. Eventually it comes up with a transformation of what is learned into the virtues expected (*zhuan zhi wei de*). Such virtues as human-heartedness and righteousness are all symbolized in the Heavenly Way and practically exercised by human beings. A synthesis in this regard exemplifies the highest form of achievement of which the human as human is capable. At the same time, however, it advises people to be both realistic in pragmatic learning and idealistic in moral cultivation. This calls for a pursuit of moral transcendence as an elementary part of character building.

C. Tianxia *and Its Cosmopolitan Ideal*

Both Daoism and Confucianism show concern for *tianxia* as a political rather than a geographical concept. Its literal rendering could be "the land under sky," but in a more narrow sense, it refers to China as it once was, divided into many states. In a broad sense, it signifies the world in its entirety. The conception of *tianxia* among the Chinese literati is deeply rooted in their minds as a noble *telos* of their life mission. The mission itself is composed of four segments abbreviated as *xiu qi zhi ping*, which means four major tasks such as cultivating the personality, regulating the family, governing well the state, and keeping the world in peace. The whole idea is elaborated in the Confucian classic *The Great Learning (Da xue)*.[18] It involves eight major steps ranging from near to far or rising from low to high in a logical sequence, thus forming a progressive process sustained by the law of cause and effect and aiming at "keeping the world in peace" as its final objective.

It is often assumed that one may read the old text and understand the current situation better, but this is only possible by extending the implications of the text in the context of the status quo. In this regard, the most appealing aspect is perhaps not the learning process itself but the conventional ideal of *ping tianxia* as "keeping the world in peace." Looking into the extended meaning of *tianxia* as the whole world, we are inclined to compare it with the widespread and often overvalued notion of the state in modern politics. Geographically and ideologically speaking, the notion of the state is usually understood to be nationality based and largely confined to a marked borderline or national territory. And even if by some chance it is not associated with a radical nationalism that does harm to other nations for the sake of national identity, the concept of the state is often utilized to justify a kind of egoistic patriotism. After all, it is usually in the name of state interests, national power, and blind patriotism that some unreasonable destruction and even war crimes are committed. By contrast, the ideal of *tianxia* is in principle world oriented and, as such, it features a more cosmopolitan horizon. While admittedly idealistic, it appears more constructive and reciprocal in the realm of international relations, and it could be employed to encourage a world outlook of high-minded cosmopolitanism.

With regard to the three derived aspects of heaven-and-human oneness explicated above, the theory of *tiandi* as nature connotes a cosmic scheme of appropriate praxis for humankind to act according to the law of reciprocity. Moreover, the doctrine of *tiandao* as the Heavenly Way implies a moral scheme of spiritual cultivation for humankind to pursue self-perfection; and the conception of *tianxia* as the "world as a whole" indicates a political scheme of cosmopolitan consciousness for humankind to develop a broader vision. This line of thought is said to function as a keystone in the formation of the cultural psychology (*wenhua xinli jiegou*) among the educated in particular. It always remains open to be rediscovered and reinterpreted with the passage of time.

III

The Two-Dimensional Orientation

IT IS WORTH MENTIONING that after the founding of the "New China" (as it is sometimes called) in 1949, the rationale of heaven-and-human oneness was brought under attack by the official ideology. Maoism went so far as to declare a kind of "civil war" against heaven or nature. This is typically evidenced in one of Mao's decrees, which reads as follows: "It [Maoism] draws tremendous delight from the battle against Heaven, and so it does from the class struggle amongst humanity" (*yu tian dou, qi le wu qiong; yu ren dou, qi le wu qiong*). As a consequence, the separation of heaven and human was politically imposed and rampantly reinforced. This situation lasted for a decade or so, during which China paid a heavy price in the late 1950s and suffered a nationwide famine resulting from "manmade natural disasters" in the early 1960s. It was not until the early 1980s that academics in mainland China resumed a reconsideration of the concept of "heaven-and-human oneness." But this time the methodology manifested a two-dimensional orientation in view of "pragmatic reason" (*shiyong lixing*), which involves *ziran renhua* as the humanization of nature, and *ren ziranhua* as the naturalization of humanity.

A. Ziran Renhua *as the Humanization of Nature*

According to Li Zehou, nature can be classified conceptually into two modes: the external and the internal. External nature stands for the living surroundings of humankind, while internal nature stands for the physical and psychic faculties of humankind. In 1999 Li made a metaphorical use of such binary terms as "hardware" and "software" to help illustrate his interpretation. Let me elaborate.

Regarding the humanization of external nature, the analogy of "hardware" refers to the re-creation or re-formation of the natural environment in which humans live. It is reflected, for instance, in manmade reservoirs, canals, artificial lakes, animal husbandry and agriculture, and so forth. Nowadays this form of practice continues, for instance, in the field of transforming the biological genes of plants and vegetables with the help of modern technology. The analogy of "software," on the other hand, points to the crucial changes that have occurred to the interrelationship between nature and humankind. As a result of the development of the "hardware" mentioned above, human fear and worship of natural elements and phenomena have gradually vanished over the course of civilization, and have been replaced by an aesthetic affinity and other utilitarian expectations. Hence, the beauty of a natural landscape is discovered and appreciated. It is on this point that Li Zehou grounds his argument on a historical ontology (*lishi benti*). As he stresses, it is this historical development that has altered the heaven-and-human relations and also made possible the humanization of nature. In this sense "humanization" is not something merely conceptual or subjective, but essentially anthropo-ontological. That is to say, the objective relationship between nature and humankind has been changed historically, thus making nature a more integral part of human existence. Eventually, nature was turned from a fearful object in-itself into an object for-itself. All this is the fundamental and objective basis of the humanization of nature in the subjective conscious of humankind.[19]

As is also noted in *The Four Lectures on Aesthetics* (*Meixue sijiang*),[20] the humanization of nature is in principle a process that goes hand in hand with the progression of human culture. It involves the historical relationship between human praxis and nature, and transforms, either directly or indirectly, natural things into aesthetic objects. In this respect, the humanization of nature in its narrow sense, which is operated through human labor and technological recreation, provides the basis for the humanization of nature in its broad sense.[21] Primitive peoples, for instance, could hardly appreciate such natural scenes as mountains, waters, flowers, and birds, simply because they had to live under the fearfulness of nature that was not humanized either in its broad or narrow sense.

In the case of the humanization of internal nature, Li Zehou again offers an analogical analysis with reference to the transformation of physical faculties, DNA structures, and so on. This involves deliberate human control and re-creation of the natural faculties and their functions (*ganguan de renhua*). As a result, the five faculties or senses, for example, are humanized or enculturated, and we humans therefore can enjoy an ear for music, an artistic hand for painting, and a literary eye for poetry, among other senses. This suggests that the instinctive and sensory utility of the faculties gradually decreases, and in turn, these faculties are modified by nonutilitarian functions including aesthetic sensibility and taste. Moreover, in this context, there comes along the humanization of desires and eros (*qingyu de renhua*). The historical process of enculturation differentiates humans from animals even though they share something in common. More specifically, the long history of making and using tools, along with social group organization, spurred the development of the human psychical functions to become significantly different from that of other animals. The difference lies chiefly in the mixture of animalness with culturalness. This leads to the cultural-psychological formation (*wenhua xinli jiegou*) in which the animal mentality and the cultural achievement are "sedimented" or stored up (*jidian*), along with sociality (rationality and culturalness) and individuality (sensibility and animalness). Among many other examples, one might cite the virtue of human love, which originated, but then further developed, from sheer animal sexuality.

From a moral perspective, human ethics or practical reason is also connected with this "humanization of the internal Nature"[22] as is the development of human taste and aesthetic sensibility.[23] All this leads to Li's assumption of historical sedimentation (*jidian lun*),[24] by which he metaphorically refers to the hidden structure of human enculturation in connection with Jung's archetypal psychology, Piaget's genetic epistemology, Bell's aesthetic hypothesis, and, above all, Marx's practical philosophy. It has been challenged and reexamined by other philosophers in recent decades, both within and outside China. Here, I shall restrict my comments to a brief description rather than a critical analysis.

B. Ren Ziranhua *as the Naturalization of Humanity*

If *ziran renhua* as "humanization of Nature" is borrowed from Karl Marx and extended from a historico- and anthropo-ontological viewpoint, then *ren ziranhua* as naturalization of humanity is chiefly inspired by the Chinese thought of heaven-and-human oneness. According to Li Zehou, the naturalization of humanity serves as the counterpart to the humanization of Nature. It aims at human fulfillment or the wholeness of human nature.

Correspondingly, the naturalization of humanity is assumed to contain at least two aspects. One of them is composed of three kinds of activities: first, establishing a co-existent and harmonized interaction between humankind and nature, and coming to perceive nature as a shelter to live and rest in; second, returning to nature for aesthetic contemplation of its beautiful landscapes and helping things grow properly by taking care of flora and fauna; third, learning how to breathe naturally (e.g., *qigong* exercise or yoga) in order to reconcile the rhythm of human body and heart with that of nature, thus achieving the heaven-and-human oneness.[25] All three activities are associated with a certain kind of aesthetic feeling or state of mind in which the rational is fused with the emotional, the subject identified with the object, and the social consciousness accompanied by individual freedom. By virtue of the naturalization of humanity, one could possibly turn back to nature for "dwelling poetically" in the world, and for emancipating oneself from the control of instrumental rationality, from the alienation by material fetishism, and from enslavement by the system of power, knowledge, language, and so forth.

The other of the two aspects lies in an aesthetic dimension. It is found in free enjoyment (*ziyou xiangshou*) stemming from the cultural psychological formation of the person who returns to nature with a humanized as well as a socialized mentality. Compared with the service of the humanized faculties and emotions, the naturalization of humanity enables man to dwell poetically in the world, and exposes him to free enjoyment in an aesthetic and spiritual sense. For this reason, Li asserts the superiority of the aesthetic to both the cognitive and the ethical. The aesthetic is neither the internalization of reason (the cognitive) nor the condensation of reason (the ethical), but the sedimentational incorporation of both reason and sense. This being the case, it works to facilitate "the rectification of seven human emotions including joy, anger, sorrow, fear, love, hate and desire" (*qiqing zheng*) and "the delight in heaven-and-human oneness" (*tianren le*). In other words, the aesthetic of "free enjoyment" is neither the ethical in which rationality dominates sensibility nor the cognitive in which rationality shapes sensibility. It is a fully open and individual creativity in which rationality and a variety of psychical factors (e.g., perception, imagination, desire, and emotion) interpenetrate and interweave with each other. This creativity is significant to both the cognitive and the ethical because it serves to "illuminate the true with the beautiful" (*yi mei qi zhen*) and "enhance the good through the beautiful" (*yi mei chu shan*).[26] In this way, the true leads to the discovery of real knowledge and wisdom, and the good to the cultivation of moral personality.

Metaphorically speaking, the humanization of nature and the naturalization of humanity can be characterized as two wheels of a moving cart, symbolizing the historical development of human culture toward a final destination of self-fulfillment or wholeness. During this process, humankind as a super-biological species achieves the humanization of external and internal nature, which then opens up both the cognitive realm (free intuition) and the ethical realm (free will). All of this is extended further, and blended with the "naturalization of humanity," to form the aesthetic realm (of free enjoyment). As a result, there arises a cultural psychological formation via historical sedimentation in the form of collective unconsciousness, and it is from this perspective of historical ontology and philosophical psychology that the new implications of heaven-and-human oneness are proposed.[27]

According to my observation, one important implication to note concerns the human expression of ideas and feelings in art. This can be broadly categorized into three basic genres in the course of human history. At the very beginning, there were no pictures and words. People therefore expressed themselves through sounds and gestures. Then there arose the audio expression in the genre of music-dance. Later on, people started to learn how to draw pictures and signs in order to keep records or express themselves. Then there arose the visual expression in the genre of drawing in particular. Eventually, words were invented and came into use, and thus there arose verbal expression, for example, in the genre of literature and poetry. In recent centuries, humankind has been verbally trapped or yoked by language. The situation has only worsened in modern times to the extent that, all too frequently, a person does not speak words but instead words speak the person, that is, the person is reluctant to think on his or her own and simply parrots back platitudes that are said by others. Moreover, the situation is also conducive to the retrogression of audio and visual capacities. This may be attributed to the "over-humanization" of the faculties and senses of modern city dwellers who are imprisoned in highrises and whose only contact with nature is by peeping out at the starry sky through windows. Under such circumstances, the "naturalization of humanity" becomes indispensable, in that it will be apt to revive the aesthetic sensibility of humans. That is to say, audio and visual sensibilities will be enhanced as one is exposed to natural sounds and scenes upon one's return to nature. All this can be seen as a favorable effect, to some extent, of heaven-and-human oneness.

IV

A Pragmatic Alternative

As we have seen, the threefold significance and the two-dimensional orientation are leagued with the rationale of heaven-and-human oneness. Hypothesized from all of this is the highest form of achievement that a human qua human can pursue. It is called *tiandi jingjie*. Its literal rendering could be "the heaven-and-earth realm," but its free translation might be "the cosmic realm of being," symbolizing the cultivation of a superior personality characterized by a more universal viewpoint and a cosmopolitan frame of mind. In principle, "the cosmic realm of being" is mainly preoccupied with the excellence (or virtue) of heaven-and-human oneness. Accordingly, the cosmic personality is capable of serving not only society and humankind but also the universe and all things in it. He or she is therefore willing to do whatever possible so as to retain all beings or things in their most proper positions. In Mencius's terms, such a personality can be said to move toward the becoming of a "heavenly citizen" (*tianmin*).[28] Such citizenship is expected to completely transcend the conventional limits of ethnicity, nationality, state territory, or political borderlines.

In brief, *tiandi jingjie* as the cosmic realm of being is based on a sense of mission to "serve Heaven" (*shi tian*) by doing the utmost to help all things grow properly in the universe. Those who share such a sense of mission will see themselves not merely as social beings but also as universal beings, claiming personal commitments to both society and nature at the same time. This being the case, they will enjoy a thorough understanding of human nature, and of the interrelationship between humankind and nature. And in a more spiritual sense, they will seem to have moved from the small "I" of finiteness to the big "I" of infinity, and thereby to live in freedom instead of necessity.

Admittedly, the "cosmic realm of being" sounds both idealistic and overly abstract, but it can be made somewhat more accessible and concrete when specified in terms of *renmin er aiwu*, or "loving people and treasuring things." So understood, it will turn out to favor both a cosmopolitan consciousness and an eco-environmental sensitivity to a certain degree. For this reason, it can be recommended as a pragmatic alternative to confront the many eco-environmental problems facing humanity today, according to the law of reciprocity between nature and humankind.

In my opinion, the applicability of this alternative is preconditioned by the motivation to know *tianli* as natural laws, and to develop *renxin* as humane mind. Here, *tianli* also stands for the universal principle, while *renxin* stands for altruistic love. The knowledge of *tianli* helps one take rational actions when making use of natural resources, and the development of *renxin* guides one to treat people and things alike with equal affinity. Relatively, the former requires great-mindedness and insightfulness into the principles of all things, whereas the latter requires human-heartedness and adherence to the virtue of sincerity. Both of them involve a sense of mission and an awareness of reciprocal relationships, primarily because we humans are part of nature. We are susceptible to the impact from other beings in the world and, in return, we have an impact on them as well by what we do in general.

After all, the mind is sure to play a vital role in conducting the virtue of loving people and treasuring things either for sociocultural or eco-environmental enterprises. By contrast, if the mind were merely confined to considerations of human welfare per se, it would be too narrow and self-centered to take into due consideration the welfare of

any beings other than *homo sapiens.* Such narrow-mindedness or
anthropocentrism would, in turn, be all too inclined to meet human
needs by overexploiting other things such as natural and maritime
recourses. When this happens, eco-development gets thrown out of
balance and the eco-environment is put into jeopardy. A good
example to be cited here is North China, where there is an environmental crisis relating both to the desertification of the grassland due to
excessive animal husbandry[29] and the subsequent increase in sand-
storms due to this widespread desertification. Facing this vicious cycle,
we hope for a decisive breakthrough by looking into the cultivation of
the mind per se.

   Thus, there arises the question about how best to cultivate the mind
to the fullest extent possible. As far I can see, this involves a three-
stage process. First and foremost, one is expected to "make the mind
broad in order to experience and understand the real condition of all
things under the sky (*da qi xin, yi ti tian xia zhi wu*)." "The real
condition" as such embodies those living and environmental conditions that affect the human condition, either directly or indirectly. "To
experience and understand" is not possible unless we have relevant
knowledge and at least some empathy. In this case, the knowledge
comes from investigating the connections among all things, and the
needed empathy comes from projecting feelings into the surroundings. With this state of mind, humans will be ready to transposition
themselves into "all things under the sky" and will naturally develop
a consciousness of treasuring them equally. The reason that the
human mind is to be broadened lies in the fact that it usually remains
small, confining itself to the narrow domain of personal gains and
losses. Such small-mindedness is conducive both to egoism and
anthropocentrism, as well as the self-proclaimed privilege that "man is
the measure of all things." Hence, the cultivation of broad-mindedness
is indispensable in this regard.

   Subsequently, efforts must be redoubled to exercise the second
strategy, for example, of "making the mind empty in order to
receive and appreciate all the good in the world (*xu qi xin, yi shou
tian xia zhi shan*)." The good of this kind is not simply derived
from human beings and social events but also from other beings
and natural things. The mind needs, therefore, to learn the merits

and lessons from others in order to do a good job for all. Meanwhile, it needs to appreciate the benefits offered by others and then do them a favor in return. The whole idea seems to be that one good turn deserves another from a reciprocal perspective. It is common sense, for instance, that no one can survive without breathing in oxygen, which is largely produced by plants. Therefore, taking care of the plants is the same thing as taking care of the people breathing. The alternative would be just as harmful as lifting up a stone and then dropping it on the toes of the lifter.

Last but not least, it is of practical value to follow the third strategy, that is, to "do the utmost through the mind in order to properly plan and conduct all the world affairs (*jin qi xin, yi mou tian xia zhi shi*)." What is to be emphasized here is bilateral regarding the service of the mind. The service as such should be good-natured and best deployed to fulfill the mission concerned. It is therefore necessary not merely to make the most of the mind but also to follow the logical order discussed above, namely, by making the mind broad enough to experience and understand all the things in the universe, by making the mind empty enough to receive and appreciate all the good in the world, and, above all, by making the mind humane enough to love people and treasure things together.

In sum, *tiandi jingjie* as the cosmic realm of being features loving people and treasuring things in view of *tianren heyi* as heaven-and-human oneness. As a hypothesis, it can be creatively developed and reinterpreted into a pragmatic alternative for human fulfillment and eco-environmental protection. Practically and ultimately, it is intended to upgrade the quality of life for humankind as a whole, providing that we humans can become more cosmopolitan and more conscious of *tian* (heaven or nature) as part of our own being.

Notes

1. Cf. Chuang-tzu, "On the Equality of Things," in *A Taoist Classic: Chuang-tzu*, trans. Fung Yu-lan (Beijing: Foreign Languages Press, 1989), 49.

2. Cf. Chuang-tzu, "Zhi bei you" ["Intelligence Traveling Northward"], in *Zhuangzi jinzhu jinyi* [*A Newly Annotated and Paraphrased Version of Chuang-tzu*], ed. Chen Guying (Beijing: Zhonghua shuju, 1983), 563.

3. Cf. Dong Zhongshu, "Xun tian zhi dao" ["Act upon the Dao of Heaven"], in *Chunqiu fanlu* [*Rich Dews in Spring and Autumn*] (Shanghai: Shanghai Classics Press, 1989), 91–93.

4. Ibid., "Wei ren zhe tian" ["Heaven Serves Man"], 64; "Wangdao tong san" ["The Kingly Way"], 67.

5. Ibid., "Yin Yang yi" ["The Meaning of Yin and Yang"], 71.

6. Cf. Mencius, *The Works of Mencius*, trans. James Legge, 13.1.

7. Ibid., 13.45.

8. Ibid., 1.4.

9. Cf. *The Book of Changes*, trans. James Legge, *Hexagram 1: Qian*, 34. See also *The Classic of Changes*, trans. Richard John Lynn (New York: Columbia University Press, 1994), 138.

10. Cf. *The Book of Changes*, *Qian* (*The Creative*). See also *The Classic of Changes*, *Hexagram 1: Qian*, 130.

11. Ibid., *The Book of Changes*, *Kun* (*The Receptive*). See also *The Classic of Changes*, *Hexagram 2: Kun*, 144.

12. Cf. Mencius, *The Works of Mencius*, 13.12.

13. Cf. *The Doctrine of the Mean*, trans. James Legge, 22.

14. Cf. Zhang Zai, *Zhangzi zhengmeng* [*The Just Enlightenment*], ed. Wang Fuzhi (Beijing: Zhonghua shuju, 1975), 94.

15. Ibid., vol. 2, 18.

16. Cf. Mou Zongsan, *Zhongguo zhexue de tezhi* [*The Ethos of Chinese Philosophy*] (Shanghai: Shanghai guji chubanshe, 1997), 20–32, 74–81, 114–117.

17. Cf. Confucius, *The Analects*, trans. D. C. Lau (London: Penguin Books, 1979), Book XIV, 35. See also Confucius, *The Confucian Analects*, trans. James Legge, 14.35.

18. Cf. *The Great Learning*, trans. James Legge, 1. The English version is offered here with some minor modifications to the original text. For instance, James Legge rendered *tianxia* as "empire" and I have changed it to "the world." He translated *tianxia ping* as "the whole empire was made tranquil and happy," while I revised it somewhat as "the world was kept in peace." Other translators prefer "the whole world was brought into peace."

19. Cf. Li Zehou, "*Shuo ziran renhua*" ["On the Humanization of Nature"], in Li Zehou, *Lishi bentilun* and *Yimao wushuo* [*Historical Ontology, Five Essays from 1999*] (Beijing: Sanlian shudian, 2003), 242–243.

20. Cf. Li Zehou, *Meixue sijiang* [*Four Lectures on Aesthetics*] (Beijing: Sanlian shudian, 1989), 88–89.

21. Ibid., 91.

22. Cf. Li Zehou, *Shuo ziran renhua* ["On the Humanization of Nature"], 248–259.

23. Cf. Li Zehou, *Meixue sijiang* [*Four Lectures on Aesthetics*], 110–125.

24. Ibid., 112–113.

25. Ibid., 95–96.

26. Cf. Li Zehou, *Shuo ziran renhua* ["On the Humanization of Nature"], 263–264.

27. Ibid., 266–267.

28. Hierarchically speaking, according to Fung Yu-lan's comparison, "the cosmic realm of being" is situated above the other three categories including "the moral realm of being" (*daode jingjie*), which is preoccupied with the values of humanity and righteousness, "the utilitarian realm of being" (*gongli jinngjie*), which is preoccupied with the gaining of merits and profits, and "the instinctive realm of being" (*ziran jingjie*), which is preoccupied with the satisfaction of desires and wants. Cf. Fung Yu-lan, "Xin yuan ren" ["On the Meaning of Human Life"], in Fung Yu-lan, *Zhenyuan liushu* [*Six Books in Zhenyuan*] (Shanghai: East China Normal University Press, 1996), vol. 2, 568–649.

29. According to official statistics, the proportion of excessive animal husbandry in China is up to 36.1 percent of the total area, including Inner Mongolia, Ningxia, Gansu, Tibet, the Xinjiang regions, and the Qinghai province.

References

Chen Guying, ed. (1983). *Zhuangzi jinzhu jinyi*. [*A Newly Annotated and Paraphrased Version of the Chuang-tzu*]. Beijing: Zhonghua shuju.

Cheng Hao, and Cheng Yi, eds. (1982). "Yu lu" ["Collected Sayings"]. In *Zhongguo zhexueshi ziliao xuanji* [*Selected Sources of the History of Chinese Philosophy*]. Beijing: Zhonghua shuju.

Chuang-tzu. (1989). *A Taoist Classic: Chuang-tzu*, trans. Fung Yu-lan. Beijing: Foreign Languages Press.

Confucius. (1979). *The Analects*, trans. D. C. Lau. London: Penguin Books.

———. (1994). "The Confucian Analects." In *The Four Books*, trans. James Legge. Changsha: Hunan Press.

Dong Zhongshu. (1989). *Chunqiu fanlu* [*Rich Dews in Spring and Autumn*]. Shanghai: Shanghai Classics Press.

Fung Yu-lan. (1996). "Xin yuan ren" ["On the Meaning of Human Life"]. In *Zhenyuan liushu* [*Six Books in Zhenyuan*]. Shanghai: East China Normal University Press.

Li Zehou. (1989). *Meixue sijiang* [*Four Lectures on Aesthetics*]. Beijing: Sanlian shudian.

———. (1999). *Lishi bentilun and Yimao wushuo* [*Historical Ontology and Five Essays*]. Rpt. 2001. Beijing: Sanlian shudian.

Lynn, Richard John, trans. (1994). *The Classic of Changes*. New York: Columbia University Press.

Mencius. (1994). "The Works of Mencius." In *The Four Books*, trans. James Legge. Changsha: Hunan Press.

Mou Zongsan. (1997). *Zhongguo zhexue de tezhi [The Characteristics of Chinese Philosophy]*. Shanghai: Shanghai guji chubanshe.

Zhang Zai. (1975). *Zhangzi zhengmeng [The Just Enlightenment]*, ed. Wang Fuzhi. Beijing: Zhonghua shuju.

Index

for

262   *The American Journal of Economics and Sociology*

CL

303.
482
INT

Printed in the United Kingdom by
Lightning Source UK Ltd., Milton Keynes
138222UK00001B/94/P

This book is to be returned on or before
the last date stamped below.

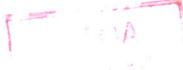